OTHER WORLDS, OTHER UNIVERSES

OTHER WORLDS, OTHER UNIVERSES

Playing the Reality Game

EDITED BY BRAD STEIGER
AND JOHN WHITE

Doubleday & Company, Inc.
Garden City, New York
1975

OCT - 8 1975

Library of Congress Cataloging in Publication Data

Steiger, Brad, comp.
  Other worlds, other universes.

  Bibliography
  1. Life on other planets. 2. Flying saucers. 3. Astral projection. I. White, John Warren, 1939–   joint comp. II. Title.
BF1999.S7214   001.9
ISBN 0-385-06448-9
Library of Congress Catalog Card Number 74-18835

*To our wives, families and
fellow travelers in the
exploration of reality.*

BRAD STEIGER likes to be thought of as a "sharer" rather than a teacher or preacher of metaphysics. He is pleased that the name given to him when he and his wife were adopted by the Repositor of Wisdom into the Wolf Clan of the Seneca Tribe, Iroquois Nation, was *Hat-yas-swas*, "He Testifies." From 1957–67 Mr. Steiger taught on both the high school and college level. Since 1967 he has been engaged in a full-time exploration of what others might term "borderland sciences," "the paranormal," or even "the world of the weird," but which Steiger calls "the greater reality which we all share but cannot always explain." His work has appeared in numerous publications and periodicals in this country and abroad, and he is a biographee in many international reference works. Among Mr. Steiger's nearly fifty books are *The Psychic Feats of Olof Jonsson; Revelation: The Divine Fire; Medicine Power: The American Indian's Revival of His Spiritual Heritage and Its Relevance for Modern Man;* and *Mysteries of Time and Space.* In 1974 Mr. Steiger received the Genie Award for Metaphysical Writer of the Year.

JOHN WHITE is a writer and teacher engaged in the exploration of consciousness. From 1972–74 he was associated with *Apollo 14* astronaut Edgar D. Mitchell as director of education for The Institute of Noetic Sciences, an organization founded by Dr. Mitchell to investigate the nature of consciousness and human potential.

Born in 1939, Mr. White has a bachelor's degree from Dartmouth College and a master's degree from Yale University. He is editor of *The Highest State of Consciousness, Frontiers of Consciousness, What Is Meditation?* and *Toward a Science of Consciousness.* He also edited *Psychic Exploration* for Edgar Mitchell. His writing has appeared in many popular and professional journals, including *Reader's Digest, Saturday Review/World Psychic, Journal of Altered States of Consciousness, Journal for the Study of Consciousness,* and *Fields Within Fields.* He has taught in high school and college. He is an editor of *Psychic* and *Human Dimensions* magazines, and is on the editorial board of *Journal of Altered States of Consciousness.* His articles have been reprinted in textbooks on linguistics, biology, and education.

He lives in Cheshire, Connecticut, with his wife and four children.

Limitations and constraints in apprehending reality are characteristic of organisms at every level of organization. The design of the human body determines our experience of reality; our biological constraints delimit what we can perceive. The central nervous system receives messages from certain portions of the ebb and flow of the natural world, but the far greater portion is infra or ultra to our "tuning." From what portions we can tune in to, our reality is constructed.

—Daniel Goleman

. . . Our normal waking consciousness, rational consciousness as we call it, is but one special type of consciousness, whilst all about it, parted from it by the filmiest of screens, there lie potential forms of consciousness entirely different. . . . No account of the universe in its totality can be final which leaves these other forms of consciousness quite disregarded. . . . They forbid a premature closing of our accounts with reality.

—William James

If I find in myself a desire which no experience in this world can satisfy, the most probable explanation is that I was made for another world.

—C. S. Lewis

Exploring the far-out spaces of human consciousness is the fastest way to social transformation.

—John C. Lilly

CONTENTS

IV. OTHER DIMENSIONS:
THE ASTRAL PLANE AND BEYOND

V. OTHER UNIVERSES: RETURN TO GODHEAD

INTRODUCTION

This book is an attempt to expand your consciousness by playing The Reality Game. The term originates with Brad Steiger in his book *Mysteries of Time and Space,* where he suggests that mankind has been challenged to participate in a kind of cosmic contest, The Reality Game. The object is to know reality, to understand ourselves and the cosmos as fully as possible. If man can apprehend the true significance of certain clues, if he can master the proper moves, he may obtain a clearer picture of his true role in the cosmic scheme of things—a role that is decidedly different from what common sense tells him it is. Steiger concludes that the rules of The Reality Game may be confusing, extremely flexible, and difficult to define, "but play man must—for it is the only game in the universe."

Why expand consciousness? Because it is the fastest way to societal transformation, and at this hour on the Doomsday Clock transformation is absolutely necessary if humanity is to survive as a species. Thus our purpose is to present information for transformation, which we hope will enlarge your conception of the universe and deepen your understanding of the intimate relation you have with it. With a new cosmology, a new picture of the universe, you automatically gain a new range of possibilities to explore in The Reality Game. By exploring these possibilities you gain experience and increase your awareness. This in turn creates a feedback situation that enables you to widen your own frontiers by discovering or devising still more avenues for reality-testing and winning another round in The Reality Game.

One of the barriers to consciousness expansion is the "reality construct" which people share. We don't experience reality directly—we construct a picture of reality. And we do it on the basis of misinformation, lack of information, and information which gets distorted through our individual sensory apparatus. Our perceptions are not as pure and direct as those of animals and infants appear to be. Our understanding of reality—of what is possible and impossible, what is ethically desirable, what is socially useful—is based on certain implicit assumptions, subtle habits of thought, and neurophysiological processes which usually operate below the threshold of awareness. These assumptions, thought patterns, and processes create a "consensual reality," a nonconscious belief system that molds our thoughts, feelings, and perceptions. This is generally overlaid by consciously held beliefs that further dictate the manner and degree to which we can know reality, and all too often our conceptions get in the way of our perceptions. The father of general systems theory, Ludwig von Bertalanffy, capsulized the situation in *General Systems Theory:*

> Man is not a passive receiver of stimuli coming from an external world, but in a very concrete sense *creates* his universe. This . . . can be expressed in many ways: in Freud's reconstruction of the building-up of the "world" in the child; in terms of developmental psychology according to Piaget, Werner, or Schachtel; in terms of the "new look in perception" emphasizing attitudes, affective and motivational factors; in psychology of cognition by analysis of "meaningful learning" after Ausubel; in zoological context by referring to von Uexküll's species-specific *umwelt;* philosophically and linguistically in Cassirer's "symbolic forms" and culture-dependent categories; in von Humboldt's and Whorf's evidence of linguistic (i.e., symbolic and cultural) factors in the formation of the experienced universe.

Our perceptions, beliefs, and reality constructs may be close approximations of truth or they may be way off base. But even when false we act as if they were true and real. Joseph Chilton Pearce points out in *The Crack in the Cosmic Egg:*

> There is a relationship between what we *think* is out there in the world and what we experience as being out there. There is a way in which the energy of thought and the energy of matter modify each other and interrelate. A kind of rough mirroring takes place between our mind and our reality. . . . We are an indeterminately large part of the function that shapes the reality from which we do our looking. Our looking enters as one of the determinants in the reality event that we see.

This is The Reality Game. Philosophers call it ontology. Carlos Castaneda's teacher, Don Juan, called it "stopping the world." By expanding consciousness, by becoming aware of how our unspoken view of the world influences our perceptions, thoughts, and actions, we can gain a clearer understanding of the nature of reality and, consequently, a greater degree of freedom by exposing previously invisible limiting factors and determining conditions. By turning our attention to the mirroring process itself, we can polish the image of reality so highly that near-clarity is obtained. In effect, we step through the looking glass to the other side and into a world of wonder—a world of direct experience rather than culturally mediated forms of thought, feeling, and behavior.

The mystic poet William Blake said that if the doors of perception were cleansed we would see everything as it is—infinite. This is quite contrary to the commonsense view of reality that most of us operate on most of the time. But common sense is mostly shared prejudice, mutually held belief systems with which we grow up. From early childhood, culture secretly builds blinders and controls in us, teaching us to direct our attention in ways that exclude awareness of certain events and experiences.

This intimate relation between our perceptions and our belief systems is vividly illustrated by psychologist Robert Ornstein in *The Psychology of Consciousness*. He points out that the familiar saying "I'll believe it when I see it" is also true in reverse. We'll *see* it only after we *believe* it! Psychic research provides a dramatic example of this in the sheep-goat effect, where the outcome of an experiment is to some degree predetermined by the mind-set (for or against) of the experimenter and the subject.

In science, the basic set of assumptions, conscious and otherwise, upon which scientists operate governs to an extraordinary degree the kind of experiments performed—*and even the data obtained and the interpretation of that data!* The prevailing world view has been termed a "paradigm" by science historian Thomas Kuhn in his book *The Structure of Scientific Revolutions.* Throughout history, Kuhn notes, scientific revolutions have occurred because the scientific establishment has been persuaded to accept a new paradigm. Previous to that, odd facts that don't fit into the accepted scheme of things simply get overlooked, ignored, or blithely labeled "anomalies" and tucked away in a corner. But, Kuhn writes, when the paradigm changes, as with Newton or Einstein:

. . . the world itself changes with them. Led by a new paradigm, scientists adopt new instruments and look in new places. Even more important, during revolutions scientists see new and different things when looking with familiar instruments in places they have looked before. . . . In so far as their only recourse to that world is through what they see and do, we may want to say that after a revolution scientists are responding to a different world.

There is a scientific revolution underway today. At this very moment facts are coming to light that present basic challenges to the world view of most scientists—facts that will require a basic restructuring of their perceptual system and the philosophy associated with it. Some theoreticians and synthesists are already at work on the necessary reformulations—another move in The Reality Game. Although most of the scientific community will consider it absurd at first, the history of science suggests that much of what was once considered occult or nonsensical has been slowly incorporated into the corpus of scientific knowledge. The emergence of paraphysics is a good example.

Paraphysics is a discipline that studies the physical aspects of paranormal phenomena, using sophisticated instruments for measuring and demonstrating the processes involved. Paraphysics has resulted from the interface between scientific technology and esoteric studies in philosophy and religion. It is taking science from physics to metaphysics by pointing to larger, previously unrecognized dimensions of physical events—gravitational, geomagnetic, lunar, solar, galactic, and even extragalactic influences—and possibly new laws and forms of energy.

The presently uncompleted scientific revolution will have enormous consequences because science is the religion of our society and scientists are our priests. What is happening is this: Ancient wisdom and spiritual concepts from traditional religious and esoteric thought are being rediscovered and validated in the language of modern science. Technology and science are paving the way for a rebirth of true religion. And it is ironic that "godless" mechanistic science should be the vehicle that at last brings us to the recognition (re-knowing) of the nonphysical underpinnings of the material world.

From physics through paraphysics to metaphysics. From orthodox science through occult science to spiritual science. That is the direction this book takes. And along the way we look at science fiction. Science fiction is often an inspired foretaste of the future because to some yet-unknown degree The Reality Game begins in imagination. From one point of view, man constructs his own reality; saying makes it so. And even though the world's holy books rightly state that in the beginning is the Word, imagination precedes the cosmological utterance. Beyond all "pragmatic" and "empirical" and "realistic" considerations are undreamed possibilities that imagination can reveal.

Truth is not stranger than fiction—truth *is* fiction, a work based on imagination. Every change, every revolution, every social transformation began as an idea, an image, in the mind of an inspired creator: Copernicus, Newton, Darwin, Freud, Einstein. Imagination is the faculty in people that comes closest to invoking the power to create which put us here in the first place. It is the meeting point for the mutual induction process of evolution between aspiring human reality and inspiring universal ideality—a process that philosopher of science Oliver Reiser vividly described in his writings: the imaging power of higher intelligence in other dimensions reaching down to humanity while at the same time humanity responds to an inherent impulse to reach up, inspired by an image of light.

Great works of art are always the result of this mutual induction process. Through the artist's imagination, sensitivity, and creativity we are brought closer to higher intelligence, the source of inspiration and, as Plato declared, eternal images. Science fiction is especially powerful in this respect. Often through science fiction life imitates art, as in the novels of Jules Verne or the film *2001,* in which the design of a spacecraft influenced NASA to actually develop a similar one.

But one can also get lost in imagination. The history of The Reality Game shows numerous false moves and dead ends. These include many forms of pseudoscience and wishful thinking. The true spirit of scientific inquiry alternates between the imaginative and the critical faculties. Many great discoveries began with an intuition, a direct insight without prior logical deductive analysis. Einstein exemplified this. He claimed that his discoveries did not come by way of logical deduction but rather from near-mystic insight and body feeling which he then had to slowly and laboriously translate into mathematical terms compatible with physics. Peter Medawar has observed that "the process by which we come to form a hypothesis is not illogical but nonlogical, i.e., outside logic. But once we have formed an opinion we can expose it to criticism, usually by experimentation." And in *The End of the Modern Age,* Allen Wheelis makes a thoughtful statement about this matter:

> Being human, we must necessarily conjecture about the world; insofar as we also are scientists we shall shape these conjectures in such a way as to expose them to the risk of being falsified. . . . The scientist will ask himself, as it were, "If this conjecture which I now believe to be true were in fact false, what are those circumstances which would most likely expose that falsity?" He will then try to achieve those circumstances, and will regard a conjecture as provisionally true only when it has survived the maximum achievable risk of such falsification, mindful that circumstances more threatening to the hypothesis may later be devised which it may then fail to survive. . . .

This is the best tradition of science—a method of knowing rather than a body of knowledge. It recognizes that new circumstances may render old "laws" obsolete, and that in attempting to fathom the depths of physical nature and our own psychological nature we must constantly perform reality testing. Fantasy, imagination, brainstorming, and so forth are useful in providing new pathways for exploring reality. But those probes must recognize that they are provisional upon the discovery of verifiable data. There must be a balance between the experimental and the experiential, the rational and the imaginative-intuitive.

The way of the scientist and the way of the mystic are equally valid, and in their best forms are one and the same. The fullest development of scientific, religious, philosophic, and artistic thought involves the use of the whole brain—the rational/analytic/logical way of knowing characteristic of the brain's left hemisphere and the intuitive/synthesizing/metalogical way characteristic of the right hemisphere. The empirical-deductive approach is integrated with the reflective-intuitive modality. There is a creative interplay between the fact-gathering senses and the life of the imagination.

Unless full due is given to both modalities, one is in danger of failing to test reality properly, completely. Dozens of examples could be given of the scientist whose understanding became dogmatized and shortsighted, based entirely on left-hemispheric experience. A sense of wonder and imagination was entirely lacking from his mechanistic, reductionistic, purposeless world view. Likewise, one can point to his right-hemispheric counterpart: the deluded person whose life is pathetically bound to a supernatural (if not illusory) world on which he places near-enslaving dependence, regardless of the data of his senses and the well-meant advice of more pragmatic friends.

The trick is to walk in balance. Or as Aldous Huxley used to say, "to make the best of both worlds." Ralph Waldo Emerson observed a reciprocal effect between reading and living. The more you read, the better you are able to understand life; the more you live, the better you are able to understand what you read. The key to not becoming lopsided—either a dry, dusty scholar or an illiterate vagabond—is, as we have said, to walk in balance.

We hope this book is balanced. In selecting material for it we tried to give proper due to scientific scrupulosity and to that quality which philosopher-science critic Theodore Roszak calls *gnosis*, "an older and larger kind of knowledge" which involves the participation of the knower so that newly gained facts may be perceived in the larger context of existence. Those with *gnosis* know how to play The Reality Game. They display the expanded consciousness of a visionary mind and a rational intellect, and employ both for the benefit of humankind. This has been a prime consideration for us in choosing excerpts from little-known works and in asking contributors to provide new material.

To play The Reality Game totally is to get in true step with time, space, and the source of being. Our tools include artistic imagination, a childlike capacity for fantasy, iconoclastic theories, and the accumulation of verifiable data by rational science, especially in areas previously deemed too sacrosanct to explore. Our goal is the expansion of consciousness and the transformation of society. We hope this book helps you master the first complex moves on the Cosmic Gameboard.

I. OTHER WORLDS: THE SEARCH FOR EXTRATERRESTRIAL LIFE

I

Our first move in playing The Reality Game involves exobiology, the search for extraterrestrial life. Exobiology is making headlines nowadays because of space probes and UFO incidents. But in some circles it is really old news. NASA Document SP-7015, published in 1965, is a huge bibliography containing thousands of annotated references to articles and books published as far back as 1900—publications which, among other things, dealt with the possibility of intelligent extraterrestrial lifeforms and ways to detect them.

What is the probability that life exists elsewhere in the universe? Cornell University astrophysicist Carl Sagan, author of *Intelligent Life in the Universe* and *The Cosmic Connection*, said recently:

> There are several hundred billion stars in our Milky Way galaxy. Many astronomers believe that a large number of them—perhaps half—have planetary systems more or less like our own. There are billions of other galaxies. The steps leading to the origin of life seem to occur easily. Most stars are older than the sun and have had more time for evolution by natural selection to produce and proliferate life on their planets. Thus the case for extraterrestrial life, even for extraterrestrial intelligence, seems to me to be a plausible one.

Shortly before, Sagan's colleague Frank Drake had stated in an article entitled "Prospects in the Search for Extraterrestrial Civilizations": "Another significant area [of study] is the ubiquity of life in space. Much theory and laboratory evidence suggests strongly that life will arise wherever conditions are not even salubrious, but only better than extremely hostile."

Sagan raised a note of skeptical caution in his statement, however. The case for extraterrestrial life is plausible, he said, but not convincing. "Perhaps the molecules of life are made easily but their combination into a system able to reproduce itself requires some very rare event. Perhaps civilizations arise rapidly, but destroy themselves soon after reaching their technical phase by nuclear weapons or pollution or exhaustion of natural resources or overpopulation."

The only certain way to know that is to make contact or to be contacted. The Soviet Union has a vigorous officially sponsored radio-astronomical search underway and there is reason to believe that in the near future other nations will initiate similar programs—routinely seeking messages sent our way by intelligent beings on other worlds.

Private efforts at contact by scientists began with Project Ozma in 1961, when Frank Drake directed the National Radio Astronomy Observatory in Green Bank, West Virginia, to observe two nearby stars, Tau Ceti and Epsilon Eridani. To date, however, despite the overwhelming probability that other lifeforms exist away from Earth, and despite several sensational reports to that effect in the news, it is still not proved in terms acceptable to science.

Extraterrestrial contact would be one of the most momentous events in modern history. (But we must allow for the possibility of contact in other times—an aspect of The Reality Game that we will examine later in other sections.) In preparation for it theologians are talking about exotheology, political theorists are considering the mechanics of intergalactic diplomacy, and linguists are wrestling with problems that surpass in magnitude the decipherment of the Rosetta Stone.

Some sober speculations on the significance of contact have been made by scientists and intellectuals. One view is that mankind is on a "quarantine list" and won't be allowed contact until our present mental condition and irrational behavior are changed—less like a virulent disease. We aren't ready for contact, the thought runs, because we would either "freak out" or spread our cultural pollution into space. Another speculative line of thought is more pragmatic: we just don't have the technology to intercept the signals of beings who are so highly evolved that we are to them as insects are to us. After all, how often do we try to communicate with ants or mosquitoes? George Wald of Harvard, winner of a Nobel prize in biology, feels that contact with an extraterrestrial civilization would take away human initiative to invent, develop, and explore on its own. Instead it would simply copy what the extraterrestrials were doing. On the other hand, Ronald Bracewell, professor of electrical engineering at Stanford, thinks extraterrestrial contact need not be feared and that we should prepare to communicate with them in a fitting manner. Wald's observations are available in NASA Document SP-328, *Life Beyond Earth and the Mind of Man*. Bracewell has NASA credentials also, however, being part of the team that performed Project Cyclops, a 1971 theoretical study of means for detecting extraterrestrial civilizations and published as NASA Document CR-114445, using the project name as its title.

So debate continues while the search goes on. It could take hundreds of years to make contact, as Project Cyclops conceives it, or it could happen tomorrow, as Soviet scientist Josif Shklovsky, head of the Department of Radio Astronomy at Moscow State University, recently suggested.

In any case, we should prepare ourselves. In the following selections a philosopher and a psychologist add their contributions to the situation. Luis E. Navia examines the metaphysical and psychological significance of discovering other intelligence in the universe. And Timothy Leary reveals his plan for contacting higher intelligence in the galaxy—a project that he feels is demanded by the evolutionary thrust of consciousness development. The countdown has begun.

LUIS E. NAVIA was born in Colombia, South America, in 1940. Since 1957 he has resided in the United States. He received his bachelor's degree in philosophy from Queens College of the City University of New York in 1963, and was elected to Phi Beta Kappa. He obtained his Ph.D. in philosophy at New York University in 1972. He has taught literature and philosophy at Hofstra University, Queens College, and New York University. He presently is an assistant professor of philosophy at New York Institute of Technology. Dr. Navia has authored several articles on philosophy, education, and history. This selection is based on a speech he delivered to the graduating class at New York Institute of Technology in 1974.

COSMOLOGY AND THE MYSTERY
OF THE UNIVERSE

In Book I of his *Metaphysics* Aristotle states that "it is owing to their sense of wonder that men both now begin and at first began to philosophize; they wondered originally at the obvious difficulties, then advanced little by little and stated difficulties about the greater matters, e.g. about the phenomena of the moon and those of the sun and of the stars, and about the genesis of the universe."[1] Then he adds, in a truly Socratic spirit, that "a man who is puzzled and wonders thinks himself ignorant," and that men "philosophized in order to escape from ignorance."

As in many other contexts, these words of the *Metaphysics* reveal a fundamental aspect of the human reality. We begin with wonder, we become aware of our ignorance, and in order to escape its cloud of darkness we speculate about the universe and about our own being. In the process of so doing we form concepts and ideas, hypotheses and theories, myths and symbols. "The lover of myth," says Aristotle in the same passage, "is in a sense a lover of wisdom, for the myth is composed of wonders." This is quite correct. At the basis of our understanding of reality there often lurks a myth which in the course of the development of thought becomes expressed in concepts and theories. This is, indeed, the true representation of philosophy and science.

Since the beginning of the history of human beings the object that has created in them the greatest wonder and perplexity has been the heavens. Man is perhaps the only living being whose eyes are persistently fixed on the realities above him. From time immemorial civilizations have existed, so to speak, in terms of that which appears in the sky. The regular course of the heavens determined the calendars by which entire cultures measured their time, and the predictable motions of the sun, the planets, and the stars were, in remote times not less than at present, the foundation of all temporal awareness. The gods of the ancients were invariably associated with the heavens: they came from the stars and it was there that they often returned. The biblical God and the divinities of the ancient Greeks shared the same origin and the same abode: the invisible regions of the universe above. Jesus himself, as we are told by Luke, was eventually "carried up into heaven,"[2] and his own mother, according to the Catholic dogma, was miraculously elevated to the higher spheres.

Even Plato's Ideal Forms were assigned, both by Plato and by later commentators, a celestial abode, and practically every system of religious and spiritual beliefs has inexorably looked up to the sky as an ultimate destination for the human race. "Within the heavens," says Plato, "are many spectacles of bliss upon the highways whereon the blessed gods pass to and fro."[3] It is, then, in the highest heavens that, according to him, true reality is found: not here, amid the noise and confusion of terrestrial affairs and distractions, but up there, where only "a pair of wings" can transport us, and where that which exists can never be adequately described by human speech.

It is interesting to observe, however, that today we are as fascinated by the mystery of the heavens as our ancestors were, and it is evident that our wonder has increased as our capacity to transcend the atmosphere of our planet has grown. Today the possibility of exploring and measuring the vastness of space, where we float on an insignificant speck of dust, is in our hands, and the metaphorical "pair of wings" of Plato's *Phaedrus* has finally acquired a sort of physical reality in the form of space vehicles.

We have surely entered an era in which we may be allowed to move freely along "the highways whereon the blessed gods pass to and fro." Space exploration has plunged us into an age of extraordinary discoveries, fantastic expeditions, and unheard-of accomplishments which are bound to eclipse by their magnitude and significance all previous human achievements. The journeys of Marco Polo, the rounding of the African continent, the voyages of Columbus, and many other past feats of humanity are beginning to appear as nothing but faint preludes to an enormous cosmic symphony of which we are sounding the initial notes. Many writers are already aware of the terrifying novelty of our times, and when they talk about "a new age," "a great change," and so on it is perhaps our future space exploration and consciousness that they rightly have in mind.

It is unavoidable, however, that such an adventure be both prefaced and followed by profound changes in our ordinary frames of thinking. The symbolism of the past, in which Plato, the Indian sages, and the biblical authors are so wealthy, will have to develop a texture of realism and verifiability, and the accounts of previous fictional writers will have to acquire a radically new meaning. Our thinking has already been disturbed, for instance, by the astroarchaeological hypotheses of Erich von Daniken and Joseph Blumrich, who maintain that the gods of antiquity may have been visitors from remote regions of the universe.[4] Our religions and cultures, and even our languages, may be nothing but deteriorated vestiges of forgotten cosmic encounters.

Astounding as this view may sound at first, one must confess that, given the knowledge obtained from our technological space feats on the one hand and, on the other, from our growing understanding of the immensity and complexity of the universe, there is nothing either meaningless or impossible in it. In fact, I would venture to say that such a view sheds much light on certain issues and problems with which we have not been able to cope scientifically. Subsequent empirical research probably will clarify the strength or weakness of the ancient astronaut theory, provided that philosophers and scientists are willing and able to approach it with a sufficiently open mind.

The ancient astronaut theory rests on a more complex and general hypothesis, namely the contention that the universe is inhabited by intelligent beings other than human beings. This contention is generally known as the ETI (Extraterrestrial Intelligence) hypothesis. Obviously, before we can logically speak of cosmic visitations or of the presence of cosmic beings in the prehistory of mankind we must be able to accept, at least as a possibility, the existence of extraterrestrial intelligent beings. The ancient astronaut theory rests logically on this hypothesis, and not vice versa, which explains the fact that some scientists who are willing to speak about a plurality of inhabited universes are unwilling to lend an ear to the advocates of astroarchaeology. It is, then, possible to examine the former without taking the latter into account.

The ETI hypothesis is by no means new. Contemporary publications, such as those of Carl Sagan (*The Cosmic Connection*) and Walter Sullivan (*We Are Not Alone*), are in reality nothing but more precise formulations of what many ancient writers firmly believed. Anaximander of Miletus (600 B.C.), one of the earliest Greek philosophers, believed in the existence of other inhabited planets which, according to him, floated in endless space at equidistant points. Aristotle himself suggests that the idea of extraterrestrial intelligent life was something which "our forefathers in the most remote ages have handed down to their posterity," and that this tradition ought to be regarded as "an inspired utterance."[5] He speaks on two occasions of the men and animals who inhabit the moon, and he remarks in this respect that they are invisible to us only because of the distance that separates us from them.[6] These Aristotelian comments are in fact restatements of an ancient Pythagorean doctrine according to which the entire universe was seen as teeming with intelligent beings.

Plutarch and Lucretius argued against the belief in the uniqueness of the earth, and for the belief in other inhabited celestial bodies. Giordano Bruno was burned by the Roman Inquisition in the year 1600 for defending, among other things, a contention which we would classify today as the ETI hypothesis. John Locke, whose influence in our political and empirical philosophy has been so vast, observed in his *Elements of Natural Philosophy* that

> . . . it is more suitable to the wisdom, power, and greatness of God, to think that the fixed stars are all of them suns, with systems of inhabitable planets moving about them, to whose inhabitants He displays the marks of his goodness, as well as to us.[7]

Then he added, as if he were anxious to debunk the anthropomorphism of the official religious doctrine, that to conceive of such an inhabited universe is more pious than "to imagine that those very remote bodies [the stars and their planets], so little useful to us, were made only for our sake."

It is true that a literal reading of certain biblical passages leaves one with the impression that the universe was created by God for the sake of the earth, and the earth for the sake of mankind. Such an account appears in many passages of the Old Testament, as in Genesis 1:14–16, 1:28–31, 9:2–3, and so on. In line with this biblical tradition, Thomas Aquinas maintained in his *Summa Theologica* that "it is not possible for there to be another earth than this one."[8] Indeed, to postulate a number of inhabited worlds would entail an interpretation of the biblical text which many religious commentators would have found difficult to accept, and a series of insoluble questions would immediately arise: Are those *other* inhabitants burdened with original sin? Has Jesus died for them, too? Are they entitled to salvation?

And yet it is interesting to remember that in the year 1277 the Catholic Church condemned the doctrine of the uniqueness of the earth. By an order of the Church "it was forbidden to teach that God could not have created a plurality of universes."[9] All things are possible for God. The rabbinical tradition went as far as to affirm that in the course of infinite time God had already created innumerable universes which underwent destruction, and that this present universe of ours is only the last one in a long series of successive creations.[10] It is therefore evident that the ETI hypothesis has found advocates even in the most orthodox religious circles.

The fact is, however, that the Thomistic view prevailed, with the subsequent belief that the earth is both the center of the universe in a physical sense and the ultimate purpose of all creation in a teleological sense. But once one becomes convinced of the truth of this anthropomorphic notion, the mystery of the universe finds a rather convenient solution, and our innate sense of wonder is weakened by a body of dogmas which does not fit within our present understanding of the immensity of cosmic space.

This brings me to my substantive point. Regardless of how many theologians, philosophers, and scientists may have supported or attacked the ETI hypothesis, we must ask whether we are justified in leaning toward such a contention and, further, whether those who at the present talk about extraterrestrial life are abandoning the confines of scientific investigation. Many academicians tend to look with suspicion upon this sort of discussion because of the emphasis they often place on the exclusive importance of readily verifiable matters. Perhaps this explains the current atmosphere of conservativism in the schools, a conservativism which was responsible in the past for the temporary stifling of revolutionary theories, such as those of Copernicus and Galileo, Lamarck and Darwin, Freud and Jung, and many others. But, as Lewis Beck has observed, we may have reached the time to lift the traditional ban on creative speculation.[11] Thus, we may be able to satisfy our inborn sense of wonder at the immensity of the universe.

The view that the earth is the only inhabited body in the universe is the result of two beliefs which have been generally accepted until recently. First, it has been maintained that we are the effect of a special act of creation on the part of God and, second, it has been believed that the earth rests at the center of the universe. Unquestionably a certain interpretation of the Bible lends abundant support to both beliefs and they stand in close interrelationship. Egocentrism and geocentrism, as we can call them, go hand in hand and to attack either one is to undermine the other. The fundamental truths of a genuine philosophical religion are, however, never affected by a rejection of them; Galileo was perfectly correct in insisting that no astronomical discovery can affect in any way a true system of religious ideas. It is only certain narrow and superficial interpretations of religious sources that suffer catastrophic earthquakes as the result of new insights into the nature of the universe.

The last few hundred years have witnessed a number of cosmological insights which have permanently altered our view of our position in the universe. Now we know that this planet of ours is in fact nothing but a minor planet which floats in space and moves around its sun, and that this sun is itself a minor star which travels through space in the company of one hundred billion stars which rotate around the mysterious center of our galactic neighborhood, the Milky Way. Our galaxy, moreover, is only an insignificant point of light within the observable universe, which contains several billion galaxies. What the universe as a totality truly contains, or what the total universe really is—these are questions to which neither astrophysics nor cosmology can give even the vaguest answer. We simply do not know and, as Kant suggested, we will never know. We must remain satisfied with questions and issues concerning the observable universe, which is probably an insignificant part of an infinitely larger whole.

But the vastness of this observable universe is in itself staggering. A few generally known figures will suffice to confirm this:

Whereas a ray of light travels from the moon to the earth in less than two seconds, and from the sun to the earth in less than eight minutes, at the speed of 186,000 miles per second, it takes a ray of light over four years to reach the star closest to the sun. It takes a ray 30,000 years to cover the distance between our solar system and the center of our galaxy, and 100,000 years to move along the entire diameter of this galaxy. But all this is not really very much. Within the observable universe there are as many galaxies as there are stars within the Milky Way, which means that astronomical calculations reveal the existence of billions and billions of galaxies. It is known, for instance, that within the Big Dipper alone there are a million galaxies. Until recently certain foggy formations in the heavens were believed to be clouds of cosmic dust, but now these same clouds have been found to be immense conglomerations of galaxies which constitute what cosmologists and astronomers designate as "island universes."

There is no logical reason to believe, however, that many of the trillions of stars which constitute this and those other galaxies in this and other "island universes" *do not* possess planets somehow similar to those of our solar system. In fact, to think otherwise would be to deny the universality of the physical laws which were responsible for the formation of our own system, and this very few scientists are willing to do. Thus by the sheer force of numbers alone we are undoubtedly obliged to say neither that this solar system is unique nor that a planet such as ours is an isolated cosmic case. It is not difficult to infer from these premises that in all probability some form of life does exist elsewhere and that, given even the most conservative statistical estimates, some form of life similar to terrestrial intelligent life has developed in a multitude of places. "Since other galaxies are believed to have, on the average, as many stars (and therefore planets) as the Milky Way, and since there are an estimated hundred billion galaxies," says science writer Kenneth Weaver, "the number of extraterrestrial civilizations could be truly astronomical."[12]

If only one in a hundred thousand stars in our galaxy had a planet with some kind of life, we would be confronted with at least one million populated earths. One must add that if such an estimate were extrapolated to the billion galaxies in the observable universe, the one million populated earths would become multiplied to incalculable numbers.

Thus, both the egocentrism and geocentrism of the past are forced into oblivion, and with them the uniqueness of the earth and of human existence becomes relegated to the category of primitive notions. Cosmology leaves us no other choice than to regard ourselves as members of a vast community of beings, and this constitutes, more than anything else, an even greater source of wonder and admiration.

Much speculation has been devoted recently to the implications which the ETI hypothesis entails for philosophy, science, technology, and religion. In philosophy, for example, it is debated whether our fundamental norms of morality would suffer a transformation in the presence of extraterrestrial beings, and whether our cognitive theories would have to undergo revisions in the event of discovering another cosmic civilization. Logicians and philosophers of language are presently working on the most simple linguistic systems which would allow for communication with beings whose linguistic and sensory apparatus may be radically different from ours. In science, a number of investigations are being conducted into the implications of ETI on the various theories of evolution, and much research is being conducted into the consequences of Einstein's Theory of Relativity for space exploration.

As most astrophysicists know, given the Einsteinian conception of space and time, vast astronomical distances do not represent an unconquerable obstacle for space travel, since as the speed of a body is significantly increased, its real time is reduced. It follows from here that the common unintelligent objection often raised against von Daniken's views—namely, that there cannot be ancient cosmic astronauts because of the enormity of galactic distances—is based both on the lack of technical imagination and on clear theoretical ignorance.

But even if we were to abandon all belief in past cosmic visitations and all hope of future galactic travel, there still remains the fruitful endeavor of developing and perfecting radiotelescopes, one of the greatest feats of science and technology. By means of these technological marvels we hope to receive and decode intelligent signals from remote corners of the universe. "There is compelling reason to believe," says Kenneth Weaver, "that faint radio signals from civilizations elsewhere in the universe may be coming our way."[13] The decoding of only one of these signals would suddenly announce the actual arrival of a new age for mankind, an age in which the mystery of the universe would become even more perplexing, in which our sense of wonder would be stimulated tenfold, and in which philosophy, science, and religion would have to reappraise their premises and tenets. Then the belief of the ancient Greeks would finally be corroborated, the estimates of astrophysicists confirmed, and, perhaps, our engrossing terrestrial affairs somewhat minimized.

For thinking people today, these and other cosmological speculations and hopes ought to represent a great source of intellectual challenge. Those who in the name of practicality denounce cosmological speculation and space exploration should be reminded of the words of Dag Hammarskjöld concerning a certain crewman in Columbus's expedition: "He kept wondering whether he would get back to his home village in time to succeed the old shoemaker before anybody could grab the job."[14]

Practicality is a commendable human inclination but the exclusive worship of practicality is not. To combine a spirit of practicality with our perennial sense of wonder about the universe may be a difficult balance to maintain. But if we want to be an integral part of the new age that is now beginning, we must maintain it and remain the fertile ground on which new and revolutionary cosmological hypotheses may grow.

NOTES

1 Aristotle, *Metaphysics* 982b.
2 Luke 24:51.
3 Plato, *Phaedrus* 247a.
4 E. von Daniken, *Chariots of the Gods?* (New York: Bantam Books, 1971); J. Blumrich, *The Spaceships of Ezekiel* (New York: Bantam Books, 1974).
5 Aristotle, op. cit., 1074b.
6 Aristotle, *On the Movements of Animals* 699b.
7 J. Locke, *Philosophical Works* (London: Henry G. Bohn, 1854), V. II, p. 478.
8 T. Aquinas, *Basic Writings* (New York: Random House, 1945), V. I, p. 463.
9 L. W. Beck, "Extraterrestrial Intelligent Life." *Proceedings and Addresses of the American Philosophical Association,* V. XLV, p. 8.
10 M. J. Cohen, *Pathways Through the Bible* (Philadelphia: The Jewish Publication Society of America, 1970), p. 5.
11 Beck, op. cit., p. 5.
12 K. F. Weaver, "The Incredible Universe." *National Geographic,* V. 145, No. 5 (May 1974), p. 625.
13 Ibid., p. 622.
14 D. Hammarskjöld, *Markings* (New York: Alfred A. Knopf, 1971), p. 66.

TIMOTHY LEARY, presently in a California prison on charges arising from his experimentation with psychedelic drugs, began his exploration of consciousness as a professor of psychology at Harvard. His expanding search for the meaning of life brought him to consider exobiology. This essay presents his concept for contacting other life. It is taken from his 1974 book *Terra II . . . A Way Out,* in which he states, "Life is an interstellar communication network . . . disseminated through the galaxies in the form of nucleotide templates (which) land on planets, are activated by solar radiation, and evolve nervous systems." Dr. Leary can be contacted through Starseed, 531 Pacific Avenue, San Francisco, California 94133.

STARSEED: A WAY OUT

Neurologic* leads to this conclusion: life is of extraterrestrial origin and of extraterrestrial destination.

This discovery is the hopeful, renewing, exalted philosophic perspective that humanity has been awaiting.

Life was seeded on this planet by astroplankton (panspermia) around three billion years ago. The nucleotide signals contained the blueprint for the gradual evolution of life through a sequence of biomechanical stages. Every living creature from the unicellular to the human is a stamped-out unit playing its part in the over-all design. The role of each living entity is to reproduce, to carry on the electrical chain of life and to contribute its body to the humus topsoil, to contribute its biological function (plants breathe [in carbondioxide] and create oxygen, etc.) to the over-all unity.

The goal of the evolutionary process is to produce nervous systems capable of communicating with the galactic network. Contacting the Higher Intelligence.

Evolution unfolds through larval stages necessary to secure life on this planet and provide the matrix from which later mutations and metamorphoses spring.

At this halfway point in the life of our solar system, it is time

* The title of one of Dr. Leary's publications, and a punning term for his thesis that profound wisdom is built into humanity through the functioning of the nervous system. *Editors.*

for humanity to address itself to the mission. The central purpose of mankind must be, from now on, to contact Higher Intelligence. If humanity continues to wrestle for spatial dominance on the planet, it will destroy itself and the evolutionary goal will be postponed until the next cycle.

This essay presents a feasible and practical plan for sending a starship city, Starseed, to the center of the galaxy to contact and exchange information with Higher Intelligence. The voyage will last hundreds of years and will necessitate the creation and maintenance of all the life-support systems and social structures now extant on Earth. The starship will be a miniature replica of Earth, within, rather than on the surface of, the space vehicle.

The Starseed plan unfolds in three stages:

1. An international committee is formed in January 1974 which works out the technical, economic, and social blueprint for the voyage, and selects the crew.

2. In 1976 the initial crew will start constructing a functional replica of the city, to be located in the Arctic region. The technical and social procedures for the voyage will be developed during this period, which will last twenty-four years. The engineered components for the actual ship will be constructed in different countries.

3. In the year 2000 Starseed will be launched. While the ship will not return within the lifetime of any living person, messages will be sent back continually to inform and enlighten mankind on the discoveries made about extraterrestrial conditions and, equally important, discoveries made within the mobile laboratory about human communication.

The Vision

Up until the present the human being has existed in a larval state with no precise answers to the basic questions: exactly how did we get here, why are we here, and where are we going? The primitive, larval religions have produced theories, rituals, and ethics which concern tribal survival, e.g., the Ten Commandments. Despite the vagueness of larval cosmologies they all share the vision of a Higher Intelligence which can be contacted "up there" in a later stage of evolution. The persistence of a "Noah myth" is also worth noting.

Thus we see that Neurologic and Starseed, far from being heretical novelties, are the current manifestations of the oldest guiding myths of our species. This is no time to be pessimistic. From the perspective of Starseed we joyously see that humanity, in spite of momentary distractions of war, dictatorships, plague, has moved directly and efficiently in the direction of its mission: to establish physical security on this planet, to develop the technology, and to liberate the nervous system to higher states of consciousness.

The malaise which now infects the world is philosophic. The ancient transcendental visions expressed in the Stone Age metaphors of Christianity, etc., have been lost or distorted. The old religions, let it be noted, kept the entire evolutionary spectrum open. The purpose of life was to contact the "Higher Intelligence in Heaven." In order to prepare for the voyage, "scientific" organizations of cosmonautical engineers (e.g., the Catholic Church) worked out and executed the earthly plans thought necessary to prepare humanity for the trip (e.g., the Ten Commandments). A thousand years ago no one questioned the cosmological purpose of life; everyone agreed that the basic goal was the voyage upward. The Renaissance focused attention on the scientific and technical steps necessary to contact the Higher Intelligence. Unhappily, mankind became fascinated by its scientific accomplishments, trapped into a technological addiction, and overemphasized the larval processes of physical survival, terrestrial power, and material skill and comfort. The heretical and diabolical power of the state caused humanity to forget, momentarily, that the aim of life is to "contact the Higher Intelligence in Heaven," a goal which can now be defined not in the accurate but poetically vague metaphors of prescientific theology, but in terms of a starship launched in the direction of the astronomically defined center of the galaxy, where, according to all statistical probabilities, we shall contact more advanced civilizations and be instructed as to the next stage in our existence.

Does Higher Intelligence Exist?

Here is the only question worth the consideration of any intelligent person. Does Higher Intelligence exist? Everyone must say a basic yes or no to this decisive probe. If your answer is negative, either explicitly or by passive, uncaring default, then nothing makes any difference except petty satisfaction of robot comforts during this brief, pointless existence. If your answer is affirmative then the most exciting, adventurous, and hopeful vista emerges. Certainly no other reward or prospect can compare.

Humanity now hungers for reassurance that the ancient aspirations were not in vain and for a reminder that there is a glorious purpose to existence on this planet. What sounds like the most far out and impractical fantasy becomes, upon reflection, the only sensible proposal.

Let us examine the logical possibilities:

1. Advanced civilizations exist on planets within our galaxy and can be contacted by means of electromagnetic messagery and timeship exploration. The similarity of our present situation to the pre-Columbian visions of other continents is haunting.

2. Higher Intelligence exists on this planet within the mysteries of the DNA code decipherable by means of the nervous system.

3. No higher intelligence exists beyond the gradual accumulation of scientific knowledge. There is no advanced life in other solar systems and no new, different levels of awareness to be discovered within the nervous system.

No matter which of these hypotheses one esthetically prefers, the fact still remains that the best investment for the human race, the most exciting, inoffensive way to pass our time is to assume, pretend, gamble that there is a Higher Intelligence and to organize an all-out search. From the history of science we learn that the only way any new energy is discovered is to look for it and, indeed, we tend to find whatever we look for. To paraphrase Voltaire, if the Higher Intelligence does not exist, it is time to invent It.

When five thousand persons from every country assemble to live and work together in the dedicated search for H.I. the results, even if negative, cannot fail to be amusing and instructive to the race.

Do Advanced Civilizations Exist in
Other Solar Systems?

"I believe, as to the question of extraterrestrial life, that it is one of the most important and exciting problems that confronts us." (Sir Bernard Lovell, director, Jodrell Bank Radio Telescope.)

"At the end of 1962 the Soviet Academy of Sciences published an entire book on the universality of intelligent life, written by Josif S. Shklovsky, one of the most brilliant theoretical radio astronomers alive." (Quoted from *We Are Not Alone* by Walter Sullivan.)

Alistair Cameron, the astrophysicist, in the introduction to his anthology on interstellar communication, describes the possibility of life on other worlds as "currently the greatest question in scientific philosophy." Already, he says, we are admitting "that there be millions of societies more advanced than ourselves in our galaxy alone. If we can now take the next step and communicate with some of these societies, then we can expect to obtain an enormous enrichment of all phases of our sciences and arts. Perhaps we shall also receive valuable lessons in the technique of stable world government." (Ibid.)

"No field of inquiry is more fascinating than a search for humanity, or something like humanity, in the mystery-filled happy lands beyond the barriers of interstellar space. . . . As far as we can tell, the same physical laws prevail everywhere. The same rules apply at the center of the Milky Way, in the remote galaxies, and among the stars of the solar neighborhood. In view of a common cosmic physics and chemistry, should we not also expect to find animals and plants everywhere? It seems completely reasonable; and soon we shall say that it seems inevitable." (Harlow Shapley, director, Harvard College Observatory.)

"Most exciting of all the prospects [of interstellar contact] are the spiritual and philosophic enrichment to be gained from such exchanges. Our world is undergoing revolutionary changes. Our ancestors enjoyed a serenity denied to most of us. As we devastate our planet with industrialization, with highways, housing, and haste, the restoration of the soul that comes from contemplating nature unmarred by human activity becomes more and more inaccessible. Furthermore, through our material achievements, we are threatened by what the French call 'embourgeoisment'—domination of the world by bourgeois mediocrity, conformity, and comfort-seeking.

"The world desperately needs a global adventure to rekindle the flame that burned so intently during the Renaissance, when new worlds were being discovered on our own planet and in the realms of science. Within a generation or less we will vicariously tread the moon and Mars, but the possibility of ultimately 'seeing' worlds in other solar systems, however remote, is an awesome prospect. 'The soul of man was made to walk the skies,' the English poet Edward Young wrote in the eighteenth century." (Walter Sullivan, op. cit.)

"Since there are about one hundred thousand million stars in the Milky Way system, this means that some thousand million stars must have planets in the appropriate condition to support long-term organic evolution.

"It may be argued that the fivefold reduction which we have already made in the original estimate is not five but five thousand times wrong. In this case we conclude that there must be still a hundred million stars in the Milky Way with planets which could support organic evolution.

"When we consider the wider aspects of the cosmos as a whole the situation becomes even more dramatic. . . . Our estimates lead us to conclude that in the observable universe there are probably some trillion stars possessing planets in a suitable condition for the support of organic evolution." (Sir Bernard Lovell, director, Jodrell Bank Radio Telescope, in *The Exploration of Outer Space.*)

Has Life Been "Seeded" on This Planet?

The basic question of human philosophy. Where did life come from? According to the ancient, prescientific religions, an extraterrestrial, celestial Creator introduced life upon the earth.

Scientific theories of evolution disproved the anthropomorphic concepts of *how* life developed, the crude engineering notions of the seven-day God. But biological philosophers and geneticists have failed to explain the origin of life.

"In looking down the long avenue of evolution, Darwin concluded that, in the dim past, there must have been some single, primitive form of life from which everything else arose. He then logically asked: Whence came that original species? In a recently discovered letter, thought to have been the last that he dictated and signed before his death, Darwin said the knowledge of that time (1882) was so meager that any serious attempt to explain life's origin would be premature. . . . The 'principle of continuity,' he wrote, 'renders it probable that the principle of life will hereafter be shown to be a part, or a consequence, of some general law.' "

Science has not yet produced any evidence or theory to improve on the biblical account that a celestial Higher Intelligence is responsible for life on the earth.

Indeed, there is a mounting wave of evidence and conjecture that provides the technical explanation of how the Higher Intelligence managed to do it.

Panspermia, a notion of Svante August Arrhenius, states that the templates of life arrived in the form of microscopic spores which escaped from the donor planet by means of air currents or volcanic eruptions. As Sullivan points out, "The trouble with the panspermia idea was that bacterial spores . . . would probably be killed soon after they left the protecting envelope of air around the [donor planet] by ultraviolet rays from the sun."

Meteorites provide a more plausible engineering explanation for the arrival of living matter on our planet. It is estimated that more than one thousand meteorites land on our planet every year. At the microscopic level there is a constant rain of material . . . it has been estimated that this dust falls at a rate of about one thousand tons a day.

On the night of May 14, 1864, a meteorite fell around the village of Orgueil, France. Twenty portions of the object were recovered which ranged in size from apples to pumpkins. In composition the objects resembled peat, easily cut with a knife, soluble in water. The Orgueil meteorite has probably been more elaborately studied than any other chunk of material on earth. These analyses have indicated that the meteoritic material contains hydrocarbons and highly varied, complex, and baffling organic molecules, including some similar to cytosine, which is one of the bases of nucleic acid. On the basis of the evidence that organic materials have reached our planet within meteorites, the hypothesis that life on Earth has been seeded from extraterrestrial sources seems, at the present time, more realistic than theories of spontaneous generation.

The psychological and practical implications of the Starseed hypothesis are fascinating. Our home base, our parental source, is extraterrestrial. From the genetic perspective of the seventh neural circuit, life originated elsewhere in the galaxy. We have, as it were, been sent to school on planet Earth to develop. When we have evolved to the point where we understand our origin and can locate our "celestial parents," we are ready to return home. During the first two billion years of our planetary childhood we have passed through the larval states necessary to produce a bilateral nervous system capable of deciphering the secret of life which is encoded in DNA.

The place to find our celestial "parents" is obviously the center of the galaxy.

The Necessity for the Voyage

Evidence has been cited that Higher Intelligence probably exists on planets most likely to be located in the direction of Galactic Center. Evidence has also been summarized that life on this planet was probably seeded from organic molecules transported from more advanced planets.

The purpose of life, it has been suggested, is to contact Higher Intelligence.

If either or both of these hypotheses are falsehoods, it does not matter. Since they are the most logical and practical and optimistic "falsehoods" available, they should be accepted and acted upon until a more effective hypothesis comes along.

It is necessary to organize the voyage to Galactic Center as a concrete act of visionary love. To demonstrate to our "galactic parents" and ourselves how good we can be. For five thousand people selected from every nationality to live together for eight years to prepare for the voyage will be in itself the greatest achievement of human history. Even if the ship never leaves, a magnificent experiment in human spirituality and practical intelligence will have been conducted.

Once Terra II is launched into time, those remaining will have a collective vision and a social model which will very likely produce a new spirit of reconciliation and renewal.

The Starseed voyage, lasting thousands of years, will cost less than the amount presently necessary to support one week of the global military budget. Once the first expedition is launched it is probable that others will follow. There is nothing competitive or elitist involved. Any group of five thousand people who wish to organize for a trip to Galactic Center is free to do so.

There is no choice. The voyage has to be made.

Phase I: The Initial Planning

In January 1974 a Starseed center will be opened. Committees will be formed to develop plans for construction of the sky-city and its total self-support and self-government during the voyage. Terra II is a miniature replica of Terra I. The sky-society will require a system of agriculture, sanitation, ecology, health, education, recreation, climate control, transportation, communication, government. In addition to the design and construction of the ship and its propulsion and life-support systems, industrial facilities for constructing all of the machinery needed during the long voyage must be designed. Research laboratories for every science now known to mankind must be included. Once the sky-city is launched it will, of course, be self-supporting. However, the financing for construction and equipping of the ship will be the responsibility of the organizing committee. Selection of the crew will also be accomplished during this phase.

The committees will divide their work into two stages: the construction and maintenance of the pilot city, and the construction of the sky-city.

To illustrate the scope of crew composition:

We shall be selecting the faculty, administration, graduate school, maintenance and ground staff of a university combining Oxford, Cambridge, and the Moscow Agricultural College. Plus families.

It is anticipated that around forty-nine committees will select one hundred crew members each. Every effort will be made to include delegations from every country in the world and from any minority group which believes it is not represented.

The specific organization of the organizing committees will not be forecast, but left to the participants.

A basic rule of the enterprise is that there shall be no secrecy. Every detail of the organization and execution of the voyage will be open to public scrutiny.

Phase II: Earth-city

In January 1976 the first contingent will proceed to the Arctic to begin construction of the replica Earth-city. Insofar as is practical, the building and maintenance of Earth-city will duplicate the steps necessary to build and operate Terra II. Since the final design of the skyship awaits decision by the technical committees, this outline of Earth-city can only be suggestive.

The first wave of colonists will be construction engineers who will build landing facilities, temporary housing for about five thousand. The replica of the skyship will be built. Nuclear energy power plants will be assembled. As soon as the first wave can live within the ship they will construct the seed modules for life support and social existence. The remainder of the crew will join in stages. Each wave will build and put into operation the systems necessary to support the subsequent wave.

This period of assemblage will be of crucial importance. Experimentation, innovation, and trial of the many technical and social issues. For example, one or more languages will have to be developed and learned. Countless technical and human decisions must be made. We are creating the ultimate utopian community, a small model world which must deal with every aspect of human life.

The model will be biological. The ship as body. The crew as nervous system. Each voyager a neuron. Biomechanics. Neurotechnics.

All the classic human problems must be solved in a way which combines the improvements we crave and the traditions to which we are addicted.

In general the crew will remain within the ship-world during this period. Reactions of claustrophobia will inevitably develop and adaptation to life enclosed in a miniature world will be an important part of the preflight training period. Some of the crew will remain in the old-world society to participate in the construction of the skyship. Crew membership will at all times be voluntary and those who wish to leave the new society can do so. It is possible that the sky-society will decide to bring along or construct in flight space vehicles which can be sent back to Earth; it is also possible that there will be no possibility of return.

By 1981 the crew will have been selected and the replica city will operate in total self-support for the three years before departure begins.

Phase III: The Flight

In 1984 the first contingent will rocket from Earth to a parking orbit where the construction of Terra II will take place. The sequence of sending the crew in phases as worked out in the Arctic replica will be repeated. It is expected that the assemblage of equipment and personnel will take no more than sixteen years. Terra II will take off for the center of the galaxy before the year 2000.

Intellectual Fusion

The skeptical reaction to this proposal: Since human beings have not been able to cooperate and establish a harmonious use of resources in the past, how can we expect them to change cooped up inside a miniature world which, like a pressure cooker, may generate explosive pressures of disharmony? Etc.

There are several hopeful answers to this realistic objection.

The population of Terra II is both self-selected and group-selected. We shall offer the galactic intelligence our best hopes, our best energies, our best people.

The Terra II population will be highly motivated, united in the greatest enterprise that humanity has ever initiated. Human beings in the past have been caught in webs of ambivalent and conflicting motivation. Class, caste, race, nationalistic, personal, familial. The Terra II population will be intimately harnessed together in a mutual survival process.

The most promising asset of the flight will derive from the *intel-*

lectual fusion which will lift the level of cognitive ability to a new, metamorphosed level. At the present time the human species has produced an astounding number of scientific and creative achievements and there is a large population of extremely evolved persons living around the globe. They are separated from each other. Each person and each group is bogged down in a social-political structure which on the one hand supports them and on the other hand limits them to the restricted visions of political bureaucracies. Research goals are deliberately shortsighted to appear practical: cure of cancer, military hardware. Social scientists in particular are limited in proposing solutions to human problems because above all they must not rock the boat. Etc. Institutes which bring scholars and scientists together such as RAND, Hudson Institute, Salk Foundation, while they encourage cross-disciplinary contact, do little to motivate.

The Starseed project can be seen as an enormous process of intellectual nuclear fusion. Five thousand brilliant human beings will be assembled on a time-ship world and they will have to produce new and successful solutions to all of the ancient human problems in order to survive. The situation will require creativity. At the present time the chemist and the psychologist work at their separate laboratories and then drive home to the suburbs. There is no pressure to integrate discoveries, cross-fertilize on a survival basis.

Terra II will more than justify its existence as an incubator of scientific discoveries in every aspect of life. Each scientific and scholarly discipline will have its research facilities aboard. The results of the ongoing research will be relayed continuously back to Terra I.

It is likely that within short years the skyship will make radio contact with other civilizations. As Terra II leaves the powerful field of solar radiation its own signals will be clearer to other scanning receivers. These first contacts with Higher Intelligence will inevitably make available great advances in our understanding of physical-chemical-biological processes, which in turn will be transmitted to Earth.

Today scientists play at the games of science. In addition to being scientists they are Democrats, golfers, adulterers, players in games which are totally removed from the high peaks of their creativity. The novelty of and continual pressure for innovative solutions on Terra II will guarantee a higher state of consciousness, a demonstration of new levels of neural effectiveness.

Financing the Voyage

The Starseed project is totally self-supporting. International in scope, it cannot ask or accept financial support from any country. Nor can it be under any outside political control.

Starseed is, of course, a nonprofit enterprise. No member of Terra II will receive any funds from Starseed for personal living expenses or for compensation. Starseed will pay outside companies who manufacture equipment and perform subcontracting tasks.

The cost of the Starseed project will be ——— billion dollars. This sum will be raised by means of a) donations, b) research contracts, and c) sale and lease of media rights.

a) *Donations:* Starseed finances will be handled by a trust which will receive tax-deductible donations. At the present time we have received pledges from ten persons who have agreed to donate a million dollars each. The enthusiasm of donors is explained by the general reaction that Starseed is the first totally sensible idea ever suggested for the use of human resources. By 1976 it is expected that a thousand million-dollar donations will be received, plus another billion dollars in smaller contributions. As the project becomes tangible and concretely realizable the flow of donations will increase geometrically.

b) *Research Contracts:* The Terra II crew will include one thousand of the most gifted scientists working on new designs and solutions for every aspect of human life. The patents on discoveries made by the various research groups will be licensed or sold for an estimated one billion dollars a year.

c) *Sale and Lease of Media Rights:* The Terra II crew will include one thousand of the most talented musicians, artists, writers, scholars, filmmakers, architects, designers, artisans, etc. The activities of the Earth-city will become of great interest to the inhabitants of Terra I. The creative productions of the crew and the news chronicling of Starseed events will bring in more than one billion dollars a year.

The Starseed trust will, in addition, sell long-term rights to the inventions, productions, and creations of the population of Terra II for the years after the launching. The value of Terra II productivity will increase as the years of the voyage pass to the extent that these expressions will become literally priceless. Terra II will have already paid its own way, recompensed Terra I for the necessary supplies and equipment before launching. During the centuries of the voyage Terra II will be freely donating back to the home planet the fruits of its discoveries.

Even though the inhabitants of Terra II will become a new mutant race, their filial indebtedness, gratitude, and concern for the parental planet will continue. The very existence of Terra II as a higher-conscious evolute from Terra I will, it is expected, serve as a model and as an inspiration, and, perhaps, even as a conscience for Terra I to emulate.

October 1973

II. OTHER CIVILIZATIONS: THE PREHISTORY OF EARTH

II

"Now, the island was called Atlantis and was the heart of a great and wonderful empire. . . . But afterward there occurred violent earthquakes and floods, and in a single day and night of rain . . . the island of Atlantis . . . disappeared beneath the sea."

This description of a legendary prehistoric civilization's catastrophic end was given by Plato in his dialogue *Timaeus*. Since Plato's time more than two thousand books have been written about Atlantis, and the lost continent seems to stand in the modern mind as one of the more exotic variants on the utopia-paradise theme. Recently, much to the dismay of the conventional thinker, serious proponents of Atlantean research have begun their quest anew, insisting that Plato was relating to his students much more than allegorical lessons in civics and government. There is steadily amassing evidence to suggest that civilization on Earth has been cyclical and that there have been highly evolved cultures before the tradition which led to our own epoch. The recurrent search for Atlantis may be a physical expression of the half-forgotten memories of glorious times which lie in mankind's collective unconscious.

Atlantis is, of course, only part of the big picture, only a piece in the mosaic of the Cosmic Gameboard. Other legendary civilizations and lost ancient cities, although not as well known, beckon with equal allure. There is, for example, the allegedly older continent of Lemuria (also known as Mu), and the kingdoms of Agartha, Shamballah, and Ultima Thule.

Another persistent idea is that a civilization of great antiquity exists below the surface of the earth, and that inside a labyrinth of lighted caves dwells the Old Man, who over eons has evolved into the New Man, biding his time to resume his mastery of ground-level civilizations. Members of the elder race—some of whom are benign, others sinister, even malignant—maintain communication with the surface of the planet through tunnels which are said to exist in Tibet and South America, among other places. Some UFO researchers have claimed that those mysterious objects which occasionally streak across our skies originate from this underground civilization.

According to the psychic Mark Probert, a civilization called Yuga existed half a million years ago in the Himalaya Mountains. Yuga was completely destroyed in an earthquake that took the lives of nearly half of its 180 million inhabitants. The citizens of Yuga—and those of other lost worlds—were supposed to be highly evolved beings possessed of an advanced technology, such as the fabled crystal energy devices said to have powered Atlantis. More recent additions to the writings on precataclysmic civilizations have suggested that many of them may have had ties with extraterrestrial cultures, such as the one said to have existed on Lucifer, a planet which destroyed itself by atomic warfare and now remains only as the asteroid belt between Mars and Jupiter.

It is somehow offensive to modern man to consider the thought that a race of men—or hominids—may have created a civilization the equal, perhaps even the superior, of his own thousands, even millions, of years ago. Even UFOs may be discussed in the halls of academia and orthodoxy with a higher degree of seriousness than that granted to an examination of such matters as Atlantis and prehistoric "lost" cultures.

In his novel *The Ice People* Rene Barjavel described this peculiar psychological state of affairs. In Barjavel's science fiction accounting, an international assemblage of scientists explores the remains of a remarkably advanced civilization that existed 900 million years ago in Antarctica. This society had mastered a technology capable of having preserved one man and one woman down through the eons. In an aside to the narrative Barjavel has one of his scientist-protagonists observe that the conviction that man-as-a-species improves with time has no doubt arisen from an unconscious confusion with man-as-an-individual: "Man is a child before he becomes an adult. We—modern man—are adult. Those who lived before us could have been nothing but children. But perhaps it is time to ask ourselves whether perfection is not in childhood, whether the adult is not a child that has already begun to decline."

The demise of many of these magnificent and mighty societies is frequently thought to involve what Edgar Cayce called "earth changes." These are gigantic global cataclysms due to a reversal of Earth's magnetic poles—the sort of catastrophes about which Immanuel Velikovsky writes in *Earth in Upheaval* in explaining the miraculous destructions and disasters (the sun stopping in the sky, the Red Sea parting, etc.) recorded in many of the world's early writings. After the destruction of these civilizations, the accounts go, survivors founded many of the societies which evolved into our "modern" period. Thus the Egyptians, the Mayans, and other so-called ancient civilizations are only degenerated remnants of the original grandeur. According to many esoteric traditions, however, certain secret brotherhoods have kept alive the knowledge and true history of these lost civilizations, and are working behind the scenes for the benefit of humanity, revealing preserved wisdom, technical and otherwise, to selected individuals. These secret societies are said to form an "inner government" which is the real power behind the outer forms of social rule.

This skeletal description of those "cradles of antiquity" is romantically appealing in its mystery. We meet it time and again with endless variations. Are those lost civilizations merely airy figments based on some perennial wishful fantasy, some impossible human yearning for a return to a golden age? Are such visions of vibrant past civilizations only man's own symbolic inner projections of his brief glory before the dust of death overtakes him? Might the gods of Atlantis be unfulfilled archetypes? Is utopia, as the Greek roots of the word imply, "no place"? Or are these images of powerful empires which have waxed strong and conquered the earth based on actual prehistoric events?

In the case of Atlantis, at least, evidence has been steadily mounting to suggest that behind the legend is a concrete reality. Brad Steiger's *Atlantis Rising* and John Michell's *The View Over Atlantis* are two recent and worthy treatments of the subject. But even if we leave that legendary land out of the question for the moment, there now appears to be sound archaeological reason for accepting the idea of a global culture that existed long before Egypt achieved eminence— at least, Egypt in the sense that modern historians think of it. (Gerald Massey's following selection presents quite another view of Egypt's true age.) Anthropologist James Bailey's *The God-Kings and the Titans* gives ample evidence that there was regular transoceanic contact between the Old and New Worlds before the time of Christ, going back nearly eight thousand years before the present.

Even more devastating in its effect on orthodox concepts of history is the work of Professor Charles Hapgood at Keene State College in New Hampshire. Hapgood's book *Maps of the Ancient Sea Kings* is subtitled "Evidence of Advanced Civilization in the Ice Age" and presents a series of discoveries that he and his students made which in his words, "tend to prove that the tradition of medieval portolan map-making has an origin dating back to the end of the last Ice Age, and that some of these maps provide almost the first hard evidence of the existence of an advanced worldwide culture long antedating the rise of Egypt." One commentator notes that the most amazing piece of evidence for Hapgood's theory is the Piri Re'is map, which outlines the coast of Antarctica buried under miles of ice for tens of thousands of years. The map is named for a Turkish admiral living in the 1500s who claimed that it was based on sources thousands of years old. Only in 1949 were scientists able to map the invisible Antarctic coastline by using seismic soundings, yet the map was discovered in 1929 and then deposited in the Library of Congress. How was the aerial perspective obtained? Was it mapped from high in the air—perhaps in Atlantean aircraft or their equivalent?

These modern discoveries come to us by way of traditional methods of scientific investigation. Recently, however, a handful of pioneering archaeologists in the United States and Canada have been using psychic channels to augment their standard procedures, and have been dramatically rolling back the veils of time. The information obtained comes through psychometry and prediction, and it deals both with the history of various artifacts and with the location of new sites for future archaeological digs.

Professor J. Norman Emerson of the University of Toronto and Professor James Radford of Lewis and Clark Community College in Godfrey, Illinois, have independently demonstrated that psychics can psychometrize objects—that is, gain detailed, accurate, and new knowledge about ancient objects simply by touching and handling them. Even more startling is the find made near Flagstaff, Arizona, by a graduate student of anthropology and some of his faculty members. This discovery, first reported in late 1974 at the American Anthropological Association convention, was made by following instructions from a psychic in Oregon. The psychic described what would be found at the Arizona location to a depth of fifty feet. In 1973, when excavation reached the twenty-foot level, artifacts were found as predicted. Chipped-stone implements were unearthed in association with organic material that could be dated by radiocarbon-14 analysis. The results? Proof of human presence in North America twenty-five thousand years ago—thousands of years earlier than had previously been known!

More extensive versions of human evolution have been given by some who claim to receive their knowledge psychically or by revelation. We have selected material from the publications of Mark-Age of Miami, Florida, to illustrate this aspect of what has been called "intuitive archaeology." The authenticity of the Mark-Age claim, or of any other, must await verification by the scientific method. This is especially important because frequently the sources of alleged revelatory information disagree among themselves both in major and in minor ways. Mark-Age claims that humanity's origins go back more than 200 million years. This may appear unlikely at first, yet some hard evidence is available to indicate the presence on this planet of humanlike creatures capable of technology 500 million years ago! One piece of data cited by Brad Steiger in *Mysteries of Time and Space* is a fossilized sandal print with a squashed trilobite in it which was found in Utah in 1968.

A more modest view of man's beginnings was given nearly one hundred years ago by Gerald Massey—a view that for its time was as radical as Mark-Age's. Massey proposed that man originated in Africa. The evidence he cited in 1881 was inferential, however. Not until half a century later would Raymond Dart and Robert Broom find the first remains of *Australopithecus* ("southern ape-man") in the Transvaal of South Africa and date it at one million years before present—far older than the nearest competitor. Since then the case for the African origin of *Homo sapiens* has been clearly shown. Massey challenged the keepers of the history of the world, and won.

Massey's victory is not yet complete, though. In one aspect his thesis seems to require modification. Massey claims that (1) man originated in Africa and (2) the first humans were black—that is, of the Negroid race. However, archaeological evidence for the beginnings of the black race goes back only seven thousand years. Anthropologist Roger W. Wescott, author of *The Divine Animal,* points out that this is an anthropological enigma. There are distinctive bone structures characteristic of the black race, but none found so far date earlier than 5000 B.C. So we have an inconsistency here that needs further examination before Massey can be wholly reconciled with the modern historical record of human evolution. But two steps forward and one step back is a familiar move in The Reality Game.

NADA-YOLANDA is the spiritual name of Pauline Sharpe, born in Brooklyn, New York, in 1925. For ten years she was a magazine editor and freelance writer for radio and television in New York. From 1953–60 she was owner-manager of a personnel agency in Miami, Florida. In the late 1950s she began to develop what she terms her elementary spiritual powers (ESP). Mediumistic communications began to come from entities who identified themselves as ascended masters from the Hierarchal Board, the spiritual government of our solar system. In 1960 Yolanda and Mark, another "light worker," began Mark-Age. For the past fifteen years the organization has published monthly periodicals, five hardcover books, and has released educational and meditational tapes to prepare the planet for the Second Coming of Jesus, whose true name is said to be Sananda. Mark-Age is located at 327 N.E. 20th Terrace, Miami, Florida 33137.

EVOLUTION OF MAN

Abel and Cain

Genesis to Revelation in the Holy Bible is an outline of man's evolution prior to the fall of part of the race into Earth incarnation, of the subsequent devolution, of the reevolution to the true status as sons of God, of prophecies concerning the latter days of the two hundred and six million years of evolutionary experimenting on Earth, and indications of the next level of evolution beginning by the end of the twentieth century.

Man of Earth operates on three levels: Christ or etheric, operating in his light body in the fourth and higher dimensions; Adam or mortal, striving in his physical body on the third dimension of the Earth plane; and Eve or soul, functioning in his astral or emotional body in the astral or psychic planes. When Adam (conscious) and Eve (subconscious) dwell together on Earth (in the physical body), they bring forth the children Abel and Cain (thoughts and deeds of good and evil). Thus, the allegorical story of Adam and Eve and of Cain and Abel is partly a spiritual and a metaphysical teaching concerning man's own nature and creations.

But also it is historical in that it is based on the long struggle between two factions of the Elder race, the golden giants spoken of in the Holy Bible and other scriptures. The conflict between the Abel and the Cain groups of fourth dimensional man concerned their responsibility toward that part of the race which had descended, or had fallen or had been entrapped, into the third dimensional or physical matter of Earth. This third dimensional segment of man had devolved into the human or the subman form to use the Earth plane as a schoolroom for experimentation and exploration. Becoming entrapped in matter, it lost the use of spiritual and psychic senses and became confined to experiencing only through the five physical senses.

The Abels, particularly their leader Sananda, desired to teach their human brothers the powers and uses of the light or fourth dimensional body so as to raise them into the spiritual consciousness of the Elder race from which they had fallen. But the Cain clan was of the opinion that those in the third dimension had been placed on Earth to serve the Els, to be slaves. Since the life of the Cains was so pleasant and easy, they believed God preferred them, and that all they thought and did was favorable to Him.

Golden Giants

The Elder brothers served as rulers and priests over man in the third dimension of the Earth plane. In their etheric or light or fourth dimensional bodies, the Els could travel interdimensionally and interplanetarily throughout the solar system. They had memory recall of their past-life experiences and places of existence in the solar system. They were able to maintain the same body or vehicle in which to express on Earth for at least two hundred and fifty years.

Their social structure was truly communistic, in that no one owned anything. But their society was a class system, separated according to spiritual evolution and talents. The seat of one of their great tropical civilizations was a planned society developed around an inland sea now known as Salt Lake and the Salt Lake desert. Their settlements were built around the sea in circles or tiers, for grading or segregating purposes. The higher mountain ranges were set aside for spiritual retreats, schools, and training centers for priests. There the golden giants, the sons of God, grew in self-esteem, self-satisfaction and conceit.

The governmental capital of the Elders was in the area now known as Lake Tahoe in California and Nevada. The capital was built in concentric rows, according to their favorite custom. This was most suitable, due to the high ranges which completely closed it off and prevented the humans from entering the seat of government. This physical inaccessibility in no way hampered the Elders, who functioned in the fourth dimensional body. They could enter or leave either physically or in the light body, since they had control over both third and fourth dimensional frequencies.

Elder Race and Human Subrace

The third dimensional or human race operated in vehicles quite similar in structure to our present physical bodies. They were able to maintain those bodies for seventy to eighty-five years, a few living to be about one hundred. They understood most of the teachings of the Elder race and benefitted from the interdimensional and interplanetary travels and exchanges the golden giants enjoyed. But they were prohibited from participating in the inner temple practices and the esoteric mysteries. The higher ranges, both literally and symbolically, were off limits to them.

Eventually, some of the Elders believed they could use, command, even suppress, the further development and spiritual growth of the human group. Inevitably this trend led those of the Cains to think of the humans as less important in the one brotherhood of man under the Father-Mother God. So, instead of developing the intended teacher-student relationship to bring about the balanced third-with-fourth dimensional form which had been the original intent and purpose of the guardians composing the Hierarchal Board or spiritual government of our solar system, the situation became more separative and restrictive in nature and the relationship became that of masters and slaves.

When the council of the fourth dimensional race determined to eliminate any representation or consideration of those on the third dimensional frequency vibration, Sananda championed the concept that the Elder race was responsible for the human race and was supposed to teach the humans higher and proper uses of their inherent spiritual nature and powers, otherwise the latter could not evolve from the density of Earth plane matter. Arguments and strategies took possibly thousands of years, developing through one or more incarnations and societies toward the actual planning and execution. But the present Lake Tahoe area is where policies were determined and decisions were enforced.

In this argumentation, Sananda was not one of the governmental leaders but was at the spiritual headquarters of this race of golden giants. This was located in what are now the Grand Tetons of Wyoming, covering the Yellowstone Park area. It was the approximate center of their spiritual retreats and schools. Like the governmental capital, it was built in concentric circles encircling a desert and an inland sea. The main source of light and energy for the Elders at that time was the Temple of Venus, located in these mountains. To this day those who are spiritually intuned can feel the special radiations of brotherly love and mortal sacrifice that emanate from this focal point.

Abel and Cain Conflict

More and more the Abels and the Cains became separated in viewpoint and purpose, until finally some of the Abels, under Sananda's leadership, determined to lead an expedition across the inland sea covering what now are Utah and parts of Nevada. They moved to the northwest, crossing the Cascade Range in northern Washington, through what is now British Columbia to what we know as Alaska, which then had a temperate to semitropical climate.

The last battle between the two dissenting forces took place near the foothills of Mount Shasta, about two hundred miles northwest of Lake Tahoe. The Cains, in the majority, tried to prevent Sananda and his band of disciples and a small group of humans from leaving their control and rulership. This so-called war was fought on a higher level than the physical as we understand it. The battle was one of spiritual talents and wills. Some of the records of this titanic struggle have been transmuted into crystals of an etheric vibration and now are locked in the third dimensional frequency inside caves or tunnels around Mount Shasta in northern California.

It was here that Sananda met and passed his great test of that period. Through divine love he discovered the key in the vibration and mantram known as *Love God and Love One Another*. Use of this key raised the crystals and hid them beyond the selfishness and the spiritual pride and ego of those who did not want this racial history preserved or made available to future generations. This initiation gave Sananda the foothold and the authority thenceforth to preside over the Seventh Ray of Divine Love, Peace and Rest for all third dimensional mankind during the dispensation which followed. Eventually it led to his Hierarchal Board appointment as Prince or spiritual ruler of Earth.

Yet, in spite of having passed through this grave trial, Sananda as leader of the Abels was overpowered; Cain slew Abel. This prevented him from taking command then and there over the future evolvement of the third dimensional race on Earth. The human subrace thus lost its opportunity for direct, in-person training in a peaceful, constructive, brotherly pattern.

The Hierarchal Board then banished all the golden giants to Venus, home of the Third Ray functions and aspects in our solar system, for their further cleansings and greater dedications. Although they had made mistakes and had lost a golden opportunity to express greater love for a less evolved race, they were not lost or punished in the mortal sense of the term.

Awaiting Sananda

This war of the golden giants is perpetuated in our racial memory through the many allegories, myths, legends and folk tales to be found in nearly all cultures and societies. Amongst the American Indians, for example, are many stories relating to this, including the coming of man from the skies to visit Earth. Tribes in the north and the west still cherish secret places of worship which commemorate the home and the temples of Earth's spiritual leader: Sananda, the golden one. Through their arts and crafts they still pass down to present generations the story of his struggles for mankind. These appear in their tribal dances, hieroglyphic tablets, tapestry and pottery. But only a few of today's Indians have been initiated in this knowledge.

The Salinas Valley, near the coast of central California north of Santa Barbara, is very holy ground. It has been protected by Indian and devic forces for the return of Sananda. It was there that the Abels had been able to find some peace and harmony, with a small segment of them solidifying their resources and implanting a number of vibratory rates for eventual resettlement.

The history there is confused because some wished to pursue their goals, whereas others decided to retreat and to declare a truce with the Cains, letting the higher forces determine balance in ages to come. But nothing was resolved except the implanting of a high rate of energy, which since that time has been felt strongly by those sensitive to higher frequency rates.

It has been a favorite base of operations for etheric spacecraft. Even during the days of the Amerindians here, huge spacecraft would land from time to time to allow conversing with the chiefs and the holy men. This did not occur at frequent intervals, but perhaps every two hundred and fifty to three hundred years. Enough source of interest was secured from these contacts to cause legends and the beginning of communication between those in the higher planes and the remnants left on Earth.

It is not easy to convey the importance of these contacts. They are part of the divine project and system of never completing a segment until it has been fulfilled via spiritual enjoyment and satisfaction. No two systems are alike. No two plans follow the same course of action. Only are there similarities and patterns projected in order to show a divine pattern of procedure in the upliftment or evolution of any specific job well done via divine fiat.

Spiritual Processing

"Uriel. Let us begin to know this sameness of pattern so we can begin to detect the schematic of spiritual processings. All are one in the Divine, and no two parts of the One can ever be separated. Therefore, no matter how highly developed a segment is, it can never lose touch or communication with another part of the whole or the one divine object.

"Let us know, therefore, that those called the Elder race are no more separable from man of Earth. But they take on different form. They know different jobs and responsibilities and they know they are obligated to their function until all are raised to the level within the same specific species or evolutionary growth pattern. This is not easy to explain, because so much time is involved in the process that man thus loses touch with all the various parts of the whole plan and the oneness which is God.

"As is indicated here, many are on Earth from the Elder race or White Brotherhood and have not fallen into the trap of three-dimensional feeling or ensnarement. But they still can take bodily form and not stand out amongst those of Earth because their nature is so similar to those in that revolting trap of three-dimensional cyclic development.

"However, every time they take on body and work within the mold of this segment of the one race, the sons of God, they change, reset, formulate new concepts and precipitate a higher action within man's racial patterns and thinking. This takes billions of years. Since man is in no rush to reach his spiritual reevolution, it is slow in turning around from mortal into immortal intunements.

"He will have to see gradually the benefits of operating spiritual vehicles at his disposal before he is willing to overcome his mortal aspects which he himself created along with devic and elemental kingdoms at his disposal and under his command. I am Uriel, lord of light and love divine. Amen."

Lemuria and Atlantis

Regrettably, the destructive motives, thoughts and acts of the Cains greatly lowered the standard or level of frequency for the Earth. But despite this they were able to maintain firm control over the planet through a series of civilizations. Among the more recent were Lemuria or Mu, in what is now mostly the Pacific Ocean and the Pacific coast of the United States, and Atlantis, from the eastern coast of the United States across the Atlantic Ocean to the western coast of Europe.

The height of their successes and developments was approximately twenty-six thousand years ago; the final and last days of their destruction were twelve to thirteen thousand years ago, which is about as far back as we have had acceptable physical documentation. Still, their approach was not based on the divine law and truth of *Love God and Love One Another*. Instead, they continued to use force, domination, control and various types of dictatorships against one another. Through such designs of destruction, the law of cause and effect brought them and their civilizations to yet another cleansing, referred to as the great flood of Noah's time.

In the hundreds of years it took for the final destruction of Lemuria, the lower grades of workers in that civilization took the seed or the pattern of their bodily forms, by means of migrations, to Alaska, the northern United States, and Canada, with many of them escaping to the islands of the Pacific which then were the mountain peaks of that sinking continent. The higher grades of fourth dimensional form no longer were operable on this planet. And until the return of Sananda to Earth, they will not be operable for the majority of mankind here now. He personally will teach greater compassion and love in the Golden Era, beginning about 2000 A.D. By then the memory scar of this advanced but degenerate society should be healed, with all spiritual conceit and pride removed from the subconscious tracks of the race.

It may seem that the transmutation of mortal into spiritual consciousness has been long and difficult. But what the Elders did achieve during the age of the golden giants was an anchoring for a future racial pattern. They succeeded in leaving their imprint on the third dimensional frequency of this planet, even though it has taken the masses of mankind millions of years of physical and spiritual evolution to rise to another peak of development that will raise the third dimensional form into fourth dimensional frequency and expression.

During the times of Lemuria and Atlantis the spiritual Hierarchy came to the sad realization that the human race on Earth still was not ready to complete its final, seventh step into fourth dimensional or spiritual consciousness. So, a new plan and strategy were conceived. Presently we are in those latter days of the greater, overall, longer ranged, two-hundred-and-six-million-year program. This Mark Age period and program therefore are the last judgment spoken of in the Holy Bible.

Return of Sananda

Each one's individualized Christ or I Am presence and the collective spiritual organization headed by the Hierarchy of this solar system force all souls, and the race itself, to return and to work out their karma. That which is sown must be reaped. So it is that Sananda, the Christ leader of the Abels, not only has earned the privilege but is obliged to lead mankind of Earth into spiritual evolution. Continually, in various roles and incarnations, he has returned to guide the humans out of their bondage in this dense, material, third dimension.

However, from the time the Hierarchy banished the golden giants to Venus, and even through the thousands of years of Lemuria's great civilization, Sananda did not take up physical incarnation on Earth. But this did not prevent him from guiding, teaching and instructing man from the inner planes in much the same manner he has been doing in these latter days, the Mark Age period.

In the last days of Atlantis, Sananda did incarnate on Earth in order to guide the cleansing and to preserve a certain amount of balance, understanding and perseverance within the remnant of that civilization. This return was in the generations of Noah. Noah was not an individual, but was that group of men on Earth which did the will of God. Through their spiritual knowledge and experience they managed to preserve one male and one female of each species. This is symbolic reference to their ability to maintain the proper balance of positive and negative polarities needed to perpetuate each type of life form on the physical plane. The leader of the Noahs was Sananda.

The last thirty or forty years of the twentieth century are the latter days. This end time is not the end of the world but is the final judgment or the final campaign of the most recent, a twenty-six-thousand-year hierarchal plan and program to raise all on Earth into the fourth dimension. All that the sons of God have worked for in this solar system for the past two hundred and six million years is about to culminate, preparing the way for a new cycle of evolution. But one of the major tasks remaining in this Mark Age or latter-day period is that of preparing the way for the return to Earth of its spiritual ruler, Sananda; who, in his last Earth incarnation, was Jesus of Nazareth.

Spiritual evolution occurs in orderly, spiraling stages. At the peak period of each age in the evolutionary struggle of man on this planet, Sananda as Prince of Earth has reappeared to lift, to instruct and to help in the gradual transmutation of man's expression on this third dimensional frequency. Each of his incarnations, for each period of evolution of man on Earth, initiated and patterned another firm step in the ladder of spiritual growth. Some of Sananda's better-known incarnations on Earth are given in the glossary of this book [*Evolution of Man*].

Finally, as Jesus of Nazareth, he fulfilled the prophecies that are found in almost all religious scriptures concerning the anointed one or the fully spiritualized man on the third dimension in the higher body, the light or resurrected Christ form. By transmuting his third dimensional body into his fourth dimensional or light body within this Earth frequency vibration, this way showed for man on this plane dramatized the pattern for all to follow in the return to being fully functioning members of the Elder race.

MAJOR EVOLUTIONARY CYCLES

206,000,000 Years Ago

• Elder race of giants, fourth dimensional man in his etheric or light body, began experimenting with the elements and forms on Earth.

• Allegory, parables, myths and legends—such as Adam and Eve in the Garden of Eden, and all such scriptural references of most religions on Earth today, including such Greek and Roman myths—refer to this period of trial and error by fourth dimensional man with third dimensional substance and form.

• Etheric man helps to form land masses of Lemuria (Mu) by experimenting with the third dimensional elements of the planet.

26,000,000 Years Ago

• Final fall of man. Many of the Elder race became entrapped in third dimensional forms with which they were experimenting.

• Two schools of thought, the Cains and the Abels, developed. The Cains wished to dominate and to enslave the fallen, third dimensional subrace of man. The Abels believed they should teach the human subrace to rise back into the fourth dimensional form and to use their inherent etheric talents as sons of God.

• Caste system formulated: (a) those who maintained their fourth dimensional body and talents; (b) those who experienced third dimensional, physical sensations and remembered fourth dimensional or spiritual energies; (c) those who lost contact with their Sonship relationship and fourth dimensional form and were lost in physical or material embodiment and reembodiment or reincarnation.

• Battle of the giants. Cains defeated the Abels, who were led by Sananda.

• Beginning of Hierarchal Board plans in our solar system to raise up the human subrace trapped on Earth between third dimensional form and astral planes.

• Lemurian societies or group civilizations began to develop, approximately from western U.S.A. through the Pacific Ocean and as far west as Mid-East and Far-East lands. Rise and fall of many groups, societies and civilizations.

206,000 Years Ago

• Hierarchal Board of the solar system, in the etheric dimensions, determined that controversy and continuation of the caste system started by Cains would not allow the Lemurian societies to achieve the goal of raising the entrapped race back to etheric forms while on third dimensional frequency.

• Elder race in fourth dimensional form withdrew from planet Earth.

• Contacts between third dimensional humans and fourth dimensional Elder race, only by etheric spacecraft and inner plane communion.

• Emotional and mental bodies of mankind in third dimensional form were anchored.

• Preparation of land mass of Atlantis, from east coast U.S.A. and Caribbean area to western Europe.

• Indian tribes, families, societies throughout South, Central and North Americas were the links between the Lemurian races and Atlantean groups.

26,000 Years Ago

• Height of Atlantean societies and civilizations. Attempt to equalize all.

• Peak of material, physical, third dimensional form for mankind on Earth.

• Determination by Hierarchal Board that superiority, domination, misuse of powers and knowledge would not allow Atlantis to succeed in spiritual goals.

• Beginning of breakup of land masses, both Atlantean and Lemurian areas; which sustained only remnants of its civilizations, such as the aboriginal societies of today.

10,000–13,000 Years Ago

• Final submerging of land masses and remnants; the period known as the Noahs and great flood.

• Beginning of recorded history of our present societies and civilizations.

• Atlantean cultures moved east to Europe and west again across the U.S.A., retracing steps of previous Lemurians two hundred and six thousand years ago who had moved east across the Americas to start Atlantis.

2000 Years Ago to Present: Piscean Age

• Sananda, leader of the Abels, returned to Earth as Jesus of Nazareth to redemonstrate fourth dimensional or etheric talents in present third dimensional matter.

• Demonstration by Sananda as Jesus of resurrection and ascension as the pattern for all men to follow equally; no exceptions, no caste system.

• Promise by Sananda to return as Jesus from the ascended or fourth dimensional state in the end days or latter-day period now known as Mark Age period and program.

2000 Years Ahead: Aquarian Age

• Return of planet, mankind and all life form into the fourth dimensional frequency vibration; the etheric form, for the race of man.

• Interchange with man of other planets, planes and dimensions in our solar system. Brotherhood, unity, seventh step of spiritual achievement. Domination of Seventh Ray of Love, Peace, Rest.

• Spiritual government on Earth under the Prince of our planet, Sananda of the Hierarchal Board. Reentry into the federation of planets in our solar system, and exchange with the Hierarchal Board or Elder brothers.

GERALD MASSEY (1828–1907) was a self-educated British social philosopher, writer, and poet. He served as the model for Felix Holt in George Eliot's novel *Felix Holt the Radical*. His life was characterized by a search for truth about the nature and origins of humanity. This led him to publish in 1881 a monumental work in two volumes, *A Book of the Beginnings*, from which this selection was excerpted. The subtitle to the work reads, "Containing an attempt to recover and reconstitute the lost origins of the myths and mysteries, types and symbols, religion and language, with Egypt for the mouthpiece and Africa as the birthplace." *A Book of the Beginnings* was recently reprinted (University Books, 1974), along with Massey's other two-volume work, *Ancient Egypt* (Samuel Weiser, 1974).

THE PREHISTORICAL PERIOD OF MAN IN EGYPT AND AFRICA

Travelers who have climbed and stood upon the summit of the Great Pyramid of Gizeh tell us how all that is most characteristic of Egypt is then and there in sight. To the south is the long Necropolis of the Desert, whose chief monuments are the Pyramids of Abooseer [Abusir], Dashoor [Dahshur], and Sakkara. That way lies the granite mountain flood gate of the waters, which come winding along from the home of the hippopotami to leap down into the Nile valley at last with a roar and a rush for the Mediterranean Sea. To the west are the Libyan hills and a limitless stretch of yellow sand. Again, there is a gray desert beyond the white line of Cairo, under the Mokattam hills.

And through these sandy, stony desert borders, Egypt runs alongside of its river in a double line of living green, the northward-flowing waters and their meadowy margin broadening beneficently into the Delta. Underfoot is the Great Pyramid, still an inscrutable image of might and of mystery, strewn round with reliquary rubbish that every whirl of wind turns over as leaves in a book, revealing strange readings of the past; every chip and shard of the fragments not yet ground down to dusty nothing may possibly have their secret to tell. . . .

Egypt is often called Kam, the Black Land, and Kam does signify black; the name probably applied to the earliest inhabitants whose type is the Kam or Ham of the Hebrew writers. But Kam is likewise to create, and this was the created land; visibly created like the gum from the tree by droppings. Kam is the root and has the value of the word *chemistry,* and the land of Kam was the result of nature's chemistry, aided by the Hatches or Dams.

The land of Egypt was reborn annually as the product of the waters was added layer by layer to the soil. Three months' inundation and nine months' dry made up the year. The nine months coincided with the human period of gestation, a fact most fruitful in suggestion, as everything seems to have designedly been in this birthplace of ideas. They dated their year from the first quickening heave of the river, coincident with the summer solstice and the heliacal rising of the Dog Star. The Nile not only taught them to look up to the heavens and observe and register there the time and tide of the seasons, but also how to deal with the water by means of dikes, locks, canals, and reservoirs, until their system of hydraulics grew a science, their agriculture an art, and they obtained such a mastery over the waters as finally fitted them for issuing forth to conquer the seas and colonize the world.

The river likewise gave them their first lessons in political economy and the benefits of barter, by affording the readiest means of exchange. Its direction runs in that of longitude, or meridian, with all the products ranged on either side like stalls in a street; so close to the waterway was the cultivated soil. It crossed through every degree of Egypt's latitude and became the commercial traveler of the whole land, carrying on their trade for the enrichment of all.

Generally speaking, the monuments offer no direct clue to the origin of the people; they bring us face to face with nothing that tells of a beginning or constitutes the bridge over which we can pass to look for it in other lands. Like the goddess Neith, Egypt came from herself, and the fruit she bore was a civilization, an art, a mythology, a topology, absolutely autochthonous.

We see no sign of Egypt in embryo; of its inception, growth, development, birth, nothing is known. It has no visible line of descent, and so far as modern notions go, no offspring; it is without genesis or exodus.

When first seen Egypt is old and gray, at the head of a procession of life that is illimitably vast. It is as if it always had been. There it stands in awful ancientness, like its own pyramid in the dawn, its sphinx among the sands, or its palm amid the desert.

From the first, all is maturity. At an early monumental stage they possess the art of writing, a system of hieroglyphics, and the ideographs have passed into the form of phonetics, which means a space of time unspanable, a stage of advance not taken by the Chinese to this day.

The monuments testify that a most ancient and original civilization is there; one that cannot be traced back on any line of its rootage to any other land. How ancient, none but an Egyptologist who is also an evolutionist dares to dream. At least twelve horizons will have to be lifted from the modern mind to let in the vistas of Egypt's prehistoric past. For this amazing apparition coming out of darkness on the edge of the desert is the head of an immense procession of life—issuing out of a past from which the track has been obliterated like footprints in the shifting wilderness of sand.

The life was lived, and bit by bit deposited the residual result. The tree rooted in the waste had to grow and lay hold of the earth day by day, year after year, for countless ages. Through the long night they groped their way, their sole witnesses the watchers on the starry walls, who have kept their register yet to be read in the astral myths, for the heavens are Egypt's records of the past.

The immeasurable journey in the desert had to be made, and was made step by step through that immemorial solitude which lies behind it, as certainly as that the river has had to eat its own way for hundreds of thousands of years through the sandstone, the limestone, and the granite in order that it might at last deposit the alluvial riches at the outlet, even though the stream of Egypt's long life has left no such visible register on Earth as the waters of old Nile have engraved in gulf-like hieroglyphics upon the stony tablets of geological time. The might and majesty of Egypt repose upon a past as real as the uplifting rock of the Great Pyramid, and the base, however hidden, must be in proportion to the building.

They are there, and that is nearly all that has been said; how or when they got there is unknown. These things are usually spoken of as if the Egyptians had done as we have, found them there. The further we can look back at Egypt, the older it grows. Our acquaintance with it through the Romans and Greeks makes it modern. Also their own growth and the shedding of the past kept on modernizing the myths, the religion, the types. It will often happen that a myth of Egyptian creation may be found in some distant part of the world in a form far older than has been retained in Egypt itself.

It is a law of evolution that the less-developed type is the oldest in structure, reckoning from a beginning. This is so with races as with arts. The hieroglyphics are older than letters, they come next to the living gesture signs that preceded speech. But less-developed stages are more often found out of Egypt than in it because Egypt went on growing and sloughing off signs of age, whilst the Maori, the Lap, the Papuan, the Fijian suffered arrest and consequent decadence. And the earlier myth may be recovered by aid of the arrested ruder form.

The Stone Age of Egypt is visible in the stone knife, which continued to be used for the purpose of circumcision, and in the preparation of their mummies. The stone knife was a type persisting from the time of the stone implements. The workers in bronze, iron, and other metals did not go back to choose the flint weapon.

The antiquity of Egypt may be said to have ended long before the classical antiquity of the moderns begins, and except in the memorials of myth and language it was premonumental. We know that when Egypt first comes in sight it is old and gray. Among the most ancient of the recipes preserved are prescriptions for dying the hair. There are several recipes for hair dye or washes found in the Ebers Papyrus, and one of these is ascribed to the lady Skheskh, mother of Teta, the first king on the monuments after Menes. This is typical. They were old enough more than six thousand years ago for leprosy to be the subject of profound concern. A manuscript of the time of Ramses II says:

"This is the beginning of the collection of receipts for curing leprosy. It was discovered in a very ancient papyrus inclosed in a writing-case under the feet [of a statue] of the god Anubis, in the town of Sakhur, at the time of the reign of his majesty the defunct King Sapti," who was the fifth Pharaoh of the First Dynasty, in the list of Abydos.

Leprosy was indigenous to Egypt and Africa; it has even been conjectured that the white Negroes were produced by it, as the albinos of the black race.

The most ancient portion known of the ritual . . . seven thousand years old, shows that not only was the Egyptian mythology founded on the observation of natural phenomena at the time established, but the mythology had then passed into the final or eschatological phase, and a system of spiritual typology was already evolved from the primordial matter of mythology. The text of chapter CXXX [in Massey's book] is said in the annotation to have been found in the reign of King Housap-ti, who, according to M. Deveria, was the Usephais of Manetho, the fifth king of the First Dynasty, and lived over six thousand years since; at that time certain parts of the sacred book were discovered as antiquities of which the tradition had been lost. And this is the chapter of "vivifying the soul for ever."

The traces of evolution and development are not to be expected upon the monuments which begin with some of the finest art yet found. Evidence of the primeval nature of the people is not likely to be found contemporary with the perfection of their art. The ascent is out of sight, and the Stone Age of Egypt is buried beneath a hundred feet of Nile sediment, but the opponents of evolution gain nothing by the negative facts. Perfect art, language, and mythology did not alight ready-made in the valley of the Nile; and if the ascent be not traceable here, neither is it elsewhere. There is not a vestige of proof that these were an importation from other lands.

It will be maintained in *A Book of the Beginnings* [from which this chapter was extracted] that the oldest mythology, religion, symbols, and language had their birthplace in Africa, that the primitive race of Kam came thence, and the civilization attained in Egypt emanated from that country and spread over the world.

The most reasonable view of the evolutionary theory—and those who do not accept that have not yet begun to think, for lack of a starting point—is that the black race is the most ancient, and that Africa is the primordial home. It is not necessary to show that the first colonizers of India were Negroes, but it is certain that the black Buddha of India was imaged in the Negroid type. In the black Negro god, whether called Buddha or Sut-Nahsi, we have a datum. They carry in their color the proof of their origin. The people who first fashioned and worshiped the divine image in the Negroid mold of humanity must, according to all knowledge of human nature, have been Negroes themselves. For the blackness is not merely mystical; the features and the hair of Buddha belong to the black race, and Nahsi is the Negro name. The genetrix represented as the *Dea Multimammae,* the Diana of Ephesus, is found as a black figure, nor is the hue mystical only, for the features are as Negroid as were those of the black Isis in Egypt.

We cannot have the name of Kam or Ham applied ethnologically without identifying the type as that of the black race.

True, the type on the earliest monuments had become liker to the later so-called Caucasian, but even the word Caucasian tells also of an origin in the Kaf or Kaffir. Philology will support ethnology in deriving from Africa, and not from Asia.

The type of the Great Sphinx, the age of which is unknown, but it must be of enormous antiquity, is African, not Aryan or Caucasian.

The Egyptians themselves never got rid of the thick nose, the full lip, the flat foot, and weak calf of the Nigritian type, and these were not additions to any form of the Caucasian race. The Nigritian elements are primary, and survive all modifications of the old Egyptians made in the lower land. The single Horus-lock, the Rut, worn as a divine sign by the child-Horus in Egypt, is a distinguishing characteristic of the African people, among whom were the Libyans who shaved the left side of the head, except the single lock that remained drooping down. This was the emblem of Horus the Child, continued as the type of childhood from those children of the human race, the Africans. Yet the Egyptians held the Libyans in contempt because they had not advanced to the status of the circumcised, and they inflicted the rite upon their conquered enemies in death, by excising the Karunata.

The African custom of children going undressed until they attained the age of puberty was also continued by the Egyptians. Princesses went as naked as commoners, royalty being no exception to the rule. At that age the children assumed the Horus-lock at the left side of the head as the sign of puberty and posterity.

Diodorus Siculus declares that the Egyptians claimed to have sent out colonies over the whole world in times of the remotest antiquity. They affirmed that they had not only taught the Babylonians astronomy, but that Belus and his subjects were a colony that went out of Egypt. This is supported by Genesis in the generations of Noah. By substituting Egypt for the mythical Ark we obtain a real starting point from which the human race goes forth, and can even utilize the Hebrew list of names.

Diodorus Siculus was greatly impressed with the assertions of the priests respecting the numerous emigrations including the colonies of Babylon and Greece, and the Jewish exodus, but they named so many in diverse parts of the world that he shrank from recording them upon hearsay and word of mouth, which is a pity, as they may have been speaking the truth. He tells us they had sacred books transmitted to them from ancient times, in which the historical accounts were recorded and kept and then handed on to their successors.

In the inscription of Una belonging to the Sixth Dynasty, we find the earliest known mention of the Nahsi (Negroes) who were at that remote period dominated by Egypt and conscripted for her armies. In this, one of the oldest historical documents, the Negroes from Nam, the Negroes from Aruam, the Negroes from Uaua (Nubia), the Negroes from Kau, the Negroes from Tatam are enumerated as being in the Egyptian army. Una, the governor of the south and superintendent of the dock, tells us how the Pharaoh commanded him to sail to some locality far south to fetch a white stone sarcophagus from a place named as the abode of the rhinoceros. This is recorded as a great feat.

"It came thence, brought in the great boat of the inner palace with its cover, a door, two jambs, and a pedestal [or basin]. Never before was the like done by any servant."

The Egyptians literally moved mountains and shaped them in human likeness of titanic majesty. "I dragged as hills great monuments [for statues] of alabaster [for carving] giving them life in the making," says Ramses III, who built a wall 150 feet in depth, 60 feet below ground, and 90 feet above. They carried blocks of syenite by land and water, weighing 900 tons. It was said by Champollion that the cathedral of Notre Dame might be placed in one of the halls of the Temple at Karnak as a small central ornament; so vast was the scale of their operations. They painted in imperishable colors; cut leather with our knife of the leather-cutters; wove with the same shuttles; used what is with us the latest form of blow-pipe, for the whitesmith. It is the height of absurdity or the profoundest ignorance to suppose that they did not build ships and launch navies. The oarblade or paddle, called the kherp, is the emblem of all that is first and foremost, excellent and surpassing, the scepter of majesty, the sign of rule. Thus to paddle and steer are synonymous with sovereignty. Shipbuilding yards were extant and are shown to be busy in the time of the pyramid builders. And here is Una, the great sailor, superintendent of the dock, going so far south that the geographical locality is out of sight. But the name shows that it was the land of the hippopotamus or rhinoceros.

At this time, then, ships of war were built in the south, of considerable dimensions, over 105 feet long, together with the Uskhs, or broad ships, in which the armies of Egypt, composed of enrolled Æthiops and Negroes, were floated down the river to fight her battles against those on the land.

Egypt, and not India, is the common cradle of all we have in common, east, west, north, and south, all round the world. The language, beliefs, rites, laws, and customs went out to India, but did not return thence by means of the apocryphal Aryan migrations. The Indian affinity with our European folklore and fairyology is neither first nor final; 'tis but the affinity of a collateral relationship. Egypt supplied the parent source, the inventive mind, the propagating migratory power. In Egypt alone, we shall find the roots of the vast tree, whose boughs and branches have extended to a worldwide reach.

The greatest difficulty in creation is the beginning, not the finishing, and to the despised black race we have at length to turn for the birth of language, the beginnings of all human creation, and, as the

Arabic saying puts it, let us "honor the first although the followers do better."

Among the Æthiops of many thousand years ago there lived and labored the unknown humanizers of our race who formulated the first knowledge of natural facts gathered from the heavens above and the earth beneath, and the waters of the wonderful river which talked to them as with a voice from out of the infinite, and who twined the earliest sacred ties of the family-fold to create cohesion and strength and purity of life; men of the dark and despised race, the black blood-royal, that fed the red, yellow, and white races, and got the skin somewhat blanched in Egypt; the men who had dwelt in the Nile valley, and by the fountains of its waters in the highlands above, so long in unknown ages past that the Negroid type of form and complection had modified into the primitive Egyptian; so long, that in this race the conical head of the *Gorillidae* had time to grow and bulge into the frontal region and climb into the human crown, until Egypt at length produced and sent forth her long-heads, the melanochroid type found in diverse parts of the world. Blackness in the beginning did not depend on, and was not derived merely from, the climatic conditions; they modified, but did not create. Once the black race is extinct it can never be repeated by climature. Its color was the result of origin from the animal prototype, and not only from nearness to the sun. On the oldest known monuments the Egyptians portray themselves as a dusky race, neither Negroid nor Caucasian. Livingstone found the likeness of these in the typical Negro of central Africa, or rather he affirms that the typical Negro found in central Africa is to be seen in the ancient Egyptians, not in the native of the west coast.

It is possible that the first intellectual beginnings of the race and of the Egyptians themselves were about the sources of the Nile. In our researches we shall find that at the remotest vanishing points of the decaying races we continually come upon the passing presence of Egypt, diminishing on the horizon in the far-off distance from the world she once engirdled round with language and laws, rites and customs, mythology and religion. Wheresoever the explorers dig deepest, in Akkad, Carchemish, Palestine, Greece, or Italy, they discover Egypt. And the final conclusion seems inevitable, that the universal parent of language, of symbolism, of early forms of law, of art and science, is Egypt, and that this fact is destined to be established along every line of research.

If we find that each road leads back to Egypt, we may safely infer that every road proceeded from Egypt.

In the very morning of the times these men emerged from out of the darkness of a prehistoric and pre-eval past from one center to bear the origins to the ends of the earth. The scattered fragments still remain, whereby they can be traced more or less along each radiating line to prove the common model, the common kinship, and the common center.

We learn from Syncellus (*Chronicon* li.) and Eusebius (*Chronicon* vi.) that among the Egyptians there was a certain tablet called the Old Chronical, containing thirty dynasties in 113 descents, during the long period of 36,525 years.

The first series of princes was that of the Auritae, the second was that of the Mestraeans, the third of the Egyptians. The first divine name in the series is one that is earlier than the sun, given through the Greek as Hephaestus, to whom no time is assigned, because this deity was apparent both by night and day. This contains matter of great moment not yet read nor readable until we have seen more of Egypt's mythology. The present point is that the Auritae princes coincide with the reign of Hephaestus as the beginning.

The Auritae are of course the Ruti of monumental Egypt, the typical name of the race of men *par excellence*. But the prefixed Au will add something to our knowledge of the premonumental Rut. Au in Egyptian means the oldest, the primordial. The word Au is the Egyptian "was," and the Au-rut means the race that was, the first and oldest race of men. Au is a modified form of Af. Both Au and Af signify "born of." The name of Africa is derived from this root Af or Au. The tongue of Egypt tells us that Af-rui-ka is the inner land, born of, literally the birthplace. They knew of no other. Thus the Auritae were the Af-ritae, people of the birthplace in Africa. But the Af in Egyptian has a still earlier form in Kaf, and the Afritae become the primordial Faf-ritae. The Kaffirs have preserved the primal shape of the word signifying the first, the embryotic, aboriginal root-race of men.

The laws of language prove that the Auritae, the first princes of this long line of descent given at 36,525 years, were Kaf-ritae; and the laws of evolution prove the primal race, so far as we can get back, to be the black people. The Kaf is the black, dog-headed, almost human monkey. Ape and Kaf are named as the first preceding man, and there was no other name known for the first than Kaf, Af, Au, or Ap. The Kaf-ruit name has the same relation to the Ruti of the monuments that the ape, the pre-man, has to man.

Egyptian monumental history begins with the name of Menes. The chronology made out by different Egyptologists is variously recorded thus:

Bunsen	3623 B.C.
Lepsius	3892 B.C.
Lauth	4157 B.C.
Brugsch	4415 B.C.
Unger	5613 B.C.
Boeckh	5702 B.C.

Brugsch-Bey makes use of the latest data, and also of the investigations of Lieblein into the pedigree of twenty-five court architects; he concludes that the year 4455 B.C. is about the nearest approximation that can be made to a correct date for the era of Menes. And, as nearly as can be calculated, the spring equinox first occurred in the sign of the Bull, 4560 B.C.

In Egyptian symbolry the celestial is primordial and continually contains the clue to the terrestrial; the earthly is but the image of the heavenly. Thus the time of Menes is none the less real, and is all the more verifiable if astronomically dated. In Egypt the only fixed or definite era was astronomical. All the reports show that prior to the period identified with the name of Menes the Egyptians reckoned vast lengths of time as "reigns" of some kind, sacred to monarchs left without human name, because representative of the divinities, and beyond these was the direct dominion of the gods.

These last reigns are mythical, but not therefore fabulous in the modern sense. The truth is that a great deal of history and mythology have to change places with each other; the history has to be resolved into myth, whilst the myths will be found to contain the only history. The ancient fables were veiled facts, and when we can get no further records on the earth, it is in the heavens we must seek for the Egyptian chronology. It is the astronomical mythology solely that will reveal to us what the Egyptians and other nations meant by dynasties of deities and the development of series and succession in their rule. It was by astronomical numbers that the Chaldeans reckoned the age of their sacred books.

"In Egypt, if anywhere," says Diodorus, "the most accurate observations of the positions and movements of the stars have been made. Of each of these they have records extending over an incredible series of years. They have also accurately observed the courses and position of the planets, and can truly predict eclipses of the sun and moon." Diogenes Laertius states that they possessed observations of 373 solar eclipses and 832 lunar; these were probably total or almost total.

The Egyptians spanned spaces so vast that nothing short of astronomical cycles could be the measure and record of time and period for them. Plato, who spent some thirteen years in Egypt trying to get into the penetralia of their knowledge, reports that they had divine hymns of songs worthy of the deity which were held in round numbers to be ten thousand years old. He tells us that he does not speak figuratively, but that they are real and credible figures. The authorship of these was assigned to the great mother Isis. These figures are not to be utilized forthwith or straightway; that can only be done by going round to work, when we shall see that such hymns probably dated from the time when the sun was in the sign of Virgo (Isis) at the spring equinox. When Plato wrote, the color of the vernal equinox was coincident with the sign of Aries, and the time was just over ten thousand years since it left the sign of Virgo.

Previous to the reign of Menes, the Papyrus of Turin and other documents assign a period of 5,613 years to twenty-three reigns. These of course are not mortal reigns. They are identified with the Shus-en-Har, the followers, servants, or worshipers of Horus. A period of 13,420 years is also assigned to the Shus-en-Har.

Nineteen Han are likewise mentioned. The Han is a cycle, and these were probably cycles of Anup or Sothis, the Dog Star, whose period was 1,461 years, nineteen of which make a total of 27,759 years. Two dynasties of gods and demigods were collected from the Temple Records and rectified by Lepsius (from the various Greek chronological writers); these begin with Ptah (Hephaistos) and end with "Bitus." Of these:

Ptah	reigned	9,000	years
Helios	reigned	1,000	years
Agathodaimon	reigned	700	years
Kronus (Seb)	reigned	500	years
Osiris	reigned	400	years
Typhon	reigned	350	years
Horus	reigned	1,800	years
Bitus	reigned	70	years

After this, says Eusebius, "came a series of reigns down to Bitus during 13,900 years"; meaning the above list ending with Horus. It is clear that Bitus has no business to be in the list of divine rulers. Nor is it necessary to assume with Bunsen that 13,800 years of reigns imply hero-worship in the modern sense. These like the preceding may have been astronomical cycles, but measured also by the reigns of sacerdotal kings, as according to Jamblichus, Bitis was a prophet of Ammon at Thebes, instead of divine names. According to Eusebius, Manetho had computed a total period of 24,900 years. Such numbers need not be rejected because they do not offer the direct means of correlating and reading them. They are quoted merely as mental eye-openers in the hope that by and by we may see a little farther and more clearly.

Herodotus says, "From the first king to this priest of Vulcan (Ptah) who last reigned (Sethon) were 341 generations of men; and during these generations, there were the same number of priests and kings. Now 300 generations are equal to 10,000 years, and the 41 remaining generations make 1,340 years. Thus they said, in 11,340 years, no god had assumed the form of a man; neither had such a thing happened before or afterwards in the time of the remaining kings of Egypt. During this time they related that the sun had four times risen out of his usual quarter, and that he had twice risen where he now sets, and twice set where he now rises."

Whatsoever truth there may be in the statement, there are no phenomenal data known to the present writer by which the assertion of Herodotus can be interpreted except those of the circle of the equinoctial precession. In no other circle or cycle does the sun ever rise at one time in the quarter it sets in at another. He therefore holds that the Egyptian priests did verily claim to have made chronological observations during a period, in round numbers, of 52,000 years.

The explanation that the priests were referring in any wise to the Sothiac cycle, a period of 1,461 years, must be rejected as not only inadequate but perfectly puerile. The speaking stones, the pictured papyri and written rolls, are all antedated by the celestial chronology of the divine dynasties, and if the present conjecture should prove correct it will drop from above the keystone into the almost completed arch of Egyptology.

My suggestion is that the divine dynasties founded on the cycles of astronomical time were continued by the era of Menes. And there is evidence to support it in the table of Abydos.

Tinis is the name of the great city of Abydos, and the name of Menes heads the first Thinite dynasty. Now the new table of Abydos, discovered 11 years ago [1870], in a corridor of the temple of Seti I, at Harabat-el-Madfouneh, gives a succession of 65 kings from Menes, the founder of the line, down to the last reign of the Twelfth Dynasty.

If we take the accepted average of human life as about three generations to the century, this succession of 65 monarchs will extend over a period of 2,166 years, leaving a fractional remainder. This is as near to the length of time during which the equinox remains in a single sign as need be, that time being 2,155 years. And this is the table of Abydos, of the Thinites, and of Menes.

Also the table comes to an end with a break so abrupt, an interregnum of some kind so marked, that it leaves us staring into a chasm, which is at present without a bridge, and we have to leap or scramble from the Twelfth Dynasty to the Eighteenth.*

In his list of the Pharaohs and their epochs, founded on the list of kings in the table of Abydos and on the regnal years actually proved, Brugsch-Bey gives the date of 4400 B.C. for Menes and 2266 for Amenemhet IV, the last king of the Twelfth Dynasty, or a total of 2,134 years for the twelve dynasties; within twenty years of the time required in the celestial reckoning!

The monuments do not come down to the time of the entrance of the vernal colure into the sign of Pisces, but the gnostics brought on the imagery, and on one of the Greco-Egyptian gnostic seals in the British Museum there is a figure of the young sun-god Horus, with the solar disk on his head carrying the fish as his latest type. He stands on the crocodile, and this illustration of the manifester as Ichthus, with the fish above and crocodile beneath, corroborates the view that the crocodile-god, with the ram's head, had represented the sun in the sign of the Ram.

The same sequence is illustrated by the types of sacrifice. The fish is now the sacrificial type, and has been ever since the equinox occurred in the Fishes. Before that the type was the Ram or the Lamb. Earlier still it was the Bull; among primitive races we can get back to the Twins as the typical sacrifice, and each of these types corresponds to the solar sign, and to time kept in the astronomical chronicles.

Also, the Egyptian month Choiak begins in the Alexandrian year, on November 27; and in the calendar of lucky and unlucky days in the fourth Sallier papyrus it is said to be unlucky to eat fish on the twenty-eighth day of the month Choiak, because on that date—our Christmas Day—the gods of Tattu assumed the form of a fish, or in other words the sun entered the sign of Pisces, at which time the

---

* Massey elaborates on the lacuna in the monumental records in his larger works. *Editors.*

equinoctial colure must accordingly have been in the sign of the Twins.

The importance of this sequence and of the identification of Menes' era with the divine dynasties, and the consequent link established with the backward past, will become more apparent when we come to consider the cycle of the equinoctial precession, or the great year of the world which began when the vernal colure left the sign of Aries for that of Pisces nearly twenty-eight thousand years ago, and ended when it re-entered the sign of the Fishes, 255 B.C.[1]

In this sketch of Egypt (and its prehistoric past) the outlines are drawn in accordance with the intended filling in. The treatment will serve to show the extended and inclusive sense in which the name Egypt has often to be interpreted in these pages as the outlet from the African center. We have not to turn and follow the track of the migrations into the north, called by the Hebrew writer (Gen. 10:5) the Isles of the Gevi or Gevim.

In Hebrew, Gev is the back or hinder part, identical with the Egyptian Khef; and the Children of Khef, the Æthiopic Genitrix, are designated the Gentiles who went northward and carried with them the primordial name of the Birthplace in the Celestial North. The race of Japheth are none other than the race of Kheft, whom we shall find in Britain as the Great Mother Ked.

NOTES

1 This is the date given by Cassini and Sir William Drummond, and adopted by the present writer on data kindly furnished by the Astronomer-Royal and the calculations of an eminent mathematician. The following is the official reply to my question as to when the vernal equinox coincided with the fixed point supplied by the first star (the last in the backward movement) in the Ram constellation:

ROYAL OBSERVATORY GREENWICH,
LONDON, S.E.
July 23rd, 1877

Dear Sir,

It appears from our computation, that the vernal equinox passed through the star y Arietis about B.C. 400, subject to an uncertainty of three or four years, or perhaps more. The uncertainty of observations at that epoch might easily produce an apparent error of thirty or forty years in the observed date of such a conjunction.

I am, dear Sir,
Yours faithfully,
W. H. M. Christie.

Gerald Massey, Esq.

III. OTHER LIFEFORMS: A LOOK AT UFOS

III

Science fact and science fiction meet in exobiology. In some ways exobiology is the cutting edge of science. In other ways it can be the lunatic fringe. We must tread carefully here, keeping an open mind without developing "a hole in the head," and remembering that at least one alleged form of extraterrestrial life—angels—may be quietly cautioning us not to rush in foolishly.

UFOs are at once the most glamorous and most mysterious aspect of exobiology. Stories of little green men from Mars and large blue ones from Venus are so common that they could be called mundane. Is there anyone who hasn't felt an easy familiarity with that amazing extraterrestrial from the planet Krypton, Superman? And who hasn't been thrilled at least once to go on a "Star Trek" and get "lost in space"? Comic books and television are among the factors leading to a dramatic shift in attitude among the American public toward acceptance of the extraterrestrial intelligence hypothesis.

Just how acceptable the ETI has become was dramatically shown in January 1974 when the Gallup Opinion Index—popularly called the Gallup poll—issued Report No. 103. Its table of contents contained listings on "Unidentified Flying Objects" and "Life on Other Planets." The section was headlined "UFO sightings by Americans have doubled in seven years."

The report went on to state that more than fifteen million Americans—11 per cent of the adult population—have seen a UFO. These percipients of UFO phenomena believe the objects to be real and not hallucinations or figments of the imagination. Nearly half of all persons interviewed (46 per cent) believe that there is intelligent life on other planets, and seven out of ten of those who think there is life on other planets believe that UFOs are real.

UFOs *are* real—despite the denials of the Air Force's old Project Blue Book and the Air Force-sponsored Condon Report. Major Donald E. Keyhoe's *Aliens from Space* is interesting reading because he documents how the U. S. Air Force has believed for years that Earth has been under intermittent observation by alien intelligence. According to Keyhoe, this surveillance has been conducted for centuries and is being intensified now that we are beginning to take "giant steps for mankind" off our home planet.

But even Major Keyhoe fails to see the big picture. A sober and unprejudiced examination of the evidence indicates that there are a number of plausible explanations for UFOs other than that they are interplanetary transportation devices. No single hypothesis thus far advanced will cover all observed evidence.

One of the most unusual findings on the UFO problem comes from Trevor James Constable, author of the 1958 book *They Live in the Sky*. "They" refers to both higher and lower orders of intelligent beings, as well as plasma-bodied atmospheric animals. Regarding the latter, these strange plasmic creatures, which Constable nicknamed "critters," have their native existence in the infrared portion of the spectrum, beyond the range of normal human sight. They consist of physical substance in its most tenuous form. Sometimes they appear in the visible portion of the spectrum, but usually are mistaken for manned mechanical spacecraft of some kind. But, Constable maintains, they are biological, not mechanical. Pictures of them, taken with infrared film, can be seen in Constable's book—a very hard fact to ignore in playing The Reality Game.

These amoebalike aerial fauna range from the size of a coin to half a mile in diameter. Bioenergetically propelled, they give a solid radar return, as do most plasmas. They pulsate, like all living substance, and when in the visible range often emit a reddish glow. They are generally discerned as discs or spheroids, although they are able to change both their form and density. They have a diaphanous, mica-like structure and consist essentially of heat-substance. They are organisms, Constable maintains, at the upper border of physical substance. In the full physical density, some of them have been seen close up and on the ground. Constable claims that these "critters" are confused with *constructs*—intelligently fashioned vehicles—manifesting to human vision in a similar manner.

Why hasn't science taken up the lead Constable offered nearly two decades ago? Constable cites Wilhelm Reich's findings on the mass neurosis as the major reason. Humanity is pathologically armored, and armoring includes distorted perceptions—a major handicap in playing The Reality Game. Says Constable, "The sterile conceptions of mechanistic science are the ultimate expression of this armoring. The living element is always neurotically resisted. Organisms in the condition of pure heat—my critters—signal the end of mechanistic cosmology. No wonder its high priests damn such findings and stare millions of miles into space instead. Their focus and their fundamental orientation are away from any higher manifestations of terrestrial life."

Critters are not the only answer indicated by the evidence. In his *Mysteries of Time and Space* Brad Steiger theorizes that UFOs may possess a kind of intelligence that enables them to influence the mind of *Homo sapiens* telepathically and to project what appear to be three-dimensional images to the observers of UFO activity. In other words, there may be no spacecraft, there may be no UFO occupants—there may be only glowing globs of pure intelligence, permitting each observer to view them in a manner that would be most acceptable to him. That may be why some UFO observers report a confrontation with beautiful, long-haired, humanlike entities; some with bug-eyed monsters; others with small, green, astronaut-type aliens. It may all depend upon what preconceptions the observer might have about alien lifeforms. But always there must be some three-dimensional image to which the percipient may relate. Not many people can handle a communication with a glowing globule of intelligent energy.*

But just as critters may not be the whole picture, neither are critters with superintelligence—"higher manifestations of terrestrial life" —the only explanation indicated by the steadily amassing evidence. As J. Allen Hynek, chairman of the astronomy department at North-

* It is my opinion—which I have offered in various places for the past seven years—that some external intelligence has been steadily interacting with mankind in an effort to learn more about us or in an effort to communicate certain concepts to us. It appears that there is a definite symbiotic relationship which exits between man and the UFO intelligences. In some manner we do not yet understand, they need us as much as we need them. The UFO phenomenon may be just a mechanism that can bring man only so far in teaching him how to get in true step with time and space. The best teachers are those who bring their eager, but sometimes silly and protesting, students just short of the solution to a problem, then step aside to permit the awkward students themselves the sense of accomplishment to be found in having solved a seemingly impossible riddle.

Whatever the guise these intelligences assume, it would seem that they have interacted with mankind on a very subtle level for centuries. The problem is that we just cannot comprehend what *their* Reality Game is! *Brad Steiger.*

western University and former consultant to the Air Force on UFOs, points out in *Science Digest,* June 1973:

> The . . . major mistake made by the Condon committee was to consider only the problem of whether UFO reports . . . supported the hypothesis that the earth was being visited by extra-terrestrial intelligences. But the real problem was—and remains —whether UFOs are something genuinely new to science, quite apart from any preconceived theory to account for the reports. We need to consider UFOs without preconceived hypotheses. . . . The solution of the UFO phenomenon . . . may not be easy to accept. It might well call for a rearrangement of many of our established concepts of the physical world that will be far greater even than the rearrangements necessary when relativity and quantum mechanics entered our cozy little world.

Ufologists—those who continually study and pursue the UFO enigma—have theorized that some of the mysterious objects may come from some other dimension and are therefore not from some planet in "outer space." The next section will look at this aspect of The Reality Game in detail. For now let us just say that UFOs may literally share our "turf" with us and may actually be our neighbors around the corner of some other plane of being. Ufologist John A. Keel sees angels, space beings, and UFO entities as one and the same thing. In his *UFOs: Operation Trojan Horse* he says that it is a mistake to put them into distinctly separate classes. "The demonologists, angelologists, theologists, and ufologists have all been steadily examining and re-examining the same phenomena from slightly different points of view."

If these entities may actually be the biblical angels from heaven, just where is heaven? The Reverend Barry Downing, a Presbyterian minister, offers a most unusual and thought-provoking answer in his book *The Bible and Flying Saucers.* Agreeing with Keel, he suggests that the angels of an earlier day may be the space brothers of today. Was the Star of Bethlehem a UFO? Could the pillar of smoke by day and fire by night that led the Israelites out of Egypt have been a flying saucer? If so, modern technology and ufologists are in a position to demonstrate that the God-is-dead-or-demythologized school of religious thought is terribly mistaken and shortsighted. Their linked efforts might produce a sensible, acceptable space age theology that could revitalize moribund religion.

Just as the Reverend Mr. Downing sees the possibility for a concrete, factual explanation of myth and miracle in the Bible, ufologist

Jacques Vallee sees that possibility for folklore. His 1969 book *Passport to Magonia* is a scholarly but provocative examination of stories from many cultures which deal with strange people who come from "other lands." Generally they are called fairies, elves, leprechauns, "little people." And they come from exotic kingdoms, mysteriously appearing and disappearing. Are these stories based on actual facts lost in the mist of history? Many modern UFO contact reports can be read as similar descriptions with the simple substitution of the term "extraterrestrial" for "fairy."

The UFO phenomenon may be only part of a larger, total picture. It may be that several types of apparently unrelated phenomena should be lumped together and shaken until everything is unified in one theory. But whatever the final explanation or explanations of UFOs may be, we must not lose sight of this perspective: Salvation comes from within, not outside. David Spangler, a member of the Findhorn Community on the edge of the North Sea in Findhorn, Scotland, emphasizes this in his essay. Within the depths of our own consciousness, not from an outside source, is the true place from which to make the cosmic connection. The Findhorn communications resulting from their "links with space" (the title of one of their publications) make this important point: *We* are the true extraterrestrials. Humanity has become so spaced out, so out of touch with the earth and the special organic relationship that life on the planet requires, that we are in danger of destroying our home and losing The Reality Game.

Our consciousness is in a bad state and we are making false idols of extraterrestrials, false "gods from outer space." But if we are ever to restore paradise on Earth, we must work on ourselves, not rely on surrogate parents from space. Depth psychology has shown that a child's parents are his first gods. But growing up, maturing, requires that we relinquish that illusion, along with the hopes and dreams of invoking magical powers and omnipotent forces to satisfy our desires. Instead, we must do the slow, hard, and often painful work of taking responsibility for our own actions.

Humanity is now at childhood's end. It stands ready, to use Carl Sagan's words, to become Starfolk and join galactic society. We should not delude ourselves with the glamour and mystery of UFOs into thinking that salvation comes from outside. Some of the races we may contact could prove hostile rather than benevolent. But the greatest enemy and the greatest ally we have are still to be found in the depths of our psyche.

TREVOR JAMES CONSTABLE is a well-known ariation historian, a radio officer in the U. S. Merchant Marine, and a longtime researcher in borderland science. His books include *Fighter Aces, Horrido!,* and *The Blond Knight of Germany.* Mr. Constable's pioneer borderland work with UFOs is documented in his *They Live in the Sky* (1958) and is extended in the forthcoming book *The Cosmic Pulse of Life.* Influenced predominantly by Rudolf Steiner and Wilhelm Reich and impelled by the planetary need to work lawfully with natural forces, he has done extensive weather-engineering research using his own variants of the "cloudbuster" invented by Reich. By synthesizing Reich's orgone energy discovery with the far-ranging etherian physics of Steiner, Mr. Constable has demonstrated technological harnessing of orgone. He has expanded Reich's basic theory of orgone flow around the globe into practical, nonpolluting methods of weather control. He published his basic findings in weather engineering in 1973 and is now moving into commercial weather engineering.

THE CASE FOR THE "CRITTERS"

> . . . the mistakes and errors are the price for the great romance of doing something for the first time.
>
> —*Sir Francis Chichester*

The concept that certain UFOs could be living organisms did not originate with me. Sir Arthur Conan Doyle and Charles Fort both hinted at the presence of etheric fauna dwelling in the unseen around us and also in the stratosphere. American occultist Gerald Light made similar inferences in the 1940s and '50s. The first modern theory encompassing this idea with specific reference to UFOs was probably the "etheric interpretation" of the flying discs, formulated in 1946–47 by the late Meade Layne, M.A. Mr. Layne published his theory in a penetrating 1950 monograph, *The Ether Ship Mystery and Its Solution.*

Mr. Layne was founder and first director of the Borderland Sciences Research Associates in San Diego, California. A former university lecturer and an outstanding writer, Meade Layne produced one of the classics of ufology in his monograph, which is still available today—with added comments—under the title *The Flying Saucer Mystery and Its Solution.** His achievement was to produce the only theoretical treatment of UFOs to survive the entire modern period.

Mr. Layne's "etheric interpretation" is also readily extensible to cover new UFO facts, and is required reading for any person with a genuine desire to break out of the bondage of mechanistic thinking. There can be no doubt that Meade Layne was a generation ahead of his time with his mobile thinking. He also emerges as easily the greatest writer of ufology's break-in period.

Methods of obtaining advanced information were employed by this pioneer at a time when UFO data were sparse.† A sample of his writings will illustrate that his work disqualifies with equal alacrity both the faint-hearted and the weak-minded:

"The aeroforms are thought-constructs, mind-constructs. As such, they are, in effect, the vehicle of the actual entity who creates them. Just as our own terrestrial minds rule and become identified with our bodies, so does the entity of the etheric world make for himself a body or vehicle out of etheric substance.

"This body may be of any shape or size, any one of a hundred mutants—such as the indefinite and changing shapes reported by observers of flying saucers throughout the world. The shapes may be a wheel, a globe, a fusiform or cigar shape, a fireball, vapor, or gases. It may have any density, any rate of vibration desired. The impenetrable steel of landed discs, is, as it were, a sort of etheric isotope of our terrestrial steel, or we may call it 'etheric steel.' The shapes and vehicles and the entity operating them form one being, just as a human being is a psychophysical mind-body unity. The body of this etherian entity is a thought-form which can go anywhere, and penetrates our earth and sea as easily as our air."

Etherian physics in all its significance for true ufology—the ufology of the future—will be enlarged upon as this article proceeds. The important point for now is that I was not the originator of the theory that some UFOs could be living organisms, and that Meade Layne—and also John Bessor—preceded me by about ten years. When Meade

---

* BSRA is now known as Borderland Sciences Research Foundation, Inc., P.O. Box 548, Vista, Ca. 92083. BSRF is under the able directorship of Dr. Riley Crabb, nationally known writer and lecturer on the borderland sciences.

† These methods are explained in Constable's forthcoming book, *The Cosmic Pulse of Life. Editors.*

Layne saw my collection of more than a hundred photographs‡ of these mutants not long before his death, he was exuberant. He termed their capture on film "the death knell of the old order."

Meade Layne's daring hypothesis—a brilliant synthesis of physics and metaphysics—was shown to be valid when I literally stumbled across these organisms in the summer of 1957. This experimental accident, and my subsequent photography of dozens of these critters *in situ,* merely confirmed the extant theories of minds far brighter than mine. This borderland breakthrough was crude, awkward, and somewhat uncomprehending, but it nevertheless threw light immediately into the darker, previously impenetrable corners of history's greatest mystery.

Endless implications ensued. Technical, theoretical, cognitional, philosophical, psychological, methodological, and scientific questions arose of staggering magnitude. Unraveling all this will take the best efforts of far better and *younger,* more functional minds than those that currently dominate world science. The response we found, outside the small circle of friends and associates who understood our work, was essentially confined to fear and anxiety. We understood some of this only too well.

When these strange, living forms burst into our ken we found it essential to be lighthearted about our work—if only to diminish the psychological impact of unknown terrors. The sight of these queer, plasmatic fauna in photographs was sufficient to repel sensitive people otherwise interested in UFOs. Motion pictures of them sometimes caused psychically sensitive persons to bolt from the room during screening. Numerous persons today who have tampered chemically with their perceptions by ingesting LSD have become aware of these strange organisms. Back in 1957–58, however, few people were willing to attempt chemical extensions of perception,* and prior knowledge of the critters was confined to learned and accomplished occultists who knew only too well how real were the things that we had been able to capture on film.

Breaking into the borderland of physical nature that they inhabit, by making of oneself a focal point for these unseen aerial denizens, carried unknown risks. Referring to them in all their diversity of form

‡ Taken on infrared film and published in his book *They Live in the Sky* (Los Angeles: New Age Publishing Co., 1959). *Editors.*

* No inference is intended here that the author in any way supports drug-induced "extensions" of perception, whether by the uneducated or by Aldous Huxley and his ilk.

simply as "critters" seemed to help. We avoided classification attempts as premature. Occasional speculation as to what any overseeing, higher intelligences might think of our gropings kept us in a mood to laugh at ourselves, which we often did and still do.

We conceived of ourselves as children, struggling to stay upright by clinging to the side of a crib. Our falls and spills and mistakes were almost perpetual and often comical. Everything we touched was new and there were no technical texts to consult. Our ability to see the funny side of our adventures never left us, and was always a counterbalance to what might otherwise have become overwhelmingly serious.

Kidding in no way diminished our curiosity. We kept on after the critters. No one had ever done anything like this before and it was a tremendous thrill. The laws of these etherian realms are essentially functional and biological, and they open themselves only to the researcher who in his experimental work *has not lost his ability to play* —to play like a child. The searching organism is almost always playful. A sense of humor is essential, for experience quickly teaches the field worker that the stupidity and cupidity of contemporary man must surely be the comedy of the gods.

The critters had even aroused the U. S. Air Force to some public theorizing as early as April 27, 1949. On that date it stated in an official release:

"The possible existence of some sort of strange extraterrestrial animals has also been remotely considered, as many of the objects acted more like animals than anything else. However, there are few reliable reports on extraterrestrial animals."

This release, which may have been originally intended as the opening wedge to further revelations of observations made by USAF aircrews, was unwelcome in ufology. Spaceships had become an *idée fixe,* and nothing biological was wanted to disturb or modify the basic extraterrestrial spaceship hypothesis. At the other extreme stood the original skeptic, Dr. Donald Menzel of Harvard University, eternally ready to discharge his self-appointed duty of debunking UFOs. He didn't like the USAF "space animals" release either.

In his book *Flying Saucers,* published by the Harvard University Press, Dr. Menzel took exception to this release. He pointed out that even *one* reliable report of an extraterrestrial animal would be sufficient, let alone a "few," as the USAF had implied were in existence. What the USAF has in its secret files in this connection will not soon be revealed. Suffice it to say that the USAF uses infrared photographic apparatus and detectors extensively, and penetrates round the clock into the stratosphere with piloted aircraft. USAF radar blankets the United States.

My opinion is that they have objectified a great many things aloft that science does not presently understand, including animal forms. I know that aircraft have chased my critters because I have personally photographed Air Force fighters, carrying infrared homing rockets, chasing them above the Mojave Desert. The USAF, like numerous agencies of the U. S. Government, lies to the American people, and only the gullible believe otherwise.

At the time of the "space animals" release there was in print at least one reliable report of an atmospheric animal form, *available since 1934*. This report was brought to my attention by Mr. Adrian Cox of London, who saw its significance after reading an illustrated article of mine in the British *Flying Saucer Review* for July–August 1960. Mr. Cox connected this article, entitled "Space Animals—A Fact of Life," with an incident recounted in the book *Everest 1933* by Hugh Ruttledge.

The Ruttledge book was published in Great Britain by Hodder and Stoughton, and in the United States in 1935 by the National Travel Club under the title *The Attack on Everest*. On p. 228 in the American version, climber Frank Smythe writes of the second assault on Mt. Everest as follows:

"The second phenomenon may or may not have been an optical illusion. Personally, I am convinced it was not. I was still some two hundred feet above Camp 6 and a considerable distance from it when, chancing to glance in the direction of the north ridge, I saw two curious-looking objects floating in the sky. They strongly resembled kite balloons in shape, but one possessed what appeared to be squat, underdeveloped wings, and the other a protuberance suggestive of a beak. They hovered motionless, but seemed to slowly pulsate, a pulsation incidentally much slower than my own heartbeats, which is of interest supposing it was an optical illusion.

"The two objects were very dark in color and were silhouetted sharply against the sky or possibly a background of cloud. So interested was I that I stopped to observe them. My brain appeared to be working normally and I deliberately put myself through a series of tests. First of all I glanced away. The objects did not follow my vision, but they were still there when I looked back again. Then I looked away again, and this time identified by name a number of peaks, valleys, and glaciers by way of a mental test. But when I looked back again the objects still confronted me. At this, I gave them up as a bad job, but just as I was starting to move again a mist suddenly drifted across. Gradually they disappeared behind it, and when a minute or two later it had drifted clear, exposing the whole north ridge once more, they had vanished as mysteriously as they had come. It may be of interest to state that their position was roughly midway between the position of the 1924 Camp 6 and the northeast shoulder. Thus they were at a height of about 27,200 feet, and as I was at about 27,600 feet when I saw them, a line connecting their approximate position with my position would not bring them against a background of sky, but against lower and distant mountains. It is conceivable, therefore, that it was some strange effect of mist and mountain magnified by imagination. . . ."

Mr. Smythe prefaces his account by saying:

"Men under physical and mental stress have experienced curious things on mountains, and instances are described in the *Alpine Journal*. Furthermore, the effects of oxygen lack on the brain are complex and but little understood."

Frank Smythe was a member of several famous expeditions of this type, and from the viewpoint of character and background he is a witness of integrity. A graduate electrical engineer, he was educated at Faraday House Engineering College, was a former Royal Air Force officer and a Lieutenant Colonel in the British Army. He was in three Everest attempts and was a member of the International Kanchenjunga Expedition of 1930. An accomplished author, he wrote several books and many articles on mountaineering. Smythe died in 1949 but will undoubtedly be counted among the earliest modern observers of biological UFOs—when in due course the determinism of those UFOs is established.

Frank Smythe's observation must be accounted a good one by any sound standard. He observed with extreme care, did everything possible to eliminate the possibility of hallucination—or to so identify it if it was an hallucination—and verified that the pulsation of the objects differed from his own heartbeat. He did all these things systematically, after the fashion of a man trained in engineering. He also established the approximate altitude and location of the objects. Most important of all, he was extremely wary at the time of the changes in perception and consciousness that can take place at high altitudes.

Skeptics eager to torpedo the obvious biological implications of this sighting might well seize on the abnormal location of the observer and the unusual physical conditions as a means of calling it all an hallucination. The surmise here would be that what Smythe "saw" was due to altitude-induced sensory changes in his organism. Now that creatures answering Smythe's general description have been photographed with materials sensitive beyond the range of the human eye, such skeptics are forced more on the defensive. Furthermore, the objectification of these extraocular regions of the spectrum is constantly progressing. The discovery of more and different critters is inevitable; scientific development will not cease.

The probability is high that Smythe perceived something objective and real, and if altitude, oxygen deficiency, and exertion happened to extend his vision just a few millimicrons beyond the normal range, then he would perceive directly this adjacent range of physical form that has since been photographed—complete with its strange critters. The role of altitude in the perception and objectification of these critters seems significant. While this role is poorly understood at present, subsequent work will elucidate much that is now murky.

The imponderables involved will probably include the diurnal "breathing" of the planet Earth. This will be dealt with in due course. From personal experience in field work I can report that observation of the human orgone energy field at an altitude of approximately eight thousand feet on Mt. Wilson, in California, shows that this field is vastly extended over its sea-level size. Perception of the borderland critters we have photographed is also much more difficult at sea level than at four-thousand-feet altitude and above.

Perhaps the extension of the orgone energy field and its lumination that we achieved via the Star Exercise† happened spuriously to Frank Smythe through his being in rarefied air near the summit of Everest and breathing oxygen.‡ Since the vacuum of the moon's surface also revealed objectively the blue orgone energy fields of the astronauts—extending far beyond their bodies and external to their spacesuits—there is independent evidence that these things happen approximately as I have described them.

The functional connections between my methods and findings, the "mysterious" blue emanation around the U.S. astronauts on the moon, and Colonel Smythe's high-altitude observation of biological UFOs are self-evident. The Smythe sighting took place when I was

---

† An occult practice for developing higher sense perception. *Editors.*
‡ There is said to be an intimate relationship between the element oxygen and the human astral body, or seat of consciousness. For details, see Rudolf Steiner. *Editors.*

six years old. I was in no position to implant my ideas "by suggestion" —a tired old bromide routinely supplied by anxious mechanists.

Colonel Smythe was not the first man to see the critters of our atmosphere in modern times. A number of years prior to the Smythe sighting on Everest, an American named Don Wood, Jr., got a closer and more terrifying look at a couple of these critters. He saw them in the full physical density and in light-reflecting negative polarity as a result of his hobby interest in flying.

The experience shook him sufficiently to make him keep his counsel about the event for several decades. Mr. Wood's story was originally published in Ray Palmer's publication, *Flying Saucers,* in October 1959. Few people have done more to advance ufology through the years than the dogged and able Ray Palmer, an individual who has sacrificed much in life in order to keep publishing material from which orthodox publishers recoil. Mr. Wood's experience found the light of day thanks to Ray Palmer's open-mindedness, which I am happy to salute by reproducing the Wood sighting here:

"I must write you of what happened to me in 1925, which I think solves most UFO reports. I have never told this to anyone, but can get a signed affidavit if needed. Four of us were flying old 'Jennies' (OX5 motors)* over the Nevada desert. One plane was a two-seater, the one I was in. We landed on Flat Mesa, near Battle Mountain, Nevada. The mesa is about five thousand square feet and the walls are too steep to climb unless a lot of work is done.

"We wanted to see what was on top of this flat place. We landed at one o'clock in the afternoon. While walking about the top of this place we noticed something coming in for a landing. It was about eight feet across and was round and flat like a saucer. The undersides were a reddish color. It skidded to a stop about thirty feet away. This next you won't believe, and I don't care but it's the truth. We walked up to the thing and it was some *animal* like we never saw before. It was hurt, and as it breathed the top would rise and fall, making a half-foot hole all around it like a clam opening and closing.

"Quite a hunk had been chewed out of one side of this rim and a sort of metal-looking froth issued. When it saw us it breathed frantically and rose up only a few inches, only to fall back to the earth again. It was moist and glistened on the top side. We could see no eyes or legs.

"After a twenty-minute rest it started pulsating once more. (We

* The "Jenny" was a World War I-vintage aircraft mainly used for training and popular in the postwar years for sport flying. *Editors.*

stayed ten feet away.) And so help me the thing grew as bright as all get out, except where it was hurt. It had a micalike shell body. It tried to rise up again but sank back again. Then we saw a large, round shadow fall on us. We looked up and ran. Coming in was a much larger animal thirty feet across.

"It paid no attention to us, but settled itself over the small one. Four suckerlike tongues settled on the little one and the big one got so dazzlingly bright you couldn't look at it. Both rose straight up and were out of sight in a second. They must have been traveling a thousand miles an hour to get so high so fast. When we walked over there was an awful stench, and the frothy stuff the little one had bled looked like fine aluminum wire. There was more frothy, wiry stuff in a thirty-foot circle where the big one had breathed.

"This stuff finally melted in the sun, and we took off. So help me, *this was an animal*. I have never told this before as we knew no one would believe us. I only write now because this animal would be one big thirty-foot light if seen at night. I don't expect belief, but I simply had to write."

History should have a place for Don Wood, Jr., for making what might well be characterized as the most important observation thus far in the history of this confused subject of UFOs. I wrote him at his home in one of the southern states of the USA, and am satisfied that he reported his experience accurately. Truly it is that one example is worth a thousand, containing all within itself—what Goethean scientific thinkers call the *ur* example.

Only a compulsive-neurotic doubter can make a spaceship out of what landed next to Mr. Wood. His story is strong and full of *life*. Since this experience runs counter to the cherished, mechanistic conceptions of flying saucers, little attention has been paid to it, despite its significance for a genuine exobiology. Sequestration of such experiences by establishment-type ufology is their typical fate, lest disturbance be caused to cosmic conceptions rooted in sterility.

Here is an example of a man viewing something close up—a full twenty-two years before the term "flying saucer" was coined—that was discoidal, pulsating, and its own light source. The object was obviously *alive* and also injured, as though it had been attacked. Metallic froth issued from the wound, not blood. The object had a micalike shell, such as today's would-be exobiologists speculate might be possessed by Martian lifeforms. Such a shell might be expected to return radar echoes, especially if it happened to be thirty feet in diameter like the rescuing critter.

There was no radar then. Radar came later. The critters were there *before* radar, and if ten years before radar, then why not millennia? A question surely of far more weighty import for current notions both of life and of reality than any thus far raised by the ships-from-other-planets advocates, who rest their case on coincidence and accident, and minus any coherent concept of the relationship between life and pulsation.

The functional connections between the Wood sighting of 1925 and a huge corpus of evidence gathered since are everywhere apparent. Ufology is very largely made up of reports of pulsating, glowing, superperforming discoidal objects precipitately conceived of as ships. Since we added to Don Wood's observation photographs of glowing, discoidal objects that appear like giant amoebas there is clearly a new and *wholly biological dimension* to ufology.

Anyone who labors under the illusion that modern scientists do not contribute to and support obscurantism in anything pertaining to genuine findings on extraterrestrial life should peruse biologist Ivan Sanderson's book *Uninvited Visitors*. Mr. Sanderson† is a scientist who has ransacked the world for evidence concerning visitation from space, and his biggest problem always appears to be getting the facts from fellow scientists. He relates an instance in Chapter 6 of *Uninvited Visitors* where an enormous object similar to that described by Don Wood was washed ashore in southwestern Tasmania in 1962.

A wealthy amateur naturalist who heard about this critter went after it when it washed ashore on the south side of Sandy Cape. He was accompanied by a government zoologist. The intention of the naturalist—a museum backer—was to obtain a sample of the flesh. He was unable to do so because *even an ax could not cut into the thing.* (Let us pause and refer back to the statement from Meade Layne's writings quoted earlier in this chapter, dealing with the hardness and density of etheric matter. This reference justifies the "hard, micalike shell" reported by Don Wood to encase the critter that landed beside him in Nevada.)

Ivan Sanderson recounts the pathetic, deplorable measures set in motion by the Australian Government and its satellite scientists to suppress the discovery of this critter. Sandy Cape was placed off limits to everyone, including the Australian press. One enterprising reporter nevertheless got to the critter and, after a husky cop again failed to cut it with an ax, touched a cigarette lighter to its edge. He

† Mr. Sanderson died in 1973. *Editors.*

noted that the thing "withdrew" from the flame, later returning to its original contour.

The case for the critters was advanced significantly by this incident and reinforced by the subsequent revelation that seven other, similar critters had been washed up on Australia's southeast coast during the previous twenty years. The critter in the incident described had been washing in and out on the tide for over two years but had not decayed. Touching it with flame indicated some kind of residual life function, reminiscent of Galvani's basic experiment with a chicken leg. On the basis of the facts presented by Mr. Sanderson, the conclusion that the critter was not a previously known species of terrestrial life seems inescapable.

Secrecy and febrile obscurantism surrounded this incident, and will be all too familiar to the student of ufology as typical of official response to UFOs all over the world. While the handling of the Australian case may be at odds with the spirit and ideals of science and scientific inquiry, realists are aware that such machinations are the norm nowadays. Spirit and ideals were trampled under long ago in the economic stampede. Science is a means of making a living, and it is the socioeconomic blackmail thereby opened that is responsible for scientific knuckling under to government edicts that suppress scientific information.

Australians should not feel that they are being put in a bad light. In the USA the courts have actually ordered—and carried out—the burning of scientific literature and bulletins that would help us understand these denizens of space.‡ American courts and jurisprudence have been corrupted and misused to silence scientific pioneers of the new cosmic biology. . . .

Fear of life is the power source for this irrationalism. Life from space is feared most of all. The fear climate has worsened as the space age has advanced, as though man has come to so love the darkness that it is the light which terrifies him. Understanding these queer peregrinations of a frightened humanity, standing as it does at the portals of a new epoch, has become an essential element in ufology. Evasive human attitudes are at present more important as space age phenomena than is the investigation of the arcane propulsion plants being used by the aliens. Man can have no access to things that his neurotic world-conception compels him to evade.

Ufology stands to receive enlightenment and extension from Don

‡ The author is alluding to the tragic case of Wilhelm Reich. *Editors.*

Wood's sighting, as well as from the corroborative Australian critters. Tolerating the critters is a crucial psychological problem, for as Ivan Sanderson so aptly remarks of ufologists in his *Uninvited Visitors,* "The mere suggestion that there could also be a biological aspect to their subject invariably seems to upset them." Mr. Wood's silence in 1925 is understandable. There was then no scientific or quasiscientific frame of reference into which his experience could be fitted. Even the way-out wilderness of ufology did not then exist. He would probably have found himself fitted into a straitjacket by the same kind of myopic mentalities who, at the same period in history, felt that a straitjacket was the correct garb for American rocket pioneer Robert Goddard.

Straddling the Wood sighting and that of Colonel Smythe is the 1926 sighting by the Roerich Expedition of the American Museum of Natural History. Expedition members saw a shining disc high over the Altai-Himalaya. Alert and diligent research will uncover more of these early-modern encounters, forcing acceptance of the presence of the critters in our atmosphere—with all their revolutionary consequences for science.

The helplessness, and sometimes the irrational opposition, of official science in the face of these pressing questions should not deter any unblocked, free person from facing up to their further investigation. Progress depends on the raising of questions. The answers will almost certainly prove disquieting to the old order in science, and utterly destructive of its central dogmas. That is why it will take *young* people—free of neurotic dependence on the mechanistic world-conception—to press these matters forward.

Critter reports such as those described enable us to accept rationally that biological forms, *capable of easy confusion with the idealized flying saucer,* have landed on the earth many times in the past. They landed at least once in close proximity to humans, twenty-two years before flying saucers were ever mentioned. Acceptance of the critters does not invalidate the spaceship hypothesis. On the contrary, we strengthen and broaden our investigation. Furthermore, we are put on our guard against two kindred sets of phenomena—sharing a common functioning principle—that are prone to mutual confusion.

By identifying his two UFOs as living organisms Mr. Wood has done ufology a powerful service. Actual observation and obvious inference tie these creatures to a *natural power of flight* using their own life energy. The critters flew naturally at one thousand miles per hour on this power, just as we have the power to walk and run on the earth using our own life energy. That conventional science has evaded and recoiled from the investigation of biological energy does not alter the facts. Man is functionally connected to UFOs of this critter variety by the animating energy—the orgone energy discovered by the late Dr. Wilhelm Reich.

The leading brains in official science, all the Nobel Prize winners of the world combined, all the resources of all the great universities combined, cannot explain to you how you are capable of walking from your chair to the door. The energy involved is *not electrical,* and all the laboratory facilities and sterile conceptions of mechanistic biology do not give us access to this energy. Clearly, if we pursue the source and nature of our own *biological power,* we will be cheek-by-jowl with a power source for space travel—such as reposes naturally with the critters.

JACQUES VALLEE holds a master's degree in astrophysics from Lill University in France and a Ph.D. in computer science from Northwestern University, where he spent four years as an associate of Dr. J. Allen Hynek, the U. S. Air Force scientific consultant on UFO reports. A Jules Verne Prize winner for his first science fiction novel in French, Dr. Vallee has published over twenty scientific articles in British, French, and American professional journals, and three books in English about UFO phenomena: *Anatomy of a Phenomenon, Challenge to Science,* and *Passport to Magonia.* Dr. Vallee is a director of the Parapsychology Research Group in Palo Alto, California, and is engaged in future studies using computer technology.

PASSPORT TO MAGONIA

Taken by the Wind

We have now examined several stories of abductions and attempts at kidnappings by the occupants of flying saucers. These episodes are an integral part of the total UFO problem and cannot be solved separately. Historical evidence, gathered by Wentz, moreover, once more points in the same direction.

> This sort of belief in fairies being able to *take* people was very common and exists yet in a good many parts of West Ireland. . . .
> The Good People are often seen there (pointing to Knoch Magh) in great crowds playing hurley and ball. And one often sees among them the young men and women and children who have been *taken.*

Not only are people taken, but—as in flying saucer stories—they are sometimes carried to faraway spots by aerial means. Such a story is told by the Prophet Ezekiel, of course, and by other religious writers. But an ordinary Irishman, John Campbell, also told Wentz:

> A man whom I have seen, Roderick MacNeil, was lifted by the hosts and left three miles from where he was taken up. The hosts went at about midnight.

Rev. Kirk gives a few stories of similar extraordinary kidnappings, but the most fantastic legend of all is that attached to Kirk him-

self: the good reverend is commonly believed to have been taken by
the fairies.

> Mrs. J. MacGregor who keeps the key to the old church-
> yard where there is a tomb to Kirk, though many say there is
> nothing in it but a coffin filled with stones, told me Kirk was
> taken into the Fairy Knoll, which she pointed to just across a
> little valley in front of us, and is there yet, for the hill is full of
> caverns and in them the "good people" have their homes. And
> she added that Kirk appeared to a relative of his after he was
> taken.

Wentz, who reports this interesting story, made further inquiries
regarding the circumstances of Kirk's death. He went to see the suc-
cessor to Kirk in Aberfoyle, Rev. Taylor, who clarified the story:

> At the time of his disappearance people said he was taken
> because the fairies were displeased with him for disclosing their
> secrets in so public a manner as he did. At all events, it seems
> likely that Kirk was taken ill very suddenly with something like
> apoplexy while on the Fairy Knoll, and died there. I have
> searched the presbyter books and find no record of how Kirk's
> death really took place, but of course there is not the least doubt
> of his body being in the grave.

Kirk believed in the ability of the Good People to perform kidnappings and abductions, and this idea was so widespread that it has
come down to us through a variety of channels. We can therefore examine in detail four aspects of fairy lore that directly relate to our
study: (1) the conditions and purpose of the abductions; (2) the
cases of release from Elfland and the forms taken by the elves' gratitude when the abducted human being had performed some valuable
service during his stay in Elfland; (3) the belief in the kidnapping
activities of the fairy people; and (4) what I shall call the relativistic
aspects of the trip to Elfland.

Hartland reports that a Swedish book published in 1775 contains
a legal statement, solemnly sworn on April 12, 1671, by the husband
of a midwife who was taken to fairyland to assist a troll's wife in
giving birth to a child. The author of the statement seems to have
been a clergyman named Peter Rahm.

> On the authority of this declaration we are called on to believe
> that the event recorded actually happened in the year 1660.
> Peter Rahm alleges that he and his wife were at their farm one
> evening late when there came a little man, swart of face and
> clad in grey, who begged the declarant's wife to come and help

his wife then in labour. The declarant, seeing that they had to do with a Troll, prayed over his wife, blessed her, and bade her in God's name go with the stranger. She seemed to be borne along by the wind.

It is reported that she came home "in the same manner," having refused any food offered to her while in the troll's company.

In another tale, the midwife's husband accompanies her through the forest. They are guided by the "earthman"—the gnome who has requested their help. They go through a moss door, then a wooden door, and later through a door of shining metal. A stairway leads them inside the earth, to a magnificent chamber where the "earth-wife" is resting. Kirk reports that in a case whose principals he personally knew, the abducted woman found the home of the Little People filled with light, although she could not see any lamp or fire.

Rev. Kirk also says that later, in the company of another clergy-man, he visited a woman, then forty years old, and asked her questions concerning her knowledge of the fairies. It was rumored that for a number of years she had taken almost no nourishment, and that she often stayed very late in the fields looking after her sheep, that she met there and talked with people she did not know, and that one night she had fallen asleep on a hill and had been carried away into another place before sunrise. This woman, says Kirk, was always melancholy and silent.

The physical nature of Magonia, as it appears in such tales, is quite noteworthy. Sometimes, it is a remote country, an invisible island, some faraway place one can reach only by a long journey. Indeed, in some tales, it is a celestial country, as in the Indian story quoted earlier. This parallels the belief in the extraterrestrial origin of UFOs so popular today. A second—and equally widespread—theory, is that Elfland constitutes a sort of parallel universe, which coexists with our own. It is made visible and tangible only to selected people, and the "doors" that lead through it are tangential points, known only to the elves. This is somewhat analogous to the theory, sometimes found in the UFO literature, concerning what some authors like to call the "fourth dimension"—although, of course, this expression makes much less physical sense than does the theory of a parallel Elfland. (It does sound more scientific, however!)

Hartland gives tales that illustrate the theory of "tangential universes," such as the following:

> In Nithsdale a fairy rewards the kindness of a young mother, to whom she had committed her babe to suckle, by taking her

on a visit to Fairyland. A door opened in a green hillside, disclosing a porch which the nurse and her conductor entered. There the lady dropped three drops of a precious dew on the nurse's left eyelid, and they were admitted to a beautiful land watered with meandering rivulets and yellow with corn, where the trees were laden with fruits which dropped honey. The nurse was here presented with magical gifts, and when a green dew had baptized her right eye she was enabled to behold further wonders. On returning the fairy passed her hand over the woman's eye and restored its natural powers.

This tale brings us to our second point, that of the gratitude shown by the elves in return for services performed by humans, and the form such gratitude takes. The gratitude itself is evidenced by many stories of elvish gifts in Scandinavian and Northern European tales, such as this one:

A German midwife, who was summoned by a Waterman, or Nix, to aid a woman in labor, was told by the latter: "I am a Christian woman as well as you; and I was carried off by a Waterman, who changed me. When my husband comes in now and offers you money, take no more from him than you usually get, or else he will twist your neck. Take good care!"

In another story, the midwife is asked how much she wants. She answers she will not take more from them than from other people, and the elf replies: "That's lucky for thee. Hadst thou demanded more, it would have gone ill with thee!" In spite of that, she received her apron full of gold.

In a Pomeranian story, the midwife similarly replies to the same question, and the mannikin says, "Now then, lift up thy apron!" and fills it with rubbish that lay in the corner of the room. He then takes his lantern and politely escorts her home. But when she shakes out her apron, pure gold falls on the floor.

Elvish gifts have a magical character, which will take very special meaning in the next chapter. Their magical quality could be illustrated with tales from practically any country. Chinese folklore, in particular, gives numerous examples of it. In one tale, the dwarf fills the woman's apron with something she must not look at before she reaches her house. Naturally she takes a look as soon as the dwarf has vanished, and sees that she is carrying black coals. Angered, she throws them away, retaining two as evidence of the dwarf's bad treatment. She arrives home and discovers the black coals have turned into precious stones. But when she goes back to find the other coals, they are all gone.

There are, in fact, numerous stories in folklore of humans who have gone to fairyland of their own will, either taking a message, or bringing one back, or performing some service for the supernatural beings who live there. But—and this is my third point—we also have numerous accounts of abductions by the fairies. They take men and women, especially pregnant women or young mothers, and they also are very active in stealing young children. Sometimes, they substitute a false child for the real one, leaving in place of the real child a broom with rugs wrapped around it or one of *their* children, a *changeling:*

> By the belief in changelings I mean a belief that fairies and other imaginary beings are on the watch for young children or . . . sometimes even for adults, that they may, if they can find them unguarded, seize and carry them off, leaving in their place one of them.

This belief is not confined to Europe. It is found in regions as remote from Europe as China and the American Pacific coast. But, in any case, once the parents have recognized their child has been taken, what should they do? Hartland says that a

> method in favour in the North of Scotland is to take the suspected elf to some known haunt of its race, generally, we are told, some spot where peculiar soughing sounds are heard, or to some barrow, or stone circle, and lay it down. An offering of bread, butter, milk, cheese, eggs and flesh or fowl must accompany the child.

The parents then retire for an hour or two. If their gifts have vanished when they come back, then their own child will be returned.

But sometimes more radical methods have been used, and we can only pity the poor children who have been ill-treated because their superstitious parents thought they looked like elves! As late as May 17, 1884, it was reported in the London *Daily Telegraph,* two women were arrested at Clonmel and charged with cruelty toward a child three years old. They thought he was a changeling and, by ill-treating him, hoped to obtain the "real child" from the fairies! And there is no question that in medieval times the same superstition has led to the death of children who had congenital defects. Sometimes the same treatment applies to adults who have been changed, and Hartland gives a very funny example of such a case:

> A tale from Badenoch represents the man as discovering the fraud from finding his wife, a woman of unruffled temper, suddenly turned a shrew. So he piles up a great fire and threatens to throw the occupant of the bed upon it unless she tells him what has become of his own wife. She then confesses that the latter has been carried off, and she has been appointed successor. But by his determination he happily succeeds in recapturing his own at a certain fairy knoll near Inverness.

Of course, the UFO myth has not yet reached such romantic proportions, but we are perhaps not quite far from it, at least in certain rural areas, where strange flying objects have become a source of terror to people traveling at night, and where the rumor that "invaders" might be around has gained interest, if not support. A recent television series has capitalized on this aspect of UFO lore. In the show, the human race has been infiltrated by extraterrestrials who differ from humans in small details only. This is not a new idea, as the belief in changelings shows. And there is a well-known passage in Martin Luther's *Table Talk,* in which he tells the Prince of Anhalt that he should throw into the Moldau a certain man who is, in his opinion, such a changeling—or killcrop, as they were called in Germany.

What was the purpose of such fairy abductions? The idea advanced by students of folk tales is again very close to a current theory about UFOs: that the purpose of such contact is a genetic one. According to Hartland:

> The motive assigned to fairies in northern stories is that of preserving and improving their race, on the one hand by carrying off human children to be brought up among the elves and to become united with them, and on the other hand by obtaining the milk and fostering care of human mothers for their own offspring.

(We shall see below what parallels can be found in recent UFO cases.)

However, such is not always the purpose of abduction, and people are often returned by the elves after nothing more than a dance or a game. But a strange phenomenon often takes place: the people who have spent a day in Elfland come back to this world one year, or more, older!

This is our fourth point, and quite a remarkable one. Time does not pass there as it does here. And we have in such stories the first idea of the *relativity of time*. How did this idea come to the story-tellers, ages ago? What inspired them? No one can answer such questions. But it is a fact that the dissymmetry of the time element between Elfland and our world is present in the tales from all countries.

Discussing this supernatural lapse of time in fairyland, Hartland relates the true story of Rhys and Llewellyn, recorded about 1825 in the Vale of Neath, Wales. Rhys and Llewellyn were fellow servants to a farmer. As they went home one night, Rhys told his friend to stop and listen to the music. Llewellyn heard no music. But Rhys had to dance to the tune he had heard a hundred times. He begged Llewellyn to go ahead with the horses, saying that he would soon overtake him, but Llewellyn arrived home alone. The next day, he was suspected of murdering Rhys and jailed. But a farmer "who was skilled in fairy matters" guessed the truth. Several men gathered—among them the narrator of the story—and took Llewellyn to the spot where he said his companion had vanished. Suddenly, "Hush!" cried Llewellyn. "I hear music, I hear sweet harps."

All listened but could hear nothing. Llewellyn's foot was on the outer edge of the fairy ring. He told the narrator to place his foot on his, and then he too heard the sounds of many harps and saw a number of Little People dancing in a circle twenty feet or so in diameter. After him, each of the party did the same and observed the same thing. Among the dancing Little Folk was Rhys. Llewellyn caught him by his smock-frock as he passed close to them and pulled him out of the circle. At once Rhys asked, "Where are the horses?" and asked them to let him finish the dance, which had not lasted more than five minutes. And he could never be persuaded of the time that had elapsed. He became melancholy, fell ill, and soon after died.

Such stories can be found in Keightley's *The Fairy Mythology* and other books, although of course the story of Rhys and Llewellyn is remarkable because it dates from the nineteenth century, thus providing a measure of continuity between fairy and UFO lore. In the tales of this type, several modes of recovery of the persons taken are offered. One of them consists in touching the abducted man with a piece of iron, and the objection of supernatural beings to this metal is one of the themes of fairy lore.

Near Bridgend, Wales, is a place where it is reported that a woman who had been taken by the fairies came back ten years later and thought she had not been away more than ten days. Hartland gives another charming story on the same theme, concerning a boy named Gitto Bach, or Little Griffith, a farmer's son who disappeared:

> During two whole years nothing was heard of him; but at length one morning when his mother, who had long and bitterly mourned for him as dead, opened the door, whom should she see sitting on the threshold but Gitto with a bundle under his arm. He was dressed and looked exactly as when she last saw him, for he had not grown a bit. "Where have you been all this time?" asked his mother. "Why, it was only yesterday I went away," he replied; and opening the bundle he showed her a dress the "little children" as he called them, had given him for dancing with them. The dress was of white paper without seam. With maternal caution she put it into the fire.

The best-known stories where time relativity is the main theme are, of course, of the "Rip van Winkle" type, patterned after numerous folk stories that allegedly concern actual events. Strangely enough, we again find the identical theme in ages-old Chinese folklore. Witness the story of Wang Chih, one of the holy men of the Taoists.

One day, as Wang Chih wandered through the mountains of Kü Chow gathering firewood, he saw a grotto where some old men were playing chess. He came in to watch their game and laid down his ax. One of the old men gave him something like a datestone and instructed him to place it on his mouth. "No sooner had he done so than hunger and thirst passed away." Some time later, one of the aged players told him, "It is long since you came here; you should go home now." But as he turned to pick up his ax, Wang Chih found that the handle had turned into dust. He reached the valley, but found not hours or days but centuries had passed, and nothing remained of the world as he had known it.

A similar tradition exists in Denmark. For instance, in a tale which is typical of the pattern, a bride thoughtlessly walked through the fields during the festivities of her wedding day and passed a mound "where the elves were making merry." (Again, we have here a description of the Little People close to the magical object sometimes described as a large, flat, round table, sometimes as a hillock. A disk or a large cone resting on the ground would fit that description. In describing the fairy knoll, Hartland writes: "The hillock was standing, as is usual on such occasions, on red pillars!")

The "wee folk" offered the bride-to-be a cup of wine, and she joined in a dance with them. Then she hastened back home, where she could not find her family. Everything had changed in the village.

Finally, on hearing her cries, a very old woman exclaimed: "Was it you, then, who disappeared at my grandfather's brother's wedding, a hundred years ago?"

At these words, the poor girl fell down and expired.

It is fascinating indeed to find such tales, which antedate Einstein's and Langevin's relativistic traveler by centuries!

The supernatural lapse of time in fairyland is often allied to the theme of love between the abducted human being and one of the fairies. Such is the pattern of the story of Ossian, or Oisin:

Once, when he was a young man, Oisin fell asleep under a tree. He woke up suddenly and found a richly dressed lady "of more than mortal beauty" looking at him. She was the queen of the legendary land of Tir na n'Og, and she invited him to share her palace. Oisin and the queen were in love and happy, but the hero was warned not to go into the palace gardens or to stand on a certain flat stone. Naturally, he transgressed the order, and when he stood upon the stone, he beheld his native land, suffering from oppression and violence. He went to the queen and told her he must return. "How long do you think you have been with me?" she asked. "Thrice seven days," said he. "Thrice seven years," was the answer. But he still wanted to go back. She then gave him a black horse from whose back he must not alight during his trip in the other world, for fear of seeing the power of time suddenly fall on him. But he forgot the warning when an incident induced him to dismount, and at once he became a feeble, blind, and helpless old man.

It is not necessary to spend time here to point out in detail the parallel traditions of the island of Avalon, Morgan the Fay, the legend of Ogier the Dane, and the magical travels of King Arthur. All these traditions insist on the peculiar nature of time in the "other world." Nor is this limited to European history, as Hartland again points out:

> Many races having traditions of a Culture God—that is, of a superior being who has taught them agriculture and the arts of life, and led them to victory over their enemies—add that he has gone away from them for awhile, and that he will some day come back again. Quetzalcoatl and Viracocha, the culture gods of Mexico and Peru, are familiar instances of this.

Similarly, Vishnu has yet a tenth incarnation to accomplish the final destruction of this world's wicked. At the end of the present age, he will be revealed in the sky, seated on a white horse and holding a blazing sword.

Such great traditions are common knowledge, like the abductions of Enoch, Ezekiel, Elijah and others in the Bible. What is not commonly known is that such legends have been built on the popular belief in numerous actual stories of the less glorious, more ordinary and "personal," type we have reviewed here. For instance, while all the books about Mexico mention Quetzalcoatl, they usually ignore the local beliefs in little black beings, the *ikals,* whose pranks we have already mentioned, and who, while their relationship with modern Latin American UFO lore is clear, also provide an obvious parallel to the fairy-faith.

In his study of the tales of Tenejapa, Brian Stross reports

> they are believed to be beings from another world, and some have been seen flying with some kind of rocket-like thing attached to the back. With this rocket they are said occasionally to have carried off people.

Similarly, Gordon Creighton reports:

> The *ikal* of the Tzotzils flies through the air. Sometimes he steals women, and the women so taken are remarkably prolific, and may bear a child once a week, or once a month, or even daily. The offspring are black, and they learn the art of flying inside their father's cave.

Brian Stross's Indian informants reported that a flurry of *ikals* was sighted "about twenty years ago"—which would take us back to 1947, a very important year in UFO history.

On June 5, 1968, the press reported that a Buenos Aires couple, Mr. and Mrs. Vidal, had a very strange adventure while driving between Chascomus and Maipu. They were surrounded by a thick cloud of mist and fell asleep. When they woke up, their car was on a dirt road they did not know, and they found out to their dismay that they were in Mexico! The paint on their car, a Peugeot 403, had entirely vanished.

The Vidals went to the Argentine consulate in Mexico, and from there called some friends of theirs in Buenos Aires to make arrangements for their return. The consulate has refused to comment on the incident. The Vidals' car has been taken to the United States for investigation, and Mrs. Vidal has been hospitalized in an Argentina clinic, in a state of nervous depression. Forty-eight hours in the lives of Mr. and Mrs. Vidal cannot be accounted for.

Beyond Reason

In the past twenty years, UFO reports have been studied not only in a sensational light by people with journalistic motives and methods but also by serious persons who have tried to place them within the framework of space science, modern physics, psychology, or the history of superstition. An increasing number of researchers—best identified with the *Flying Saucer Review* in Great Britain and with the groups such as APRO and NICAP in the United States—have made systematic efforts at responsible data-gathering, at the same time attempting to discover one or several consistent "patterns" in the reports. But these efforts at rationalization of the UFO phenomenon have so far failed.

The most appealing of the theories proposed, which would regard the UFOs as probes from another planet, falls short of explaining the phenomena in their historical development. Present-day saucers cannot be evaluated without reference to the 1897 airship or to earlier sightings of similar objects. Then, too, the theory of simple visitation must be combined with the assumption that the visitors know far more physics than we do—so much more, in fact, that an interpretation in terms of physical concepts known to us is bound to end up in failure and contradiction. A second major flaw in all the theories proposed so far is found in the description of the entities and their behavior. Any theory can account for *some* of these reports, but only at the expense of arbitrary rejection of a much larger group.

The recognition of a parallel between UFO reports and the main themes of fairy-lore is the first indication I have found that a way might exist out of this dilemma. And although it is still too early for us to pick up the scattered pieces of our old theories in a new attempt at explanation, I would like to conclude this chapter with a more precise review of the most difficult cases we have before us. Of the "reasonable" sightings there is little that can be said. The real problem begins when we find witnesses who are typical of the average population and who tell a story that, though not inconsistent with the spectrum of UFO reports, still stands out because of a few specific details that are so unbelievable that our first reaction is to reject the entire story.

The thought that the story must be disregarded because it is a challenge to our reason is a reaction I am very familiar with, and it has led me in the past to select for analysis only those sightings that seem amenable to scientific criticism. Similarly, major groups such as NICAP or APRO and the official investigators working for Project Blue Book have devised some more or less conscious standards for the automatic rejection of "unbelievable" stories. To be sure, many of these reports do deserve the "crackpot" label, but such stories are usually accompanied by numerous signs of the witness's lack of mental balance. But when no such psychological context is evident, we must appraise the story very carefully.

October 12, 1963. It was raining hard between Monte Maiz and Isla Verde, in Argentina, as Eugenio Douglas drove his truck loaded with coal along the road. Dawn was coming. Suddenly, Douglas saw a bright spot on the road ahead, like the headlights of an approaching vehicle, except that it was a single, blinding light. To avoid a collision, Douglas slowed down. The light became so intense he had to lower his head and move to the side. He stopped the truck and got out. The light had disappeared.

Through the rain, Eugenio Douglas could now see a circular metallic craft, about thirty-five feet high. An opening became visible, making a second area of light, less intense, and three figures appeared. They looked like men, but they were wearing strange headdresses with things like antennae attached to the headpieces. They were over twelve feet tall. There was nothing repulsive about the entities, said Douglas, but he was terribly scared.

As soon as he was seen by the figures, a ray of red light flashed to the spot where he stood and burned him. Grabbing a revolver, he fired at the three entities and ran off toward Monte Maiz. But the burning red light followed him as far as the village, where it interfered with the street lights, turning them violet and green. Douglas could smell a pungent gas. The beauty and dramatic character of that scene is impressive, and in a screen illustration of the UFO saga this is probably the sighting that would best carry its total meaning.

Douglas ran to the first house and shouted for help. Ribas, the owner, had died the previous night, but his family, gathered around the body, reported that at the same time they heard Douglas's call the candles in the room and the electric lights in the house turned green, and the same strange smell was noticed. They rushed to open the door: there was Douglas in the pouring rain, his overcoat over his head and a gun in his hand. The street lights had changed color. It must have been one of the most fantastic scenes in the rich archives of ufology.

Eugenio Douglas was taken to the police station, where the burns on his face and hands were clearly seen. The police, it turned out, had received a number of calls about the lights' color change, but they had attributed the change to irregularities in the local power plant—which, however, would hardly account for the change in the candle lights, if that particular observation was not an illusion. Douglas was examined by a doctor, who stated the burns had been caused by a radiation similar to ultraviolet (according to Douglas, he had felt a burn when exposed to a *red* beam). When villagers went to the site where the truck was still parked, they found large footprints, nearly twenty inches long, but they were shortly afterward washed away by rain.

In late August, 1963, near the town of Sagrada Famila, Brazil, three boys, Fernando Eustagio, eleven, his brother Ronaldo, nine, and a neighbor named Marcos, went into the Eustagio garden and started to draw water from the well. Suddenly they became aware of a hovering sphere above the trees. They could even see four or five rows of people inside the sphere. An opening under the sphere became visible, and two light rays shot downward. A slender, ten-foot-tall being came down, as if gliding on the two beams of light. He alighted in the garden and walked for twenty feet or so in an odd fashion: his back seemed stiff, his legs were open, and his arms outstretched. He swung his body from left to right as if trying to find his balance and then sat down on a rock.

The three boys observed that the giant wore a transparent helmet and had in the middle of his forehead what they described as a dark "eye." He wore tall boots, each of which was equipped with a strange triangular spike, which made a peculiar impression in the soft ground and could be seen for several days afterward. His garment was shiny and had inflated as soon as the entity had touched the ground. The trousers seemed to be fastened tightly to the boots. He had a peculiar square pack on his chest, which emitted flashes of light in an intermittent manner.

Inside the sphere, still hanging motionless above the garden, the three boys could see occupants behind control panels "turning knobs and flicking switches."

When the giant in the garden made a motion as if to grab one of the boys, Fernando picked up a stone—only to find himself unable to do anything with it as the spaceman looked straight into his eyes. The giant then returned to the sphere, still using the light beams as an "elevator" but holding his arms close to his body this time. The boys were no longer afraid, although they could not account for their new feeling. As the sphere left, they were sure the giant spaceman had not come to hurt them, and somehow, in the same irrational fashion, they knew he would come back again.

In Brazil, six years earlier, an incident had taken place that has gained in UFO literature the place it certainly deserves, thanks to an excellent investigation by the late Professor Olavo Fontes, of the National School of Medicine in Rio de Janeiro, who interviewed and examined the witness, A. Villas-Boas, of Sao Francisco de Salles, Minas Gerais.

On the night of October 5, 1957, Antonio and his brother went to bed about 11:00 P.M. The night was hot, and as he opened the window, Antonio saw a silvery light in the corral similar to the spot made by a powerful searchlight. Later that night, the two brothers observed the light was still there. Then it moved toward the house, sweeping the roof before going away.

About 10:00 P.M. on October 14, Antonio was plowing with his tractor when he saw a blinding white light at the northern end of the field. Every time Antonio tried to approach it, the light moved away. This happened about twenty times, though the light always appeared to "wait for him." His second brother was watching the scene as Antonio finally gave up. The light simply vanished.

The next evening Antonio was alone at the same spot. The night was cold, clear, and starry. At 1:00 A.M. he saw something like a red star, which grew larger and became an egglike, bright object, which hovered above his tractor, then landed softly. Antonio tried to drive away, but the engine of the tractor died. He jumped down and took two steps, but someone caught his arm. After a short struggle, four men carried him inside the craft. The beings communicated among themselves in slowly emitted growls, unlike any sound the witness could reproduce, although they were "neither high-pitched nor too low." In spite of his resistance, the creatures stripped him, washed his body with something like a wet sponge, and took him into another room through a strangely lettered door.

It is not my purpose here to record all the details of the experience reported by Villas-Boas: they have been adequately documented first in the *Flying Saucer Review* by Fontes and Creighton and later by the Lorenzens, who provide a complete reprint of the testimony as recorded by Fontes and J. Martins, along with the professional opinion of Dr. Fontes after his medical examination of the witness, in their book *Flying Saucer Occupants*. Fontes's conclusion that Villas-Boas is not mentally unbalanced and that he is sincere in reporting his story is what prompts me to include the story here. And the story does provide a link between such tales as the story of Ossian and the general question of the genetic context of the UFO myth, which will be the object of the next section of this chapter.

Antonio remained alone in the room for what seemed to him a very long time. When he heard a noise at the door, he turned and received a "terrible shock": the door was open and a woman came in, as naked as he was. Her hair was blonde, with a part in the center. She had blue eyes, rather longer than round, slanted outward. Her nose was straight, her cheekbones prominent. Her face looked very wide, "wider than that of an Indio native." It ended in a pointed chin. Her lips were very thin, nearly invisible, in fact. Her ears were small but ordinary. She was much shorter than he was, her head only reaching his shoulder. She quickly made clear to him what the purpose of her visit was. Soon after, in fact, another man came in and beckoned to the woman, who, pointing to her belly, smiled, pointed at the sky, and followed the man out.

The men came back with Antonio's clothes, then took him to a room where the other crew members were sitting, growling among themselves. The witness, who felt sure no harm would come to him now, carefully observed his surroundings. Among other things—all his remarks here are of interest—he noticed a box with a glass top that had the appearance of an "alarm clock." The "clock" had one hand and several marks that would correspond to the 3, 6, 9, and 12 of an ordinary clock. However, although time passed, the hand did not move, and Antonio concluded that it was no clock.

The symbolism in this remark by Villas-Boas is clear. We are reminded of the fairy tales quoted above, of the country where time does not pass, and of that great poet who had in his room a huge white clock without hands, bearing the words "It is later than you think." It is the poetic quality of such details in many UFO sightings that catches the attention—in spite of the irrational, or obviously absurd, character of the tale—and makes it so similar to a dream. Antonio must have thought so, because he reflected that he must bring some evidence back and tried to steal the "clock." At once, one of the men shoved him to the side angrily. This attempt to secure evidence is a constant feature of fairy tales, and we are also reminded of the efforts by Betty Hill to convince her captors to let her take a peculiar "book" she saw inside their craft. As in the Villas-Boas incident, the men denied her the opportunity to convince the world that the experience had been real.

At last, one of the men motioned Antonio to follow him to a circular platform. He was then given a detailed tour of the machine, taken to a metal ladder, and signaled to go down. Antonio watched all the details of the preparation for take-off and observed the craft as it rose from the ground and flew away in a matter of seconds. He noticed that the time was 5:30; he had spent over four hours inside the strange machine.

It must be noted that the witness volunteered information about the sighting in general terms when a notice appeared in a newspaper calling for UFO reports. He was extremely reluctant to discuss the more personal aspects of his experience and related them only when questioned with insistence by Fontes and Martins. Like Maurice Masse, Villas-Boas suffered from excessive sleepiness for about a month after the incident.

Demonialitas

When folklore becomes degraded to a minor literary form, as the fairy-faith was degraded to the fairy tales we know today, it naturally loses much of its content: precisely those "adult" details that cannot be allowed to remain in children's books. The direct result of the censorship of spicy details in these marvelous stories is that they really become mere occasions for amazement. The Villas-Boas case is hardly appropriate for nursery-school reading, but to eliminate the little lady from the story would turn it into a tale without deep symbolic or psychological value. The sexual context is precisely what gives such accounts their literary influence. It is what provides impact to the fairy-faith.

Without the sexual context—without the stories of changelings, human midwives, intermarriage with the gentry, of which we never hear in modern fairy tales—it is doubtful that the tradition about fairies would have survived through the ages. Nor is that true only of fairies: the most remarkable cases of sexual contact with nonhumans are not found in spicy saucer books, nor in fairy legends; they rest, safely stored away, in the archives of the Catholic Church. To find them, one must first learn Latin and gain entrance into the few libraries where these unique records are preserved. But the accounts one finds there make the Villas-Boas case pale by comparison, as I believe the reader will agree before the end of this chapter.

Let us first establish clearly that the belief in the possibility of intermarriage between man and the nonhuman races we are studying is a corollary to the apparitions in all historical contexts.

This is so obvious in biblical stories that I hardly need elaborate. The sex of the angels is not the most difficult—on the contrary, it is the clearest—of all theological questions. In Anatole France's *Revolt of the Angels* it is Arcade, one of the celestial beings, who says:

> There's nothing like having sound references. In order to assure yourself that I am not deceiving you, Maurice, on this subject of the amorous embraces of angels and women, look up Justin, *Apologies* I and II; Flavius Josephus, *Jewish Antiquities,* Book I, Chapter III; Athenagoras, *Concerning the Resurrection;* Lactantius, Book II, Chapter XV; Tertullian, *On the Veil of the Virgins;* Marcus of Ephesus in *Psellus;* Eusebius, *Praeparatio Evangelica,* Book V, Chapter IV; Saint Ambrose, in his book on *Noah and the Ark,* Chapter V; Saint Augustine in his *City of God,* Book XV, Chapter XXIII; Father Meldonat, the Jesuit, *Treatise on Demons,* page 248 . . .

Thus spoke Arcade, his guardian angel, to poor Maurice, as he tried to apologize for having stolen his mistress, pretty Madam Gilberte. And he added shamelessly,

> It was bound to be so; all the other angels in revolt would have done as I did with Gilberte. "Women, saith the Apostle, should pray with their heads covered, because of the angels."

This is clear enough. But fairies and elves? Are they subject to such carnal desires? Consider the following facts.

In the Preface of the *Saga of Hrolf,* Torfeus, a seventeenth-century Danish historian, records statements made about the elves by Einard Gusmond, the Icelandic scholar:

> I am convinced they really do exist, and they are creatures of God; that they get married like we do, and have children of either sex: we have a proof of this in what we know of the love of some of their women with simple mortals.

William Grant Stewart, in *The Popular Superstitions and Festive Amusements of the Highlanders of Scotland,* devotes the second part of his discussion to fairies. In a chapter entitled "Of the Passions and Propensities of the Fairies," he has this to say on sexual intercourse with them:

> The fairies are remarkable for the amorousness of their dispositions, and are not very backward in forming attachments and

connections with the people that cannot with propriety be called their own species.

This is a beautiful example of convoluted phraseology. Stewart is less obviously embarrassed when he reports that such events no longer seem to take place between men and fairies:

> We owe it, in justice to both the human and the fairy communities of the present day, to say, that such intercourse as that described to have taken place betwixt them is now extremely rare; with the single exception of a good old shoemaker, now or lately living in the village of Tomantoul, who confesses having had some dalliances with a "lanan-shi" in his younger days, we do not know personally any one who has carried matters this length.

If Stewart came back today, he would have to revise this statement after reading UFO material. Kirk stated the case more clearly when he said: "In our Scotland there are numerous and beautiful creatures of that aerial order, who frequently assign meetings to lascivious young men as succubi, or as joyous mistresses and prostitutes, who are called Leannain Sith or familiar spirits." I hardly need to remind the reader of the importance of such "familiar spirits" in medieval occultism, particularly in Rosicrucian theories. Nor do I need to mention the number of accused witches who were condemned to death on the evidence that they had such familiar spirits.

There is no gap between the fairy-faith and ufology regarding the sexual question. This is apparent from the study made by Wentz, who records, for example, the following story:

> My grandmother Catherine MacInnis used to tell about a man named Laughlin, whom she knew, being in love with a fairy-woman. The fairy-woman made it a point to see Laughlin every night, and he being worn out with her began to fear her. Things got so bad at last that he decided to go to America to escape the fairy-woman. As soon as the plan was fixed and he was about to emigrate, women who were milking at sunset out in the meadows heard very audibly the fairy-woman singing this song:
>
> > What will the brown-haired woman do
> > When Lachie is on the billows?
>
> Lachie emigrated to Cape Breton, landing at Pictu, Nova Scotia; and in his first letter home to his friends he stated that the same fairy-woman was haunting him there in America.

The comments by Wentz on this case are extremely important:

> To discover a tale so rare and curious as this . . . is certainly of all our evidence highly interesting. And aside from its high literary value, it proves conclusively that the fairy-women who entice mortals to their love in modern times are much the same, if not the same, as the succubi of middle-age mystics.

This allows us to return to the religious records mentioned above, one of which offers one of the most remarkable cases of apparition I have ever come across. It is difficult to believe that stories exist that surpass, for their amazing contents or shocking features, some of the reports we have already studied, such as the Hills case or the Villas-Boas report. But, remarkable as they are, these latter two accounts refer only to one aspect of the total phenomenon; they can be interpreted only after being placed within the continuum of hundreds of lesser-known cases, which provide the necessary background. The following case stands alone, and it is unique in that it relates the apparition of an incubus with the poltergeist phenomenon.

The authority upon which the case rests is that of Fr. Ludovicus Maria Sinistrari de Ameno, who reports and discusses it in his manuscript *De Daemonialitate, et Incubis, et Succubis,* written in the second half of the seventeenth century. Who is Fr. Sinistrari? A theologian-scholar born in Ameno, Italy, on February 26, 1622, he studied in Pavia and entered the Franciscan Order in 1647. He devoted his life to teaching philosophy and theology to numerous students attracted to Pavia by his fame as an eminent scholar. He also served as Councilor to the Supreme Tribunal of the Inquisition and as Theologian attached to the Archbishop of Milan. In 1688, he supervised the compilation of the statutes of the Franciscan Order. He died in 1701.

Among other books, Fr. Sinistrari published a treatise called *De Delictis et Poenis,* which is an exhaustive compilation *"tractatus absolutissimus"* of all the crimes and sins imaginable. In short, Fr. Sinistrari was one of the highest authorities on human psychology and religious law to serve the Catholic Church in the seventeenth century. Compared to his *De Daemonialitate, Playboy* is a rather innocent gathering of mild reveries. The good father writes:

> About twenty-five years ago while I was a professor of Sacred Theology at the Holy Cross Convent in Pavia, there lived in that city a married woman of excellent morality. All who knew her, and particularly the clergy, had nothing but the highest praises

for her. Her name was Hieronyma, and she lived in the St. Michael Parish.

One day, Hieronyma prepared some bread and brought it to the baker's to have it baked. He brought it back to her, and at the same time he brought her a large pancake of a very peculiar shape, made with butter and Venetian pastes, such as they use to make cakes in that city. She refused it, saying she had not prepared anything like it.

"But," said the baker, "I have not had any bread to bake today but yours. The pancake must come from your house too; your memory probably fails you."

The good lady allowed herself to be convinced; she took the pancake and ate it with her husband, her three-year-old daughter, and a servant girl.

During the following night, while she was in bed with her husband and both were asleep, she found herself awakened by an extremely fine voice, somewhat like a high-pitched whistling sound. It was softly saying in her ear some very clear words: "How did you like the cake?" In fear, our good lady began to use the sign of the cross and to invoke in succession the names of Jesus and Mary.

"Fear naught," said the voice. "I mean no harm to you. On the contrary, there is nothing I would not do in order to please you. I am in love with your beauty, and my greatest desire is to enjoy your embraces."

At the same time, she felt that someone was kissing her cheeks, but so softly and gently that she might have thought it was only the finest cotton down touching her. She resisted, without answering anything, only repeating many times the names of Jesus and Mary and making the sign of the cross. The temptation lasted thus about half an hour, after which time the tempter went away.

In the morning, the lady went to her confessor, a wise and knowledgeable man, who confirmed her in the ways of the faith and appealed to her to continue her strong resistance, and to use some holy relics.

The following nights: similar temptations, with words and kisses of the same kind; similar opposition, too, from the lady. However, as she was tired of such lasting trials, she took the advice of her confessor and other serious men and asked to be examined by trained exorcists to decide whether or not she was possessed. The exorcists found nothing in her to indicate the presence of the evil spirit. They blessed the house, the bedroom, the bed, and gave the incubus orders to discontinue his

importunities. All was in vain: he went on tempting her, pre-
tending he was dying with love, and crying, moaning, in order to
invoke the lady's pity. With God's help, she remained unmoved.

Then the incubus used a different approach: he appeared to
her in the figure of a young boy or small man with golden, curl-
ing hair, with a blond beard gleaming like gold and sea-green
eyes. To add to his power of seduction, he was elegantly dressed
in Spanish vestments. Besides, he kept appearing to her even
when she was in company; he would complain, as lovers do; he
would send her kisses. In a word, he used all the means of seduction to obtain her favors. Only she saw and heard him; to all
others, there was nothing.

This excellent woman had kept her unwavering determination
for several months when the incubus had recourse to a new kind
of persecution.

First, he took from her a silver cross full of holy relics and a
blessed wax or papal lamb of Pope Pius V, which she always had
on her. Then, rings and other jewels of gold and silver followed.
He stole them without touching the locks of the casket in which
they were enclosed. Then he began to strike her cruelly, and
after each series of blows one could see on her face, arm, or
other areas of her body bruises and marks, which lasted one or
two days, then vanished suddenly, quite unlike natural bruises,
which go away by degrees.

Sometimes, as she suckled her daughter, he took the child
from her knees and carried her to the roof, placing her at the
edge of the gutter. Or else he would hide her, but without ever
causing her harm.

He would also upset the household, sometimes breaking to
pieces the plates and earthenware. But in the blink of an eye he
also restored them to their original state.

One night, as she lay in bed with her husband, the incubus, appearing to her under his usual form, energetically demanded that
she give herself up. She refused, as usual. Furious, the incubus
went away, and a short time later he returned with an enormous
load of those flat stones that inhabitants of Genoa, and of
Liguria in general, use to cover their houses. With these stones
he built around the bed such a high wall that it reached almost
to the ceiling, and the couple had to send for a ladder in order to
come out. This wall was built without lime. It was pulled down
and the stones were stored in a corner, where they were exposed
to everyone's sight. But after two days they vanished.

On the day of St. Stephen, the lady's husband had invited
several military friends to dine with him. To honor his guests

he had prepared a respectable dinner. While they were washing their hands according to the custom—hop!—suddenly the table vanished, along with the dishes, the cauldrons, the plates, and all the earthenware in the kitchen, the jugs, the bottles, the glasses too. You can imagine the amazement, the surprise, of the guests. There were eight of them, among them a Spanish infantry captain who told them:

"Do not be afraid. It is only a trick. But there used to be a table here, and it must still be here. I am going to find it."

Having said that, he went around the room with outstretched hands, attempting to seize the table. But after he had made many turns, seeing he was only touching air, the others laughed at him. And since dinner time had passed, everyone took his coat and started for home. They had already reached the door with the husband, who was politely accompanying them, when they heard a great noise in the dining room. They stopped to find out what it was, and the servant girl ran and told them the kitchen was full of new plates loaded with food, and the table had come back in the dining room.

The table was now covered with napkins, dishes, glasses, and silverware that were not the original ones. And there were all kinds of precious cups full with rare wines. In the kitchen, too, there were new jugs and utensils; they had never been seen there before. The guests, however, were hungry, and they ate this strange meal, which they found very much to their taste. After dinner, as they were talking by the fireplace, everything vanished, and the old table came back with the untouched dishes on it.

But, oddly enough, no one was hungry any longer, so that nobody wanted to have supper after such a magnificent dinner— which shows that the dishes which had been substituted for the original ones were real and not imaginary.

This persecution had been going on for several months, the lady consulted the Blessed Bernardino of Felter, whose body is the object of veneration in St. James Church, some distance outside the city walls. And at the same time, she vowed to wear for a whole year a gray monk's gown, with a rope as a belt, like those used by the minor brothers in the order to which Bernardino belonged. She hoped, through his intercession, that she would be freed from the persecutions of the incubus.

Indeed, on September 28—which is the Vigil of the Dedication of Archangel St. Michael and the Feast of the Blessed Bernardino—she took the votive dress. The next morning was the Feast of St. Michael. Our afflicted lady went to the church of that saint, which was, as I have said, her own parish. It was about ten o'clock, and a very large crowd was going to mass. Now, the poor woman had no sooner put her foot on the church ground than all of a sudden her vestments and ornaments fell to the ground and were carried away by the wind, leaving her as naked as the hand. Very fortunately, it so happened that among the crowd were two knights of mature age who saw the thing and hurriedly removed their coats, to hide as well as they could that woman's nudity. And having put her in a coach, they drove her home. As for the vestments and jewels stolen by the incubus, he returned them six months later.

To make a long story short, although there are many other tricks that this incubus played on her, and some amazing ones, suffice it to say that he kept tempting her for many years. But, at last, perceiving he was wasting his efforts, he discontinued these unusual and bothersome vexations.

As a theologian, Fr. Sinistrari was as puzzled by such reports as most modern students of UFO lore are by the Villas-Boas case. Observing that the fundamental texts of the Church gave no clear opinion on such cases, Sinistrari wondered how they should be judged by religious law. A great part of his manuscript is devoted to a detailed examination of this question. The lady in the above example did not allow the incubus to have intercourse with her. But there are numerous other cases in the records of the Church (especially in witch trials) in which there was intercourse. From the Church's point of view, says Fr. Sinistrari, there are several problems. First, how is such intercourse physically possible? Second, how does demoniality differ from bestiality? Third, what sin is committed by those who engage in such intercourse? Fourth, what should their punishment be?

The earliest author who uses the word "demonialitas" is J. Caramuel, in his *Theologia Fundamentalis*. Before him, no one made a distinction between demoniality and bestiality. All the moralists, following St. Thomas Aquinas, understood by bestiality "any kind of carnal intercourse with an object of a different species." Thus Cajetan in his commentary on St. Thomas places intercourse with the demon in the class of bestiality, and so does Sylvester when he defines *luxuria,* and Bonacina in *De Matrimonio,* question 4.*

There is here a fine point of theology, which Sinistrari debates with

---

* In this respect, Villas-Boas's remark that lying with the woman gave him the impression that he was lying with an animal, because of her "growls," is striking.

obvious authority. He concludes that St. Thomas never meant intercourse with demons to fall within his definition of bestiality. By "different species," Sinistrari says, the saint can only mean species of living *being,* and this hardly applies to the devil. Similarly, if a man copulates with a corpse, this is not bestiality, especially according to the Thomist doctrine that denies the corpse the nature of the human body. The same would be true for a man who copulates with the corpse of an animal. Throughout this discussion, the great intelligence and obvious knowledge of human psychology of the author is remarkable. It is quite fascinating to follow Fr. Sinistrari's thoughts in an area that is directly relevant to UFO reports. And relevant it is indeed; for Villas-Boas or Betty and Barney Hill would certainly have had a hard time before the Inquisitors if they had lived in the seventeenth century.†

The act of love, writes Sinistrari, has for an object human generation. Unnatural semination, that is, intercourse that cannot be followed by generation, constitutes a separate type of sin against nature. But it is the subject of that semination that distinguishes the various sins under that type. If demoniality and bestiality were in the same category, a man who had copulated with a demon could simply tell his confessor: "I have committed the sin of bestiality." And yet he obviously has not committed that sin.

Considerable problems arose, however, when one had to identify the physical process of intercourse with demons. This is clearly a most difficult point (as difficult as that of identifying the physical nature of flying saucers!), and Sinistrari gives a remarkable discussion of it. Pointing out that the main object of the discussion is to determine the degree of punishment these sins deserve, he tries to list all the different ways in which the sin of demoniality can be committed. First he remarks:

> There are quite a few people, over-inflated with their little knowledge, who dare deny what the wisest authors have written, and what everyday experience demonstrates: namely, that the

† Benoit de Berne, at age seventy-five, confessed he had had intercourse for forty years with a succubus named Hermeline. He was burned alive.

In passing, let us remark that the most eminent of our scientists choose, with Condon, to ignore such reports, which they label "crackpot" material. Yet, a few centuries earlier, the best minds saw in similar accounts an occasion to increase their knowledge of human nature and did not feel it was beneath their dignity as philosophers to spend considerable time in this study. If, as a twentieth-century scientist, I need an apology to write the present book, this should be as good a precedent as any.

demon, either incubus or succubus, has carnal union not only with men and women but also with animals.

Sinistrari does not deny that some young women often have visions and imagine that they have attended a sabbat. Similarly, ordinary erotic dreams have been classified by the Church quite separately from the question we are studying. Sinistrari does not mean such psychological phenomena when he speaks of demoniality; he refers to actual physical intercourse, such as the basic texts on witchcraft discuss. Thus in the *Compendium Maleficarum,* Gnaccius gives eighteen case histories of witches who have had carnal contact with demons. All cases are vouched for by scholars whose testimony is above question. Besides, St. Augustine himself says in no uncertain terms:

> It is a widespread opinion, confirmed by direct or indirect testimony of trustworthy persons, that the Sylvans and Fauns, commonly called Incubi, have often tormented women, solicited and obtained intercourse with them. There are even Demons, which are called Duses [i.e., *lutins*] by the Gauls, who are quite frequently using such impure practices: this is vouched for by so numerous and so high authorities that it would be impudent to deny it.

Now, the devil makes use of two ways in these carnal contacts. One he uses with sorcerers and witches; the other with men and women perfectly foreign to witchcraft.

This is a point of paramount importance. What Sinistrari is saying is that two kinds of people may come in contact with the beings he calls demons: those who have made a *formal pact* with them—and he gives the details of the process for making this pact—and those who simply happen to be "contacted" by them. The implications of this fundamental statement to occultism for the interpretation of the fairy-faith and of modern UFO stories should be obvious to the reader.

The devil does not have a body. Then, how does he manage to have intercourse with men and women? How can women have children from such unions if they specifically express the desire? All the theologians answer that the devil borrows the corpse of a human being, either male or female, or else *he forms with other materials a new body* for this purpose. Indeed, we find here the same theory as that expressed by one of the Gentry and quoted by Wentz: "We can make the old young, the big small, the small big."

The devil then is said to proceed in one of two ways. Either he first takes the form of a female succubus and then has intercourse with a man. Or else, the succubus induces lascivious dreams in a sleeping man and makes use of the resulting "pollution" to allow the devil to perform the second part of the operation. This is the theory taught by Gnaccius, who gives a great number of examples. Likewise, Hector Boethius, in *Historia Scotorum,* documents the case of a young Scot who, for several months, was visited in his bedroom, the windows and doors of which were closed, by a succubus of the most ravishing beauty. She did everything she could to obtain intercourse with him, but he did not yield to her caresses and entreaties.

One point intrigued Sinistrari greatly: such demons do not obey the exorcists. They have no fear of relics and other holy objects, and thus they do not fall into the same category as the devils by which people are possessed, as the story quoted above certainly shows. But then, are they really creatures of the devil? Should not we place them in a separate category, with the fairies and the elementals they so closely resemble? And then, if such creatures have their own bodies, does the traditional theory—that incubi and succubi are demons who have borrowed human corpses—hold? Could it explain how children are born from such unions? What are the physical characters of such children? If we admit that the UFO reports we have quoted earlier in this chapter indicate the phenomenon has *genetic contents,* then the above questions are fundamental, and it is important to see how Sinistrari understood them. Therefore, I give in the following a complete translation of his discussion of the matter.

> To theologians and philosophers, it is a fact, that from the copulation of humans (man or woman) with the demon, human beings are sometimes born. It is by this process that Antichrist must be born, according to a number of doctors:‡ Bellarmin, Suarez, Maluenda, etc. Besides, they observe that as the result of a quite natural cause, the children generated in this manner by the incubi are tall, very strong, very daring, very magnificent and very wicked. . . . Maluenda confirms what has been said above, proving by the testimony of various classical authors that it is to such unions that the following owe their birth:
>
> Romulus and Remus, according to Livy and Plutarch.
>
> Servius-Tullius, sixth king of the Romans, according to Denys of Halicarnassus and Pliny.

‡ Le Brun's comment throws more light: "If the body of these children is thus different from the bodies of other children, their soul will certainly have qualities that will not be common to others: that is why Cardinal Bellarmin thinks Antichrist will be born of a woman having had intercourse with an incubus."

Plato the philosopher, according to Diogenes Laertius and St. Jerome.

Alexander the Great, according to Plutarch and Quinte-Curce.

Seleucus, king of Syria, according to Justin and Applian.

Scipio the African, according to Livy.

The Emperor Caesar Augustus, according to Suetonius.

Aristomenes of Messenia, the illustrious Greek general, according to Strabo and Pausanias.

Let us add the English Merlin or Melchin, born of an incubus and a nun, the daughter of Charlemagne. And finally, as writes Cocleus, quoted by Maluenda, that damned heresiarch whose name is Martin Luther.

However, in spite of all the respect I owe so many great doctors, I do not see how their opinion can stand examination. Indeed, as Pererius observes very well in *Commentary on Genesis,* Chapter Six, all the strength, all the power of the human sperm, comes from spirits that evaporate and vanish as soon as they issue from the genital cavities where they were warmly stored. The physicians agree on this. Therefore, it is not possible for the demon to keep the sperm he has received in a sufficient state of integrity to produce generation; for, no matter what the vessel where he could attempt to keep it is, this vessel would have to have a temperature equal to the natural temperature of human genital organs, which is found nowhere but in those same organs. Now, in a vessel where the warmth is not natural, but artificial, spirits are resolved, and no generation is possible. A second objection is that generation is a vital act through which man, from his own substance, introduces sperm through the use of natural organs, into a place proper for generation. To the contrary, in the special case we are now considering, the introduction of the sperm cannot be a vital act of the generating man, since it is not by him that it is introduced into the matrix. And, for the same reason, it cannot be said that the man to whom the sperm belonged has engendered the fetus that is procreated. Neither can we consider the incubus as the father, since the sperm is not of his own substance. Thus here is a child who is born and has no father—which is absurd. Third objection: when the father engenders naturally, there is a concourse of two causalities: a material one, for he provides the sperm that is the material of generation; and an efficient one, for he is the main agent in the generation, according to the common opinion of philosophers. But, in our case, the man who does nothing but provide the sperm simply gives material, without any action tending toward generation. Therefore he could not be regarded as the child's father, and this is contrary to the notion that the child engendered by an incubus is not his child, but the child of the man whose sperm was borrowed by the incubus. . . .

We also read in the Scriptures (Genesis 6:4) that giants were born as a result of intercourse between the sons of God and the daughters of Man: this is the very letter of the sacred text. Now, these giants were men of tall stature, as it is said in Baruch 3:26, and far superior to other men. Besides their monstrous size, they called attention by their strength, their plunders, their tyranny. And it is to the crimes of these giants that we must attribute the main and primary cause of the Flood, according to Cornelius a Lapide in his *Commentary on Genesis*.

Some state that under the name of sons of God we must understand the sons of Seth, and, under that of daughters of men, the daughters of Cain, because the former practiced piety, religion, and all other virtues while the latter, the children of Cain, did exactly the opposite. But, with all the respect we owe Chrysostom, Cyril, and others who share this view, it will be recognized it is in disagreement with the obvious meaning of the text. What do the Scriptures say? That from the conjunction of the above were born men of monstrous corporeal proportions. Therefore, these giants did not exist previously, and if their birth was the result of that union, it is not admissible to attribute it to the intercourse between the sons of Seth and the daughters of Cain who, of ordinary size themselves, could have children only of ordinary size.

Consequently, if the intercourse in question has given birth to beings of monstrous proportions, we must see there not the ordinary intercourse of men with women but the operation of the incubi who, owing to their nature, can very well be called sons of God. This opinion is that of the Platonist philosophers and of Francois George of Venice, and it is not in contradiction with that of Josephus the historian, Philo, St. Justin Martyr, Clement of Alexandria, and Tertullian, according to whom these incubi could be angels who had allowed themselves to commit the sin of luxury with women. Indeed, as we shall show, there is nothing there but a single opinion under a double appearance.

What we have here is a complete theory of contact between our race and another race, nonhuman, different in physical nature, but biologically compatible with us. Angels, demons, fairies, creatures from heaven, hell, or Magonia: they inspire our strangest dreams, shape our destinies, steal our desires. . . . But who are they?

BARRY H. DOWNING is pastor of the Northminster Presbyterian Church at Endwell, New York. He serves on the advisory staff of the Midwest UFO Network as a consultant in theology. The Reverend Mr. Downing, a physics major as an undergraduate, earned a doctorate from the University of Edinburgh. His dissertation concerned the relation between science and religion, and the concepts of time and space in the science and theology of Isaac Newton. He recently completed a forthcoming book on religion and mankind's future, *God's Game*.

WHERE IS HEAVEN?

To be consistent with the method we have employed in evaluating the biblical material up to the present time, to ask the question "Where is heaven?" is also to ask the question, "Where do flying saucers come from?" The present consensus of most writers is that since there are perhaps millions of inhabitable planets in the universe, flying saucers probably come from one such planet, and the nearer to earth the better. A *Time* magazine essay, "A Fresh Look at Flying Saucers," points out how difficult long-distance space travel becomes. "Even the nearest star, Proxima Centauri, is 4.3 light-years away. And because presumably no spaceship—or any matter—can travel at or beyond the velocity of light, which is the universal speed limit according to the Einstein theory of relativity, it would take considerably longer than 4.3 light-years to reach the earth from its nearest stellar neighbor. At the 17,500 m.p.h. that astronauts travel, it would take nearly 170,000 years."

We are still in the stone age of space travel, so that it is probably quite misleading to compare the speed of our spaceships with those of beings who are really advanced in space travel. But *Time*'s essay raises an important question: What does Einstein's theory of relativity have to do with space travel, and what sort of possibilities does the theory contain concerning our search for heaven? Although I am no authority on relativity, I will try to examine some of the issues.

One of the basic assumptions of Einstein and Eddington and others who have developed the general "theory of relativity" is that space, time, and gravitation are interdependent, not independent. In fact, gravitation came to be understood as either a property of space, or of matter which permeated and influenced all space. Thus any point particle is in effect under the influence of the whole universe. Furthermore, non-Euclidean geometry had been developed, and it was suggested that space may not be "straight" or "flat," but rather curved, and that all objects traveling in space follow a curved path.

Einstein predicted that the gravitation of the universe would even deflect light rays, and this was later experimentally verified. He was led to conclude that the universe might be "finite, but unbounded," meaning that although there is no physical boundary to the universe, the gravitational field of the universe would act as a "fence," so that any point particle traveling in space—even a ray of light—would be bent in an arc and would never escape a certain volume or area of space. Thus the force of gravitation would cause our usable space to be finite. Matter in space is something like a dog on a leash, tied to a stake. The dog can wander in a circle around the stake—his world does not appear to be bounded, but it is finite. He is limited by the leash (force of gravitation) which pulls him in toward the center stake.

Another aspect of Einstein's thinking, which has been verified to some extent by experimental observation, is that any mass which is accelerated takes on an additional apparent mass, and as the mass approaches the speed of light, this increase in apparent mass becomes greater. This is one of the reasons scientists were led to conclude that it would be impossible to accelerate any mass—including a spaceship—to a velocity which would equal or exceed the velocity of light.

Since gravity provides resistance to acceleration, we have to have rockets to send our spaceships into orbit. The rockets counteract the resisting force of gravity. As we have already pointed out, however, many of the flying-saucer reports suggest that saucer activity is so unusual that some have come to the conclusion that the beings who developed the saucers have somehow developed a technology which has set them free from the effects of gravity. Major Donald E. Keyhoe, in his book *The Flying Saucer Conspiracy,* devotes a full chapter to the idea of an antigravitational field. He points out that saucers have been seen to make right-angled turns at high speeds, and to accelerate from a velocity of zero to eighteen thousand miles an hour almost instantly. Saucers have apparently on occasion caused electromagnetic interference, such as shorting out the electrical systems of automobiles. We assume that saucers have some kind of propulsion system, and yet they usually make no noise. These are some of the reasons that have led men such as Keyhoe, Edwards, and Vallee to conclude that saucers are propelled by generating some kind of anti-gravitational field or shield. Whether or not the term *antigravitational* is the best term to describe the phenomenon is not clear. But in any case, we have asked the question: If the civilization behind the saucers has found a means to escape the effect of gravity, what does this mean?

We have mentioned that according to Einstein, our visible universe is "finite, but unbounded." Our universe is finite to us because we are bound to our universe by gravitation like a dog tethered to a stick. If we were to be set free from the effects of gravity, however, I can see no reason why we would not be free to move beyond our universe into a new space, much as if a dog had been cut free from his tether. Scientists have been discussing the possible existence of "antimatter"; there is no logical reason why only one type of matter could exist. Some material substance might exist outside our universe if it were somehow unaffected by the gravitational field of our universe. It might be possible for several universes to coexist, much as several boats sail the ocean, provided that each universe has a *different type of gravitational system* so that none are attracted toward any others. If gravity is the property of the curvature of space, it might be possible for several universes to coexist separately, provided they were governed by different spatial curvatures. But this still leaves us with the problem that since according to the relativity theory the speed of light is the universal speed limit, it would take millions of years traveling at the speed of light to reach any possible universe outside our own. Perhaps, however, since our concepts of relativity are still being explored by science, there is a yet undiscovered way to overcome this "speed limit." Then almost infinite speeds might become possible.

This is of course speculation, but I do believe the present concepts of space, cosmology, and the whole question of the nature of the universe are so open that we do have the freedom to speculate in this way; however uncertain our conclusions, we can still explore the biblical framework without having to feel intellectually guilty about doing so. Although science has made fantastic discoveries about the universe, many of these discoveries have simply opened brand-new fields which need to be explored.

If the theory of relativity permits us to imagine heaven as a universe separate from and beyond our own universe, this is by no means the only possible solution to the problem, and I will now suggest another. Our own space may be curved, either in a negative or positive direction, or it may have a zero curvature. Scientists have not decided which type of curvature is characteristic of our own universe, but given the idea that our space is curved, it is interesting to consider concepts in mathematical space topology such as Jordan's Curve Theorem which states in effect "that there are an inside and an outside of a simple closed curve in a plane." This idea seems to imply that if our universe is similar to a closed curve, then there might be an "inside" and an "outside" universe coexisting *in the same space* with our own universe. We are led to ask the question: Would it be possible for the universes of different spatial curvatures to coexist in the same space? Could you move from one universe to another provided you understood the spatial curvature, or gravitational formula for each space?

This reads like science fiction, but it is interesting to examine one flying-saucer report recorded by Keyhoe. He points out that there seem to be at least two types of UFOs: the "flying-saucer" type, and a cigar-shaped "mother ship" into which flying saucers have been seen to fly. Keyhoe records this report by Captain James Howard and the crew of a BOAC air liner:

> As Captain Howard was checking his arrival time, a dark object appeared a few miles to the left. Flying parallel to the plane, it was clearly visible in the light from the setting sun. Manoeuvring around this mysterious craft were several small, round objects. For a few moments Captain Howard and his co-pilot, First Officer Lee Boyd, watched in amazement. Until then Howard had been sceptical of flying-saucer reports, and Boyd had been only half convinced.
>
> The small saucers appeared to be flying in and out of the larger ship, though the pilots could not be sure.
>
> Suddenly the mother-ship changed its position, making it appear to change shape, just as an aeroplane, seen from different angles, assumes varying shapes.
>
> Both Captain Howard and Boyd were convinced that the objects were solid. And from the way the six small UFOs manoeuvred, circling and apparently boarding the mother-ship, they were obviously under intelligent control.
>
> Calling Goose Bay Air Force Base, Boyd reported the strange formation. Within seconds two U.S. Sabrejet fighters were scrambled to meet the *Centaurus*.
>
> By now all the crew and some of the passengers had seen the saucer formation. Had this been a cargo flight, Captain Howard might have risked a closer approach. But with the lives of the

crew and the fifty-one passengers to consider, he decided against it.

The mother-ship and its smaller saucers were still flying parallel to the *Centaurus* when one of the Sabrejet pilots radioed the airliner from a point twenty miles away. The saucers, Captain Howard told him, were still pacing his plane.

"I'll be there in two or three minutes," the Air Force pilot answered.

Then a strange thing occurred.

Quickly the six smaller craft merged with the mother-ship. Accelerating at tremendous speed, the larger machine vanished in a matter of seconds.

It is possible to conclude with Keyhoe and the pilots that the dark object was a mother ship and that it disappeared quickly because a gravity-free spaceship would have the property of extremely rapid acceleration. But given the idea of the "curvature" of space, and of an "inside" and "outside" universe, it would be possible to speculate that the so-called mother ship into which the saucers flew was in fact a bend or warp in the space-time continuum, some kind of space "tunnel" from the "middle" universe to either the "inside" or "outside" universe. One can well wonder why the saucers seemed to be bright while the mother ship was "dark." Were they made of different material, or was the mother ship in fact not a ship, not material, but rather some kind of strange void? This dark object appeared to change shape. Is this because the "mother ship" changed position as Keyhoe suggested, or might this have been the natural result of stress placed on the space "tunnel" due to the changing position of the planets in our solar system, causing a variation in the density of the gravitational field? Keyhoe reports that the mother ship appeared to accelerate very rapidly, and of course this is possible. But if the space tunnel were suddenly to close, it would probably close like a camera shutter, giving the appearance of an object moving rapidly away, and finally diminishing to a point. Thus given the idea of the curvature of space, and the fact that space and gravitation are interdependent, it is possible to conjecture that more than one universe might coexist in the same space, and if you knew how to control gravity, you might also know how to control your space and move from one spatial curvature to another.

Whether the pilots in the BOAC liner saw the saucers disappear into a mother ship, or into some sort of space tunnel leading to another invisible universe right in the midst of us, I do not know. But given the various cosmological possibilities which seem to be inherent within the general theory of relativity, I think that the idea of the space tunnel cannot be ruled out immediately on theoretical grounds. On the basis of the report recorded by Keyhoe, I believe that a space tunnel is a possible interpretation of what was observed. It is *easier,* I think, to believe Keyhoe's interpretation, that the dark object was a mother ship. But it would be a mistake at this point in our understanding of cosmology, or in our understanding of the point of origin of flying saucers, to rule out any possibility before more evidence is available.

UFOs have been seen to change shape, going through something like a "folding" process, and to disappear so rapidly that they have been described as going "out like a light." Since UFOs and beings associated with them apparently have unusual control over gravity (in the Bible, everything from the parting of the Red Sea, or the Jordan River, to Jesus' walking on water), and since modern science has suggested that gravitational forces may be linked with curvatures of space, we must remain flexible in regard to the problem of where UFOs originate. It is important to realize that in the past half-century concepts of space have become much more fluid, much more open than those accepted by science before 1900. It is perhaps best at this point to remain undecided about the truth value of my "space tunnel" interpretation. It does not seem too probable, but scientific concepts seem to be fluid enough that we cannot automatically rule it out. In this "undecided" frame of mind let us examine some of the biblical concepts of the nature and location of heaven.

The "Spirit of God" and the "Opening of the Heavens"

When Jesus was baptized, he saw "the Spirit of God descending like a dove, and alighting on him" (Matthew 3:16). Where did this UFO come from, according to the biblical account? After Jesus was baptized, "the heavens were opened" and the Spirit seems to have descended from this "opening." This idea of an "opening" represents an example of the "mythological" expression of the biblical cosmology against which Bishop Robinson and others have written. The "opening" suggests that in our "three-decker universe" "a door" leads from our world below to the world above where the angels live in heaven. In the first chapter of Genesis we read that God created "a firmament in the midst of the waters, and let it separate the waters from the waters" (Genesis 1:6). The early biblical people seem to have believed that there was something like a glass sheet which held water up in heaven (apparently outer space was thought to be mostly water); when rain was needed, various doors were opened in heaven to let the rain come down. Thus when the great flood came upon Noah, we read that "on that day all the fountains of the great deep burst forth, and the windows of the heavens were opened" (Genesis 7:11).

We have to admit that there is here a primitive cosmology, and certainly something like it may have prevailed during the whole biblical period. But the idea which the "firmament" expresses may be useful, if somewhat modified, in order to understand our own relation to heaven. Our visible universe seems to be essentially homogeneous and created. It seems unlikely that no matter how far one traveled into outer space, one would find heaven. But there may be something like a "glass sheet" which separates our created universe from both "heaven" and "hell." I am suggesting that by using the concepts of the curvature of space in Einstein's universe, there may be something like a "three-decker universe." In [the] "three-decker universe" heaven is simply the "third story" on a house, the earth is the second story, and hell is the first (or the cellar), each stacked one on the other; this may have represented the primitive biblical view, as Bultmann, Robinson, and others have argued. But what about a three-decker universe in which the stories are not so much vertical to each other as horizontal to each other? The universes are separated by "walls" rather than by floors and ceilings, although this analogy is not adequate, because heaven, hell, and our visible universe may in fact occupy a "one-room house," but by means of a variation in the curvature of space, whether positive, negative, or zero, we are able to have three universes occupy the same volume of space. One would perhaps move from one universe to the other by "bending space" so that an opening would be made.

Keyhoe, as we have seen in his *Flying Saucer Conspiracy,* has shown that UFOs of the saucer type have been seen to fly in and out of some dark object which we have suggested was a "space tunnel." If those present at the baptism of Jesus saw the "Spirit of God" (the bright cloud) emerge from some dark opening above, then perhaps we have here the link between our world and the next. This of course stretches scientific knowledge, proper biblical exegesis, and the imagination to a limit which perhaps cannot be justified, but it is a useful model by which further to examine biblical thought. One

interesting fact about the use of the Greek word for *opening* is that
it refers to opening places which otherwise would be closed to man.

When Stephen was about to be stoned, he "gazed into heaven and
saw the glory of God, and Jesus standing at the right hand of God;
and he said, 'Behold, I see the heavens opened, and the Son of man
standing at the right hand of God'" (Acts 7:55–56). The reference
to God's "glory" might indicate the presence of a "bright cloud" type
of UFO, and we find Stephen apparently seeing in some kind of vision
the "opening" or bending back of space. None of the other persons
present seems to have had this vision, which shares something of the
apocalyptic character of the Revelation of John. Whether the experience of Stephen was psychological, physical, a combination of
both, or neither is difficult to say. But it is interesting that Stephen
seems to have sensed that God was present as if he were in the "next
room," so to speak. The door to the next room was momentarily
opened to him.

Why did Stephen "gaze into heaven"? The passage says that
Stephen, "full of the Holy Spirit, gazed into heaven" (Acts 7:55).
The Holy Spirit in the Bible is usually *invisible,* but nevertheless
present to each person. The Holy Spirit seems to be an invisible
power from another universe which is right in the midst of our universe. At Pentecost the disciples "were all together in one place. And
suddenly a sound came from heaven like the rush of a mighty wind,
and it filled all the house where they were sitting. . . . And they
were all filled with the Holy Spirit" (Acts 2:1–4). I will not even
begin to attempt to explain what happened at Pentecost, but one gains
the impression that the Holy Spirit seems to have "broken through"
the space of the room where the disciples were gathered. The "breakthrough" was reported to have caused a physical disturbance, "like
the rush of a mighty wind," an effect that might result from the
"bending" or "opening" of space. When the Holy Spirit came upon
Stephen, he did not gaze "up" to heaven; he gazed "into" heaven,
as if it were in the next room. Jesus did not ascend "up" to heaven;
he ascended "into" heaven, to the "inner sanctuary" of the presence
of God. Perhaps the use of the preposition "into" is more important
than we have realized in expressing the location of heaven.

On another occasion the Apostle Peter fell into some sort of trance,
and he "saw the heaven opened, and something descending, like a
great sheet, let down by four corners upon the earth. In it were all
kinds of animals and reptiles and birds of the air." (Acts 10:11–12)
Peter was told that he should kill and eat the contents of the sheetlike

UFO which was lowered in front of him. Peter, a Jew, had never eaten unclean food, and he was told to eat to prepare him for his meeting with the Gentile Cornelius, who had heard an angel in a vision tell him to send for Peter. Both Peter and Cornelius reacted as if they made contact with a strange world which was somehow in their midst, but was usually invisible.

"The Kingdom of God Is in the Midst of You"

On one occasion Jesus told his disciples, "Where two or three are gathered in my name, there am I in the midst of them" (Matthew 18:20); how could Christ be present to the disciples, yet invisible? Although it is not clear what happened, Luke records that Jesus was led by the villagers of Nazareth "to the brow of the hill on which their city was built, that they might throw him down headlong. But passing through the midst of them he went away" (Luke 4:29–30). This passage implies that Jesus passed through their midst without effort. One of the more debated passages in Scriptures is the answer Jesus gave to the Pharisees concerning the coming of the kingdom of God. "Being asked by the Pharisees when the kingdom of God was coming, he answered them, 'The kingdom of God is not coming with signs to be observed; nor will they say, "Lo, here it is!" or "There!" for behold, the kingdom of God is in the midst of you'" (Luke 17:20–21).

The first question must be, What is meant by the phrase *the kingdom of God?* It must be remembered that Matthew almost never uses the phrase *the kingdom of God;* rather, he speaks of the equivalent *kingdom of heaven.* Luke, on the other hand, almost always speaks of the *kingdom of God.* The kingdom of God (or heaven) would necessarily be a place where God reigned. Would this be on earth or in heaven, or both? It is clear from the teaching of Jesus that there is a distinction between heaven and earth. In the "Lord's Prayer" we read "thy will be done, on earth as it is in heaven" (Matthew 6:10). The Jews believed that indeed someday the kingdom of heaven would come to earth, and it was this belief which motivated the question the Pharisees raised concerning the coming of the kingdom.

The answer Jesus gave can be given a number of interpretations:

The kingdom might be "in the midst of you" in the sense that God is concerned with man's heart or mind, and he seeks to come into the "midst" of the life of every person. Thus the idea of the "kingdom" is given a spiritual or mental interpretation. But this interpretation is unsatisfactory because Jesus, knowing his opinion of the Pharisees, would not have been likely to tell them that the kingdom was within *them*. One would not expect the kingdom to be found in the minds of the hypocritical Pharisees.

The generally more acceptable interpretation is that Jesus was referring to himself. He was standing "in the midst" of the Pharisees, and the kingdom of God was embodied in Jesus. When Jesus says that the kingdom is not coming with "signs to be observed," he could have been referring to the fact that in the coming of Christ the power of God was underplayed; Jesus here acknowledges his "undercover agent" role which had been defined in the scenes in the wilderness during his temptations. The kingdom was hidden in an innocent-looking carpenter's son, standing in the midst of them. John the Baptist came preaching that "the kingdom of heaven is at hand" (Matthew 3:2), which was the biblical way of pointing to the coming of Christ. The main difficulty with saying that the kingdom was fully present in Christ is that Luke, after recording this incident with the Pharisees, moves on to describe an apocalyptic passage which Jesus relates to his disciples, and this passage speaks more directly to the question the Pharisees raised. Jesus says, "For as the lightning flashes and lights up the sky from one side to the other, so will the Son of man be in his day" (Luke 17:24). Jesus taught that some aspect of the kingdom will be consummated in the future. He suggests that the Son of Man (i.e., himself) will someday in the future return with the suddenness and brightness of lightning flashing across the sky. In the final chapter we shall deal with the "second coming of Christ," but it is important to notice that the early Church believed that someday Christ would return with a power even greater than that wielded by Moses. Thus for Jesus to say to the Pharisees that the kingdom is already—now—in the midst of them in its most powerful aspect is not quite true to much of the biblical material.

The third alternative is to distinguish between the kingdom of God on earth and the kingdom of God in heaven. The kingdom of God in heaven is fully obedient to the will of God, which is why we are to pray that God's will may be done on earth as it is done in heaven. If when Jesus answered the Pharisees he was referring to the kingdom of God in heaven, and if there is some validity in my speculation that Einstein's curvature of space provides the clue to the "place" where heaven is, then perhaps Jesus meant quite literally that the kingdom of God or of heaven is "in the midst of" us, although it is invisible. *Heaven may be an entirely different universe right in the midst of us.*

From an exegetical, and also from a scientific, point of view I may be stretching the implications of the ideas of "in the midst of you" and "the curvature of space." But if we are to take the idea of heaven seriously, then we have to attempt to reconcile two difficult facts: "the things that are seen are transient, but the things that are unseen are eternal" (II Corinthians 4:18); and just as angels seem to be physical, and as the resurrection body of Christ seemed to be physical, it would seem to follow that we need a "resurrection universe" *which is invisible and yet allows for bodily existence.* The Bible comes close to saying that this invisible universe is in the midst of us, invisible due to its different spatial curvature.

The Locked Rooms and the Space Tunnel

On at least two occasions after his Resurrection Jesus came and stood in the midst of the disciples when the doors of the room had been shut, and presumably locked, "for fear of the Jews" (John 20:19). On the first occasion Thomas was not with the disciples, but "eight days later, his disciples were again in the house, and Thomas was with them. The doors were shut, but Jesus came and stood among them, and said, 'Peace be with you.' Then he said to Thomas, 'Put your finger here, and see my hands; and put out your hand, and place it in my side; do not be faithless, but believing.' Thomas answered him, 'My Lord and my God!' Jesus said to him, 'Have you believed because you have seen me? Blessed are those who have not seen and yet believe'" (John 20:26-29).

The disciples seemed to have had no explanation of how Jesus could have come and stood in the midst of them while the door was closed. Scholars have sometimes suggested that the resurrection body of Christ was able to go through closed doors, which perhaps it could, but the disciples did not report "seeing" his body somehow move through a closed door. The Gospel of John simply says, "Jesus came." It strikes one as peculiar that the body of Jesus could move through a door and yet be touched by Thomas, as the Gospel reports in the same sequence. If we can suppose, however, that we live in the "midst" of an invisible spatially curved resurrection universe, then perhaps Jesus "came" through a "space tunnel" into the room where the disciples were gathered with the door locked. The implication would then seem to follow that Jesus did not need a UFO or "space cloud" to take him to heaven, but rather that the Ascension was a special event staged for the benefit of the disciples to let them know that there was something "final" about the way Jesus left on this occasion.

When Jesus appeared to Mary, he said to her, "Do not hold me, for I have not yet ascended to the Father; but go to my brethren and say to them, I am ascending to my Father and your Father, to my God and your God" (John 20:17). Later Jesus invited the disciples to touch him, so that it seems strange that Jesus would have forbidden Mary to "hold" him, although he may have meant, "Do not detain me." But Jesus is reported to have said that he was preparing to ascend to his Father, when in fact the Ascension did not take place for some forty days. On the basis of the resurrection appearances of Jesus one could argue that Jesus actually "moved back and forth" between our world and the resurrection world for the "forty-day" period, appearing to the disciples for short periods of time and then "ascending" or returning to the resurrection world. Jesus was *seen* to ascend on only one occasion, which was his final appearance except for his brief visit to Paul on the Damascus Road. If we can suppose that there is an invisible resurrection universe in the midst of us, then we have a possible explanation of the unusual features of the resurrection appearances of Christ.

There are at least two other occasions reported in the Bible which, while not duplicating the "closed door" resurrection appearances of Christ, may be related to them. On one occasion the apostles were being kept in a guarded prison, and an angel came and set them free. When the officers came for their prisoners, they said they found "the sentries standing at the doors, but when we opened it we found no one inside" (Acts 5:23). The disciples were found teaching in the Temple.

On a second occasion Peter was imprisoned, and "was sleeping between two soldiers, bound with two chains, and sentries before the door were guarding the prison; and behold, an angel of the Lord appeared, and a light shone in the cell; and he struck Peter on the side and woke him, saying, 'Get up quickly.' And the chains fell off his hands" (Acts 12:6–7). Peter dressed, thinking all the while that he must be dreaming. "When they had passed the first and the second guard, they came to the iron gate leading into the city. It opened to them of its own accord, and they went out and passed on through one street; and immediately the angel left him" (Acts 12:10–11). Peter was on his own, standing alone in a street in the middle of the night. He finally came to his senses and went his way.

One cannot help wondering how the angel and Peter could get by the sentries undetected, but one also wonders how the angel entered the prison. We read that the iron gate opened to let Peter and the angel out of the prison. Did the angel close the gate when he came in, or did he get in some other way? Did he come in through a space tunnel from the resurrection universe?

Perhaps this is unfounded speculation, but it appears that if we are going to explain much of the biblical data, the idea of an invisible resurrection universe in the midst of us is an extremely useful idea by which to interpret, or at least make some sense of, much of the biblical material.

DAVID SPANGLER is president of the Lorian Association, a nonprofit educational organization working in affiliation with other groups to assist the processes of planetary transformation and the birth of a planetary culture. Mr. Spangler is also a director of the Findhorn Foundation and its community, and was the principal of the Findhorn College. He is the author of *Revelation: The Birth of a New Age* and a number of booklets, including one on the subject of extraterrestrial communication, *Links with Space,* published by the Findhorn Foundation. Mr. Spangler travels about the planet lecturing and working with different groups, but has residences both in Findhorn, Scotland, and in the San Francisco Bay area of California.

PLANETARY TRANSFORMATION AND THE MYTH OF THE EXTRATERRESTRIAL

In the late 1940s new phenomena began to appear in the skies of Earth. These were silent flying craft unlike any people had seen before. They were called unidentified flying objects, or UFOs, though their disclike or oval shapes earned them the popular name of "flying saucers." To many, these phenomena had no existence except in the imaginations of science fiction writers and newsmen drawing for filler copy upon the sensational stories of pranksters. Others, their minds conditioned by the memories of the recent world war, wondered if these craft might not be some new kind of secret weapon, while still other individuals, noting the advanced technology that such craft seemed to represent, speculated that they might not be an earthly phenomenon at all but rather the appearance on our planet of visitors from outer space.

The harsh realities of a world plunging into the tensions of the Cold War that threatened to become much hotter beneath the clouds of nuclear bombs relegated the UFOs to a back corner of human affairs. The Fifties and early Sixties were a time of one crisis following another in the arena of world politics and global confrontation. Armed with increasingly sophisticated weapons of mass destruction, the leading nations of East and West played games of brinkmanship as the populations of the world waited in seeming helplessness for war to erupt. Books and films of that period mirror the fear and sense of resignation that seemed to shadow people as they dug their fallout shelters and tried to face the realities of surviving a planetary holocaust.

The challenge was primarily one of consciousness. Humanity is undergoing change as it seeks to externalize a new image of itself which can be the basis for new patterns of behavior; the processes of this transformation were mirrored in the tensions of the Fifties and Sixties as people began increasingly to see that the attitudes of nationalism, industrial competitiveness, and racial intolerance provided trigger points for catastrophe. The qualities of fear, greed, ambition, and hatred had not been eliminated from human behavior but instead continued to dominate the practice of domestic and international politics. Force, power, subversion, all remained acceptable tools for implementing the national will and bolstering the national ego. When such power was measured in terms of soldiers and their personal weapons and its use relegated to distant battlefields, the situation was bad enough; when such power became augmented by energies of nuclear destruction aimed at large population centers and threatening the very existence of humanity as a species, it became intolerable.

A consciousness that could think in terms of domination and power politics and could justify the use of a nuclear arsenal as a means toward an end could only be called insane by the standards of an atomic age. What was frightening to people was that while almost everyone agreed that this was so, such attitudes continued to be exhibited in the highest levels of government, science, and culture. It was as if a perverse weakness of the will-to-change existed or a strange double vision wherein people perceived and reacted to these challenges with a twentieth-century mind but medieval emotions. Everyone agreed that survival depended on humanity's success in truly developing a consciousness of love, of trust, and of a willingness to serve the best interests of the whole of life. The question was how to foster such a consciousness in the face of centuries-old habits of fear, of competition, and of limited understanding of the nature of man.

Since the end of World War II thousands of groups and millions of individuals have been working to effect just such a change of consciousness within humanity. The greatest number of these people are working out of a sincere effort to promote goodwill on Earth; many of them, however, are further inspired by a definite vision of a new evolutionary cycle unfolding for humanity and for all the world. Though expressed in different ways, this vision claims essentially that man is a divine being, that he has potentials of consciousness which he is not tapping, that a new energy is unfolding everywhere which will stimulate those potentials into actuality and that work must be done to facilitate the impact of that energy. The result of this will be the emergence of a new kind of individual, one who is attuned to himself and to his world in a very synergic and holistic fashion, one who can blend with others to form creative combinations of group consciousness and who can thus release into society sufficient new creativity to transform it and bring to birth a new planetary culture.

To change the consciousness of a people is no easy task; it has challenged reformers, educators, and spiritual leaders for centuries. One time-honored technique is to convince people of the necessity for change if disaster is to be averted. This is the change-or-die approach and has been used with various degrees of success, particularly in the Judeo-Christian traditions. During the Fifties and Sixties the logical consequences of humanity's direction were so apparent and so appalling that this technique quickly came to dominate the movements for consciousness transformation. Emphasis was put on dangers of racial and planetary suicide from causes ranging from nuclear warfare to irreversible ecological disruption due to pollution. A new prophetic tradition began to emerge, calling on humanity to change its ways and to make radical inner and outer changes lest the visions of holocaust come to pass.

During these years the prophets of Earth discovered a strange new ally. Like the Jews awaiting a messiah during the times of the Roman occupation of Israel, many individuals felt that the problems confronting humanity were too great to be dealt with unless there was some form of outside intervention. Prophecies of a Second Coming proliferated, but in the West, at least, where the greatest problems of survival lay anyway, religion had ceased to be a compelling power. Science and technology formed the basis of new myths of power and salvation; since technology was largely responsible for the plight of humanity, however, and since a certain fatalism had arisen about the nature of man and his inclinations toward violence, the promise of science was diluted by doubts of the capability of human beings to use knowledge and technology constructively. Thus, in subtle ways, the idea developed that if technology was the instrument for salvation, it would have to be wielded by superhuman wisdom. As no earthly institution seemed to be expressing such a wisdom, the visions and expectations of many began to turn outward and they rediscovered the UFOs.

While for years the reports of sightings had either been ignored or ridiculed, the sightings had continued nevertheless. In fact, individuals in many countries reported that they had been contacted by the intelligences responsible for such craft. These beings claimed to be representatives from various advanced extraterrestrial races, identifying themselves for the most part as "space brothers" whose interest and desire was to help humanity through its time of crisis into a new level of consciousness. Such messages and contacts found only a small acceptance at first, but as the years went on the sightings increased. As men walked on the moon, as the idea of extraterrestrial civilizations became less fantastic, and as the sense of need for deliverance grew within people, the phenomenon of communication with beings from other worlds or other universes gained a certain respectability. Books describing such communications proliferated and described a spectrum of contacts ranging from prehistoric days to modern scientific experiments with radio telescopy and ESP. From the lunatic fringe to the cultural center, the idea of extraterrestrial contact had come into its own, fueled in part by a valid curiosity and a recognition that something was happening in the skies of Earth and in part by a deep desire for help in meeting the problems humanity had created for itself. The myth of the extraterrestrial was born.

Within this context the word "myth" does not mean a fantasy or an untruth. There is nothing untrue about the myths of mankind; rather, they are descriptions of aspects of reality which are too vast or complex, or too fragile, to be subjected to strict analytical processes of classification and presentation—aspects which have power on the deepest levels of our individual and collective beingness. Myths describe processes which must be understood but which defy ordinary verbalization; they are glimpses into causal dimensions where the ruling impulses of a people or of an era are operative. An event, a person, or an era becomes mythic when he or it becomes a focus through which these deeper impulses can emerge and can impact more directly upon the consciousnesses of people; in a sense, such a person or event becomes a vessel whose contents extend far beyond the form.

In this regard, the phenomenon of the UFOs and of contact with extraterrestrials becomes a vessel embodying at least four deep impulses moving through human consciousness; it becomes a myth describing a process of transformation of consciousness, a movement from one state of being to another, and it illuminates our rite of passage. Two of these impulses are causes of this time of transformation and may be called the impulse toward the cosmic and the impulse toward communion and community; the other two impulses are manifestations of the processes of transformation and are aspects of what might be called the "will to express the essence." These are the impulse of destruction and transformation and the impulse of creativity.

The will toward essence is simply a way of saying that every quality of existence will seek to express its essential nature as fully and as purely as possible. In so doing it embarks upon a process of growth in expression; the quality or idea will take on a form which appears to express itself as best as is possible under the circumstances. When the form ceases to do so it is destroyed or transformed by an impulse arising from the seed-center or essence-center of that beingness, an impulse which also stimulates the creation of a new form which will reflect the inner nature more effectively. This process is evident in all living systems. In an individual the forms that are destroyed are usually mental and emotional; we change our ideas, our modes of behavior, our environment in order to create new forms of expression that more adequately meet our needs for self-actualization. In a society the forms of a culture are destroyed or transformed when they no longer meet the requirements for growth and for expression of the essential human identity behind that society. Changing understanding of the nature of man, therefore, leads to transformations in the cultural forms we have created to reflect that nature.

Sometimes these transformations occur easily; more often than not they conflict with the habitual expressions and the inertia of long-established customs, institutions, and beliefs. The prophetic tradition is a way of clarifying and focusing this conflict. It portrays the alternatives and sounds the note of the will toward the essence: either attune to a new way and change or face the necessary destruction of all your forms, with the risk of greater destruction beyond what is necessary. Usually the prophetic word concentrates on what is wrong and on the consequences of that wrongness; a person who is aligned with such a tradition or point of view will see the events of his time within such a perspective. Out of a range of possible perceptions he will choose those which focus on the impulses of destruction and transformation, often gaining the reputation of being a pessimist, of being negative, of spreading "doom and gloom." His motives may be good, filled with an intent to educate people as to the destructiveness of their present course in order to help them to change; on the other hand, many people align with the prophetic tradition out of a sense of righteousness, a divisiveness of attitude that seeks to separate humanity into the "saved" and the "lost," a morbid interest in destruction itself, a desire to see the present order destroyed, or in response to the fear that such doomsday prophecies can generate. Whatever the motivation, such prophecies exist and are made by individuals ranging from scientists and government officials to psychics and clairvoyants.

With such a prophetic tendency moving among humanity it was only natural that the phenomenon of extraterrestrial contact would become a conduit for its expression. The communications from occupants of UFOs over the years have covered many subjects but those that have received the greatest publicity and circulation, particularly in the late Fifties and early Sixties, were those messages that emphasized the prophetic warning. According to the "space brothers" and their contacts, man indeed teetered on the brink of holocaust which only a concerted effort at transforming human consciousness might avoid. In fact, many prophecies said that disaster could not be avoided. Plans were made, it was revealed, for large craft to evacuate segments of the human population to places of safety beyond Earth in order to preserve remnants of the human race who could then rebuild the world. However, only those who had made a change of consciousness could be thus evacuated. Whatever the essential truth of these claims might have been, they quickly became part of a revised Christian mythos in which the UFOs became the equivalent of the angels of the Lord proclaiming the Day of Judgment and promising that the elect would be saved and taken up into heaven while the lost were damned to be destroyed in a great cleansing of Earth through nuclear fires or natural catastrophes. Such an identification of the UFOs with this aspect of a mythic vision of the transformation of human culture and of apocalypse reduced their credibility in some circles; it also tended, paradoxically, to weaken the greater function of the prophetic tradition, which is to catalyze change. When the prophecies are of planetary cataclysm or cultural disintegration the scope of the problem may seem too large for the individual to cope with; outside help seems necessary. When the prophecies are coupled with a vision of such help coming in the form of advanced extraterrestrial technologies, the ability of individuals to identify with inner resources becomes further weakened. Fear is born, impotency is subtly communicated, and helplessness results. Thus, instead of galvanizing efforts toward transforming the situation, the impact of the UFO-backed prophecies upon the people who envisioned the new cycle humanity was entering was one of encouraging an indrawn, negative response, a response of waiting until the day of the great evacuation while insuring in the meantime that one's personal consciousness was properly attuned.

Preparation for evacuation, which occupied the attention and energy of countless UFO groups and other "New Age" oriented groups during the early Sixties was essentially an elevation of the impulses of destruction to an irresistible level of activity; it was an affirmation that nothing could be done, that the world needed to "go through a cleansing," and that was that. Needless to say, this response was primarily among people who subscribed to the basic premises that transformation was occurring and that UFOs were a reality; these people, however, were also often the ones who were making the first steps toward a new consciousness and it was these steps that opened them to the wider vistas of cosmic awareness and planetary vision. These were people who were moving toward positions of true influence in effecting a change of consciousness within the corporate body of humanity. It was tragic that in many cases this influence was blunted through a capitulation to a passive kind of waiting and through a limited perspective of the impact of the UFOs that caused the myth of the extraterrestrial to be played out within a much narrower myth of damnation and salvation. Rather than being vanguards of a truly new awareness, they became unwitting participants in a rerun of ancient memories of destruction and of apocalypse dressed up in modern technological garb.

However, during this same period many other people also believed in the dawning of a new cycle of planetary evolution and in the transformation of human consciousness attuned to a different impulse, the impulse of creativity. For these people the need was to identify as clearly as possible the qualities of consciousness that a new culture might express, as indicated by the highest of human thinking and by spiritual revelation, and to begin embodying those qualities in personal and collective action. These people believed that while environmental influences could assist change, true transformation had to proceed from within each person and had to be essentially self-generated. The growth of humanity could not be accomplished by outside forces—only by efforts of humanity itself to externalize its deeper and greater nature. The New Age would not be born in destruction but out of a natural evolutionary process as man rose to meet the challenges of his time, aided by an increasing understanding of higher levels of his own being and consciousness on which he could draw. Such individuals were often turned off by the messages of forthcoming destruction being received, it was claimed, from outer space; this tended to cause many of them to bypass investigation into the UFO phenomenon entirely, for in the projection of thoughtforms of destruction and salvation for a special few they saw an energy that interfered with creative, practical efforts to resolve human difficulties and that interfered with a clear recognition and affirmation of the spiritual abilities of human beings.

In some circles this division between these two approaches was extreme, leading to lack of communication between the respective adherents. In other cases it simply led to confusion, particularly as there were groups and individuals who were also receiving messages from space that affirmed the creative approach, that spoke little if at all about destruction, and that gave assurances of extraterrestrial help in clarifying the vision of humanity's spiritual potentials. It was as if the UFOs were mirrors in which humanity could see its various faces, including the faces of fear, suspicion, hostility, and aggression which were reflected in lurid stories of invasion, hostile craft, kidnappings, experimentation on human beings, and so forth, mirroring similar tendencies on the part of many humans. Yet the myth of the extraterrestrials expresses something deeper than simply reflecting human character types and modes of transformation; it also expresses two causal impulses working within humanity at the present time: the impulse toward the cosmic and the impulse toward communion.

In ages past, humanity lived in contact with the wonder and mystery of the cosmic. Everything that existed had a special dimension to it. Rocks, trees, plants, animals, places, and events had their obvious aspects, but in addition they possessed a cosmic dimension, a level of mystery. Anything could be a portal into the infinite. With the advent of descriptive science, technology, the industrial state, and objective education this dimension was lost. The cosmic ceased to be a part of everything and became instead a place that was "out there" somewhere; it ceased to be a quality inherent in all things and became a quantity, a measure of vastness. Instead of being *in* the cosmic, we must move *toward* it. This movement may be psychospiritual, as in meditation or in yoga, or it may be technological, as it usually is in the Western culture. We gain the cosmic dimensions through launching our spacecraft and vicariously looking back upon Earth through the cameras of our astronauts; and through the UFOs the cosmic reaches back to us. Our imaginations are stimulated by the idea of intelligences traveling across the vast distances of the cosmos, forgetting that the greatest distance in the universe is the gap between two consciousnesses that are not attuned to each other.

The second impulse, that which moves toward a deeper understanding of community, thus reflects the first, for community is the product of bridging the gap between consciousnesses. It is based on communion and the ability to communicate. The forces acting upon our world and upon our culture are forces of convergence toward communion; whether they are expressed through planetary communications, modern transportation and travel, multinational corporations and the interrelationships of a global economy, these forces are working to overcome traditional barriers between segments of the human family. One reality faces us above all others: If we are to survive we must learn to communicate with each other. We must learn to recognize the community of life which we share, whether we like it or not, with all our fellow humans and with all other forms of life and substance on Earth; we must learn to serve that community through discovering our communion with it and acting accordingly.

One of the barriers to such communication has been our tendency to give greater prominence to our differences than to our commonalities; we live in fragments of a world and call it the whole thing. Now, through the instrumentality of the UFOs, we are confronted with a unity greater than our earth; the cosmos arrives on our doorstep. How are we to communicate with it if we cannot communicate with ourselves? How can a fragmented world act in wholeness toward the infinite? If we are invited to participate in cosmic community, must we not find community with ourselves first? And if we are to truly understand the cosmos and not be rendered impotent by its vastness, is it not imperative that we rediscover the presence of the cosmic within ourselves? In the presence of the extraterrestrial we are faced with the need for our own unity; it is focused for us in a way that more graphically demonstrates the need for human communion and oneness with our world, which other challenges have demonstrated as well.

In pondering these questions we may ask ourselves another: What is an extraterrestrial? Is it only a being from beyond the earth, an entity from another world, another universe? Certainly that is the correct verbal definition. When we enter the realm of myth, however, we must of necessity transcend words and deal with images, symbols, and their many ramifications. What is the earth, the world, the universe? To a great extent it is an objective, multileveled reality, but it is also our subjective interpretation of that reality; a world is a product of consciousness as well as of soil and water and cosmic matter. Each of us represents a universe of his own, at least at this level of reality where we walk around clothed in bodies of dense matter, cloaked in shrouds of dense thought. Every act of communication is an act of cosmic travel, of interplanetary exploration; it is fraught with hazards of distortion that can be overcome only by the intensity of our communion with each other and with the cosmic levels that we share. The problem of communicating with a being from Alpha Centauri is not essentially different from that of communicating with your neighbor, your wife or husband, or the stranger on the street; perhaps it is less challenging, for we expect to have difficulties with a being from a different cultural background, while we take for granted that we can communicate with our friends and thus overlook the distances between us as individuals.

What about communicating with other species on our world? Ancient cultures used to talk to plants, to animals, to rocks and stones, to the wind, to the rain. Were these just fables? Or were these expressions of a language of communion and of community which our present culture has lost? Can we ever have harmony on a human level unless we can commune and communicate with our world and come back into harmony with and understanding of the psychic reality and wholeness of that world? In other words, the myth of the extraterrestrial implies the necessity of communicating with beings from other worlds, which in turn brings into focus the whole challenge of the essence of communication as the key to the processes of life, growth, and the transformation of consciousness.

From this perspective, the individuals who view the UFOs strictly as visitors from elsewhere, travelers through space who are here with either benevolent or hostile intents, are limiting themselves to a fragment of a greater truth. They become observers of an event rather than participants in a myth. The Plains Indians held their vision quests through which an individual from the tribe would go off into solitude until he received a spiritual vision; even then, the power of that vision was not released into his life until he had "danced the vision" with the help of others from his tribe. He had to externalize it, acting out its elements through the vision dance. In this respect the extraterrestrials bring us a cosmic vision, a vision of ourselves, but we lack its power of transformation until we can "dance" it, externalizing the cosmic and communal impulses inherent within it. They represent but one aspect of a universe that reaches out to us both from space and from the inner spaces around and within us on this world. Perhaps we cannot relate fully to them until we have learned to relate to the greater wholeness of the universe.

The externalization of the myth of the extraterrestrial leads us to the portals of cosmic consciousness where space and time, infinite and finite, past and future, human and nonhuman, all merge into a nexus of pure being and the essence of reality is touched. From that point a person can truly say he is ready for planetary and extraplanetary life; until then he is only a fragment moving through a dream.

One of the entry points to the cosmos, to other worlds and universes, is, strangely enough, on a windswept beach in northern Scotland. Twenty-five miles east of Inverness is the Findhorn Peninsula, jutting into the Moray Firth, which in turn opens into the North Sea. At the tip of the peninsula is an old fishing village; where it joins the mainland is the Royal Air Force base of Kinloss and, a couple of miles further on, the medieval burgh of Forres. This is the country where Macbeth met his three witches, the site of Cawdor Castle, of the battle of Culloden Moor, where Bonnie Prince Charlie's hopes for Scottish independence were smashed, and of the Loch Ness Monster. It is a beautiful rural area filled with the kind of unchanging European and British charm and solid, friendly people who draw tourists and postcard photographers. Its rivers offer outstanding salmon fishing and in the summer the beaches of the peninsula are filled with vacationers from the industrial cities of Scotland. It is an unlikely spot to find a gateway to a new world.

Even more unlikely is the Findhorn Bay Caravan Park, a holiday trailer park midway between the fishing village and the RAF base. Yet here, on land occupying not more than five acres—about one half of the trailer park—is a community of about 170 people actively engaged in contact, communication, and communion with nonhuman intelligences. They are dancing the cosmic vision, releasing its power into their lives, actively researching and demonstrating the cosmic nature of man and of his world and the birth of a new planetary culture.

In November 1962 Peter and Eileen Caddy, their three sons, and Dorothy Maclean, a friend, were forced by circumstances to settle themselves in a single small trailer on the only site then available in the caravan park, a site located next to the park's garbage dump. Peter had recently lost his job and they were living on welfare. The bleak Scottish winter was approaching but they had confidence that all would be well. In the first place, all three of the adults were highly attuned sensitives. Eileen and Dorothy, through years of training in meditation, had learned to establish a very accurate attunement to their inner divinity; Peter, on the other hand, was not meditatively oriented but had developed a very sensitive intuition which guided him in moments of action. Using his wife's guidance as a source of confirmation of his own intuition, he acted as an externalizer, using his initiative and a well-trained will to implement what was received from higher levels. For years they had lived their lives in harmony with their inner direction, and all had gone well until, without warning or reason, Peter lost his job. However, he was a capable administrator and none of them had any reason to suspect he might not soon be working again.

The winter came and passed and Peter did not find work. Instead, inner direction instructed them to begin a small garden on the land around them. This would be a simple task under most circumstances, even though none of them had ever planted a seed before. However, the Findhorn Peninsula, and the Findhorn Bay Caravan Park, are not the most usual of circumstances. The land had only an inch or so of what could pass for soil, and it was deficient in several key nutrients; instead, the ground was almost entirely sand and gravel. There was little or no shelter from the salt-laden winds that blew in at forty miles an hour from the North Sea. Trying to meet these conditions, Peter read every gardening book he could lay his hands on, but they proved of little help. They were written for more temperate conditions and often the information one book contained would be contradicted by another book; nothing was said about trying to grow things in the sand and gravel of a beach.

This impasse was broken by Dorothy Maclean. While in meditation she received the insight that all of nature was infused with a divine intelligence which was embodied by beings living on a vibratory dimension higher than the physical. These beings, to whom she gave the name of *deva,* a Sanskrit word meaning "shining ones," were an order of evolution existing parallel to humanity; they wield vast, archetypal formative forces that energize and externalize the processes and forms of nature. She was told that Western man had lost contact with these beings and had lost his oneness with his world. As a consequence he was in danger of destroying that world. However, in the new cycle that was dawning humanity would again learn to live in harmony with all lives upon the planet. A first step in this process was the recognition that the *devas* existed and a demonstration of willingness to cooperate with them. Dorothy was instructed to contact these beings to seek their help in the garden, for they possessed the energies required to make the barren soil fertile and productive.

Dorothy's immediate reaction was one of incredulity. However, she did make the attempt, using as a point of meditative focus a vegetable which they had been trying to grow in the garden. She was rewarded with an immediate telepathic and empathetic contact with a *deva* who identified itself as the embodied intelligence behind that vegetable species. It was a short communication, with the *deva* expressing surprise and pleasure that a human being was trying to communicate with it. Out of it, though, came the beginning of specific instructions for the cultivation of that vegetable. In time, as they were instructed to plant many more varieties of vegetables, Dorothy developed an intensive program of "talking to plants," or rather to the invisible kingdom of life of plant forms. They received specific guidance for gardening: how to plant the seeds, how to water, how to make compost, and so forth. Much emphasis was placed on the quality of consciousness and of work that went into the garden, for it was stressed that the human being was a generator and a transformer of life energies which had a direct impact on his environment on many levels. He needed to be a sensitive part of the psychic ecology as well as of the physical one.

The results of this cooperation between human and *deva* were astounding. As if to demonstrate just what could be done, the garden flourished and demonstrated a vitality which soil experts who came to investigate said was impossible using all known methods of organic husbandry. In that first year they grew sixty-five different vegetables, twenty-one different fruits, and forty-two different herbs; plants reached amazing proportions, including a cabbage that weighed in at forty-two pounds when picked. Furthermore, the garden remained immune from insects and blights that hit other local farms and orchards.

The renown of the garden attracted people from around the world and the Caddys and Dorothy Maclean found themselves becoming the nucleus of a developing community of people. By 1970 this group numbered 15 and the garden had grown to include flowers and shrubs, including tropical and hothouse species growing quite happily though exposed to the brunt of the northern Scottish climate. By the beginning of 1972 the community had grown to 150 people and had expanded to include a number of activities such as publishing, fine arts and crafts, performing arts and educational work, in addition to the work with the garden.

Humanity, and, by extension, the earth itself, is reaching for its maturity. Within its collective soul humanity knows that its destiny is in the cosmos, and it is this deep subjective knowing that gives such impact to the idea of extraterrestrial visitation. It is a reflection of humanity's future. To reach that future, though, requires the birth of a truly planetary consciousness and culture for mankind. It means overcoming the fragmentations, the divisions, the separations and conflicts of the infancy and adolescence of the race, and integrating the parts of man into a wholeness, individually and collectively. This is the aim of planetary transformation: to restore on a higher level of the evolutionary spiral the integral wholeness, the oneness, the synergy of the world within which all kingdoms of life and consciousness interrelate in mutually supportive and beneficial ways, and through that interrelatedness help to externalize the cosmic presence within each life itself.

One of the startling revelations of the mirror of the extraterrestrials is that humanity itself has become an extraterrestrial, moving through its own artificial world of thought and ideation and becoming increasingly out of touch with the psychic, ecological, and physical realities of its planet. We ourselves must reestablish contact with Earth and learn again how to communicate with it, how to commune with it, how to establish a community with it. We are adrift in dreams, in personal and collective ambitions, in fantasies and ego trips. It is time to land, for it is only by coming back to Earth that we will rediscover the cosmos which we have lost and for which we are seeking.

Extraterrestrial visitation becomes a focal point through which the impulses of new consciousness seeking emergence can collect and impact upon us. The thought of contact with cosmic voyagers causes us to examine ourselves more fully; the promise of extraterrestrial involvements brings into relief the need for planetary transformation and integration. A place like the Findhorn community is a focus where these impulses and needs are being externalized and worked out. It is built on a vision of the cosmic divinity within each person; it is built on the need to communicate and to establish communion between individual human beings and between humans and other species of life, so that the greater planetary and cosmic community of being can be revealed. Findhorn is manifesting what the UFOs are suggesting. It is acting on the impulses of wholeness which hold the keys to the cosmos. It is "dancing out" the vision and the myth of the extraterrestrial so that within its experience individuals can reintegrate with the oneness of life and can cease to be "extra-" anything, cease to be apart from anything. *This is the key. Consciousness, not time or space, is the only separating factor in creation; it is also the only linking factor.* If we can share the same "consciousness space," we are together, even though we may physically be on opposite ends of the universe. To communicate we must establish communion, which is in turn a product of a consciousness dynamically attuning itself to its world and ever transcending the barriers of its own perceptions of identity.

This principle is reflected in messages received from extraterrestrials which suggest that their craft do not travel through space as we know it but through dimensions of consciousness, that they are in contact with intelligences far removed from us and that they can travel anywhere with the speed of thought. We see them as extraterrestrials, beings from outside; apparently, many of them see us as aspects of a single cosmic community, not separated, not "extracosmic." How can we gain such a vision unless we start by overcoming the barriers to communication, communion, and community right here on Earth, in our society, with our neighbors, with our environment, with ourselves?

A myth describes a deep collective process; it portrays the state of a culture. The myth of the extraterrestrial describes the confrontation with the cosmic which is occurring in our generation. It suggests where we have been, where we are, and where our future may lie. To reach that future, though, we must understand the myth, integrate its several levels of communication and insight, and allow its energy to work within and through us into actions of transformation. The impulse to turn the phenomenon of the UFOs into a purely technological one or to use it to back up prophecies is to limit the power of what is happening on levels of consciousness. The Prophet may seem to foretell the future, but in reality he is describing the present. On the other hand, the individual who can take that description, that vision, and use it to catalyze a release of creative energy to implement the emergence of new patterns is truly the futurist. He is the Priest, mediating between the timeless divinity in which all promise is held and the creative opportunities of the present. This individual holds the positive vision. He offers the creative alternatives. He becomes the Way, the integration of the myth, the embodiment of the impulses of transformation. He becomes the portal of contact and communication between worlds and universes, those that have been, those that are, and those that have yet to be.

Humanity reaches for the cosmic and the cosmic seeks to reflect its pervasive and imminent presence back to him through many means. That is why the vision of the extraterrestrial is an idea whose time has come. It reflects the essence of man's search and offers an opportunity not only for contact with beings from other worlds but for contact with man's own unidentified nature. It can catalyze planetary transformation but only when viewed in its full mythic dimensions and not only as modern technological and science-fictionlike phenomena. It has much to teach us of ourselves, but only when we can listen fully and not just to the parts that interest us, whether those parts are of destruction and salvation, of advanced technologies, of the excitement of space travel, or of whatever.

The myth of the extraterrestrial reflects the promise and the opportunity of planetary transformation and the birth of cosmic consciousness, but we, as humanity, must embody and be its reality.

IV. OTHER DIMENSIONS: THE ASTRAL PLANE AND BEYOND

IV

In playing The Reality Game we have come up against a complicating twist—the possibility of extra*dimensional* beings. As Trevor James Constable says in his book, "There are indeed spiritual realms, peopled with beings and replete with civilizations as real on their level as we are on ours. To us, in our present earthbound state, 'They Live in the Sky.'"

Earthbound though we may be, some people claim to be recipients of communications from discarnate extradimensionals such as Ashtar, Koot Hoomi, Melchizedek, Lord Maitreya, Seth, Moroni, and Gabriel of Salvington. These entities, it is said, do not cross space as the astronauts did in going to the moon. Rather, they emerge from the depths of space itself, from hyperspace. They materialize into our world—reality as perceived in our ordinary state of consciousness. But their sudden, mysterious appearance and disappearance from ordinary perception does not necessarily mean a person has had an hallucination or is simply imagining something. It is not "regressive behavior." Nor is it due to believing in fairy tales, fantasies, and myths (except, as we have just seen, insofar as they are based on an unknown aspect of physical reality). It may have been a true perception of a real event, but an event belonging to a class or order of experience presently outside the knowledge of orthodox science. Some clairvoyants say that they regularly see this way. To them, spirits of the departed and other forms of noncorporeal life are seen as commonly as are trees and buildings.

Guardian angels, spirit guides, etheric masters—whatever man chooses to call them—the concept of ultraphysical, extradimensional beings who materialize to aid man in times of crisis appears to be universal. Most often these teaching-preaching entities function in precisely the manner that the name "angel" implies: as messengers of God, intermediaries who deliver personal or group messages. In other instances they serve as rather militant entities who seek to protect the spiritually vulnerable from the forces of disharmony.

Conceptualizing the higher dimensions which these entities allegedly inhabit is difficult. The ancient Greeks had become conscious of three dimensions of space, but it was not until Einstein's time that awareness of a fourth dimension to real space was achieved by orthodox science. More recently there has been an accelerated investigation of this area by people such as philosopher-mathematician Charles Musès, who writes of hypernumber and metadimension theory in his *Journal for the Study of Consciousness* and the book he co-edited, *Consciousness and Reality*.

Prior to the mathematical formulation of other dimensionalities, however, occult science had long been aware of higher worlds. These dimensions are variously termed the astral and etheric planes, as Yogi Ramacharaka's selection shows, or they may be referred to in terms such as those in the Arthur Ford-Jerome Ellison selection. The psychologist Wilson Van Dusen, who writes about Swedenborg in the last section, views space not simply as the distance between objects but in its more fundamental meaning as the medium of existence. In an article called "Mind in Hyperspace" (*Psychologia,* 1965) he notes that different orders of existence can thus take place in different mediums, and suggests that the nature of mind can be explained as phenomena existing in at least three levels of real hyperspace. Similarly, Mark-Age writes in their brochure *Spiritual Space Program:*

> Man came from a higher state of evolution, became enmeshed in the third dimension of materiality and consciousness, and has been making his way back to his true spiritual status. Many have made it already and have gone on to live in physical worlds of the fourth through the eighth dimensions or ranges of frequency vibration in this solar system, or to live even beyond this system. These ranges of physical expressions are beyond the five physical senses and instruments of Earthman today.

Although these two examples use the term "dimension" in different senses, it is clear that they share a common view. In that view, psychology and physics come inexorably together. In playing The Reality Game our questions about cosmology and ontology bring us slowly but surely into theology and spiritual knowledge. The closer we come to understanding the essence of ourselves by exploring personal consciousness, the closer we come to understanding the nature and structure of the cosmos. Science and religion converge to reveal what may be termed the moral foundations of the universe. Ultimately a person may attain a state of awareness called "cosmic consciousness," or, to anticipate the final section of this book, "return to Godhead." En route you pass through different levels of consciousness. In Hindu thought these are called "lokas." In Christian theology, they are "the heavens." The terminology differs from culture to culture but the underlying unity of experience cannot be mistaken.

These levels of consciousness are the realms of angels, spirit guides, space brothers, *devas,* and other evolutionarily advanced beings reported throughout history as interacting with humanity to guide and protect it. Such beings may be orders or kingdoms of creation wholly different from humanity, but they may also be the products of continued human evolution from the world of matter into the world of spirit. Swedenborg said that both angels and demons are evolving forms of humanity. The scientist John Lilly, in his book *The Center of the Cyclone,* reports his own encounter with extradimensional beings in hyperspace:

> In my own far-out experiences in the isolation tank with LSD and in my close brushes with death I have come upon the two guides. These two guides may be two aspects of my own functioning at the supraself level. They may be entities in other spaces, other universes than our consensus reality. They may be helpful constructs, helpful concepts that I use for my own future evolution. They may be representatives of an esoteric hidden school. They may be concepts functioning in my own human biocomputer at the supraspecies level. They may be members of a civilization a hundred thousand years or so ahead of ours. They may be a tuning-in on two networks of communication of a civilization way beyond ours which is radiating information throughout the galaxy.

Wherever or whatever these guides, guardians, and extradimensional entities may call home, we wish to mention again the as-yet undetermined symbiotic relationship which appears to exist between these ethereal beings and mankind. In his *Revelation: The Divine Fire* Brad Steiger quoted the words of Ishkomar, an entity who began channeling through a blue-collar worker of modest formal education. Ishkomar claimed to be speaking from a craft that had been brought to the vicinity of our planet more than thirty thousand years ago.

Among his comments pertinent to the interaction between his species and our own, Ishkomar said:

> You must reach a high level of mental development and knowledge to be able to understand our purposes. We have attempted to gain your cooperation for thousands of years. . . . We must achieve our goal by guidance of your kind, but you must desire guidance for us to be of assistance to you.
>
> Our work is beyond your present level of understanding, and yet you will eventually be of great assistance to us by cooperating with us in the study of lifeforms and conditions on your planet. The results of these studies will be intercorrelated with other studies being conducted on other worlds; and they will benefit your own planet, our people, and the inhabitants of other worlds. . . .
>
> Our need of your cooperation involves habitation of your world by your own people—under more suitable conditions than you now realize. Following the climatic upheavals on your world, we will provide guidance to bring about desired conditions of . . . mutual benefit. Seek us and you will find us. We only await your call. . . .

If the universe is conceived as existing in different but interpenetrating levels of consciousness, we can say this: Viewed from the bottom up, it seems that matter is being rarefied or spiritualized; and viewed from the top down, it is the materialization of spirit. Both descriptions are correct and refer to simultaneous aspects of The Reality Game. This was the view of Sri Aurobindo, the Indian mystic. If we give serious consideration to what he and innumerable other explorers of consciousness have told us in all times and climes, then it seems that the study of human consciousness leads surely to the possibility of superhuman and nonhuman consciousness in the form of more highly evolved entities whose existence may be on a similarly grander scale from which they influence and guide human affairs. (One astrophysicist recently speculated that pulsars, neuron stars, are intelligent beings, bringing to mind Edgar Cayce's statement that the sun may be an angel in another dimension.) If this is so, there may exist a hierarchy of consciousness in which humanity's future already exists to some unspecified degree.

Thus the concept of our future beginning in imagination would be better understood as beginning through the reception of images from higher intelligence in other worlds—images normally considered self-generated but which are really psychically or intuitively received messages from other dimensions. It is not surprising, then, that many of the world's great artists, musicians, writers, etc. looked on themselves as functioning like Greek oracles—simply as channels through which the words or music passed from on high. Beethoven said that he didn't compose music; he simply listened and wrote down what he heard. And Plato remarked that all good poets do not compose their poems by art but by possession. "There is no invention in him [the poet] until he has been inspired and out of his senses and the mind is no longer in him. . . . For not by art does the poet sing, but by power divine." It would seem, then, that the muses which the Greek artists sought to invoke were considered to be extradimensional entities who were summoned by the receptivity of those who had properly "tuned in" by fasting, meditation, dancing, or some other psychic mechanism. No work of Greek poetry omits the invocation to the muse with its holy breath and its divine madness of the soul. Perhaps the process has not changed all that much today, as the creative personality seeks its inspiration from uncharted dimensions of time and space.

Where are these hyperspaces, these other dimensions? All sources agree: They are within us, even though they seem to be without; and at the same time they are without, even though we arrive there by going within. Jesus explained that the kingdom of heaven is immanent, indwelling. But paradoxically—and this is a crucial move in The Reality Game—as one moves into those spaces the boundary between inside and outside events dissolves. Subjective experiences become objective and verifiable. This is why there has been unanimity of reports from "soul travelers" to the highest regions throughout the ages. John White examines this matter in his anthology, *The Highest State of Consciousness.*

How does one get there? How does one "tune in"? There are many doors to the same room, as many paths as there are people. The world's major religious and spiritual traditions have all developed time-honored techniques for the exploration of inner space: meditation, prayer and contemplation, singing and chanting, breathing techniques, bodily disciplines that alter awareness. *What Is Meditation?*, edited by John White, is a useful compendium of meditative techniques.

But be forewarned: Playing The Reality Game can be hazardous to your health. John Lilly points out that in going from orthonoia (commonsense reality, everyday mind) to metanoia (beyond consensual reality to a new state of consciousness), you pass through paranoia (a necessary stage of derangement and rearrangement of your mental structures). Some, however, never make it through due to lack of preparation and expert guidance. Asylums are full of them.

Nevertheless, the words of Philip Brooks, a nineteenth century Episcopal bishop, offer a useful guide in the matter: "Hold fast to yourself the sympathy and companionship of the unseen worlds. No doubt it is best for us now that they should be unseen. It cultivates in us that higher perception that we call 'faith.' But who can say that the time will not come when, even to those who live here upon Earth, unseen worlds shall no longer be unseen?"

D. Scott Rogo is a parapsychologist, educator, and writer. He has done graduate work in the psychology of music and its relation to altered states of consciousness, and has coordinated an experimental course in parapsychology under the auspices of the University of California. As a researcher Mr. Rogo has published five books, including *An Experience of Phantoms,* a two-volume study of paranormal music entitled *NAD,* a book on life after death, *The Welcoming Silence,* and several educational texts on parapsychology. His articles have appeared in various research and popular journals. He is book-review editor for *Psychic* magazine and has been a research consultant at the Psychical Research Foundation in Durham, North Carolina, one of the primary centers for research on out-of-the-body experiences.

OUT-OF-THE-BODY DIMENSIONS

Due to our very matter-of-fact way of looking at our day-to-day living we often take for granted that our "consciousness" is a product of the brain. We experience the world through our sense perceptions, which relay messages to the brain. When we sleep or wake, our brain waves show specific rhythms. If the brain is damaged it usually affects our entire ability to function in the world. Our "consensus reality" is rather rigid in its view of man and his place in the universe. Each of us is a physical being governed by a physical brain living in a physical universe.

Of all man's follies, this materialistic belief is perhaps his greatest. For ESP shows that our perceptions go beyond the nervous system and brain. A few people have been born with horrendous brain damage—yet survived and lived perfectly normal lives.*

The view that man's consciousness is tightly locked within the brain can be challenged as well, for many people have experienced a separation of consciousness from the physical body:

In 1918 I was operated on in the Presbyterian Hospital in Chicago. Several days after the operation I began to lose ground. Late one night I took a turn for the worse. Suddenly I became

* Vincent Gaddis, "With Brains Destroyed They Live and Think," *Fate,* Vol. I, No. 2, 1948.

conscious that "I" was not "in" my body, which was on the hospital bed, but was over it, above everyone's head. I had an astonishingly vivid view of the scene: several doctors and nurses were working around the "me" that was on the bed; I distinctly heard one doctor ask, "Have you sent for her family?" and the other doctor replied, "Yes, but there is no time for them to get here; she's too far gone!" The "I" that was above the scene felt a great surge of anger and resentment that the doctors thought that I'd die, and then I felt a struggle and realized that I was "back" on the bed.

Mrs. Taylor, who sent this experience to Dr. Louisa Rhine of the Foundation for Research on the Nature of Man, reported that upon waking she quoted the doctor's words back to him, much to his astonishment.

In her own brief way Mrs. Taylor had contacted a new dimension. This new dimension seemed to be a replica of the physical world, but was it? Many persons who have undergone the out-of-the-body experience (OOBE) use the experience as a vehicle to contact new universes, dimensions, and beings.

Mr. J. W. Skilton was one such inadvertent adventurer. A railway engineer working in Jacksonville, Florida, he was hardly the type of man whom one would suspect would contact "other-worldly" beings by leaving his physical body. Yet one day while he was loading crates with some fellow railway workers he suddenly saw a medium-sized, brilliantly clad being who put his hand on Skilton's shoulder with the comforting words, "Come with me." Suddenly Skilton was out of his body, gliding over the lush countryside below him. Skilton recorded, "As we passed on, this glorious being that was with me told me he was going to show me that bright heavenly world. We soon came to a world of light and beauty, many thousand times larger than this earth, with at least four times as much light. The beauties of this place were beyond any human being to describe."

Skilton saw many beings in this new world. Music cascaded around him. Ultimately he recognized his deceased mother, two sisters, and a lost child among the beings he saw. Skilton's radiant attendant reappeared, urging that he return to his own world and body. Again he found himself whisking over familiar terrain and approaching the railway car. Instantly he was back in his body. His coworkers were perplexed, for during the past several minutes the "physical" Skilton had not uttered a single word and had gone about carrying on the tedious and straining physical work with unbelievable ease. They rather sneered at his story. Luckily, Skilton found a more sympathetic listener in F. W. H. Myers, a Cambridge philosopher and one of the first explorers of the mind, who placed the account in his *The Human Personality and its Survival of Bodily Death* as a case of "ecstasy."

Skilton's account is not unique among out-of-the-body chronicles. Many percipients have reported that they seemed to be helped out of their bodies by other-world beings.

While only fourteen years old Mrs. J. Watkin had such an experience: "I had gone into bed, when my attention was arrested by a soft whirlwind sound coming through the window. Yet it was a still summer's night, with no wind at all. Then two robed men, as solid in appearance as we are to each other, were standing at my bedside. I felt no fear. They gave me a most penetrating look, at and through me, and suddenly I found myself standing between them, and the three of us looking now at my lifeless body on the bed." (From Robert Crookall's *More Astral Projections*.)

Mrs. Watkin and the two figures quickly started to travel over incredible landscapes. Upon returning to her home she slipped quietly back into her body.

Not all out-of-the-body encounters with other-world beings are as pleasant as those of Skilton and Watkin.

Sylvan Muldoon was perhaps the most famous of all out-of-the-body travelers. When he was a sickly youth he discovered that he had the ability to leave his body. He kept notes of these experiences, which he relayed to the famous psychic researcher Hereward Carrington. Muldoon reported that he once had a very harrowing encounter with an out-of-the-body creature.

Muldoon wrote in his autobiography that one night after he had gone to bed he deliberately induced an OOBE. Walking a few steps beyond his physical body he was confronted by a figure representing the form of a recently deceased man about town: "I shall never forget the savage look upon his face as long as I live," wrote Muldoon. The figure leaped upon him and he was automatically drawn back toward his body, dragging along the unwelcomed intruder, and finally escaping back into his body.

One of the most experienced out-of-the-body travelers to new dimensions was Oliver Fox. Fox (whose real name was Hugh Callaway) was an English occultist. While still a young man he began to have inclinations toward OOBEs, which led to brief encounters with some rather unusual beings. Before developing the ability to leave his body almost at will, Fox had some peculiar incipient projections. Just before falling asleep he would see moving, vibrating orbs. These orbs would turn into faces, menacing and mocking. Fox discovered that by mental control he could keep the circles from turning into faces. As he writes in his autobiography, *Astral Projection,* "But I had to be quick about it or the grinning faces would get in first." Years later Fox would learn that during his full-fledged OOBEs these vibrating circular cells would constantly invade the scene peripherally.

Fox was not alone in encountering beings that seemed to try to hinder his OOBEs. Many OOB travelers have had similar experiences.

When Fox finally achieved full-fledged OOBEs he soon learned that he could contact new dimensions. His discovery was accidental. At first he thought he was actually projected to Earth scenes, but later realized that his OOB state was really existing in a *semblance* of the "real" world while in fact it was a new dimension. By examining this new dimension subtle differences could be observed. One is reminded of *Alice in Wonderland* and her looking-glass room. Fox made this discovery on one of his first OOB essays when he found himself out of his body and outside his lodgings:

> In the magic of the early sunshine the scene was beautiful enough even then. Now the pavement was not of the ordinary type, but consisted of small, bluish-gray rectangular stones, with their long side at right angles to the white curb. I was about to enter the house when, on glancing casually at these stones, my attention became riveted by a passing strange phenomenon, so extraordinary that I could not believe my eyes—they had seemingly all changed their position in the night, and the long sides were now parallel to the curb! . . .

This second of enlightenment catapulted Fox into a new world of consciousness even beyond the OOB state. Suddenly his entire surroundings became more radiant and he went into a state of ecstasy before returning to his body.

Before going on with Fox's narratives it should again be pointed out that this type of observation—that the OOBE world is not the physical world but is instead some sort of parallel but not exact replica of the real world—is not rare in astral-projection lore. One account was given to me by a noted parapsychologist (who requests anonymity) who had a series of OOBEs as a young man. He reported, ". . . At one time while I was living in Oxford, England, I had an apparent out-of-the-body experience during the night. As in most of my other experiences I only moved around in the room in which I was sleeping. The case was somewhat unusual in that the windows had a different set of curtains in my experience than the curtains which were in fact in the room and which I knew to be there. . . ."

The slight differences between the physical world and the out-of-the-body state indicate that the OOBE might be a key to new dimensions of the universe.

Fox apparently realized this also, for soon he began to explore these new horizons. During one adventure he had great difficulty in leaving the body. But finally liberating his consciousness from the body after two unsuccessful attempts, he walked up to a wall of the room but found he could not pass through it. This was puzzling for in his preceding OOBEs he never had any difficulty in moving right through physical obstructions. This wall seemed to be a barrier to a new world:

> I stood facing the wall, gently pressing against it, and steadily willed to pass through it. I succeeded and the sensations were most curious. Preserving full consciousness, I seemed to pass like a gas—in a spread-out condition—through the interstices between the molecules of the wall, regaining my normal proportions on the other side.

Instantly Fox sped away at a lightning pace, but then, stopping for a moment, realized that he had not yet broken into the new dimension:

> And now it seemed to me that there was a sort of hole or break formed in the continuity of the astral matter; and through this, in the distance—as though viewed through a very long tunnel—I could see something indistinct which might have been an entrance to a temple."

Fox tried to move through the hole but failed and ultimately returned to his body.

Many OOB voyagers find that they are linked to new dimensions by a hole in space. While Fox wrote about these connecting tunnels to new worlds back in 1916, one OOB traveler today has claimed to have made similar observations.

Robert Monroe deserves credit as being one of the few habitual projectors to have demonstrated the OOBE in a scientific laboratory. These experiments were carried out in conjunction with Dr. Charles Tart, presently a psychology professor at the University of California at Davis. Like Fox before him, Monroe's first OOBEs were in the immediate vicinity of his physical body and then later to other earthly environments. However, as he became more accustomed to his OOB state he began to explore new depths of the universe.

In 1958 Monroe had his first encounter with a new dimension. Lifting himself out of his body by mental effort, he turned around and beheld:

> . . . there was a hole. That's the only way to describe it. To my senses, it seemed to be a hole in a wall which was about two feet thick and stretched endlessly in all directions. . . .

Peering through the hole, Monroe could see only darkness, and venturing though it he still could see nothing more. Monroe then darted back to his body.

A week or so later Monroe once more began to explore the hole. He reached his hand through and it was clasped by a human hand.

His third adventure with the hole came shortly after. Inch by inch, he began to venture beyond the peripheries of the hole. At first his hands would be clasped and helped through, but Monroe could see only endless black space. Finally things began to clear. In 1959, after a few months of exploration, Monroe darted through the hole and found himself near a building similar to a barn. Searching around, he saw a meadow, into which he ventured. It seemed to Monroe, as he walked away from the building, that the "hole" was actually a window of the other-dimension building. He reapproached the building but everything became dark, and he popped through back into his own world and entered his body.

Professor J. H. M. Whiteman is an ardent student of mysticism, a professor of mathematics, and a parapsychologist. These various academic and intellectual pursuits ideally permit him to analyze his own experiences as a habitual projector. Whiteman is the third projector to have made detailed records of these bizarre holes in space. Unlike Fox and Monroe, who came across these apertures while in the OOBE state, Whiteman sees them while still in his body and projects through them to get into the OOB state and into new dimensions at the same time.

Resting on his back to induce the OOB state, Whiteman often sees holes, usually circular, opening before him, revealing a new world panorama. He writes in his autobiography, *The Mystical Life,* that he pops right into the scene of the vision by willing himself to move through the hole. The following is a typical experience of what White-man calls the "spatial openings" of his "separations" (OOBEs):

> The separation began with a "spatial opening" in which the surface of a whitewashed wall, two feet away, was studied, with a full clarity of perception and the visual impression of pre-cise spatial position . . . the opening then changed to one in which heathlike country was seen in a wide panorama, with steep ground in front, and almost at once I was conscious for a few moments of being catapulted amid that scene.

As has been hinted at in this article, very few people who have spontaneous OOBEs seem to explore new dimensions or meet new beings. Percipients having once-in-a-lifetime OOBEs seem inhibited, attached to their body and to their concept of "reality." As Whiteman has written, the OOBE is a key to new vistas and universes and levels of consciousness. Unfortunately we can only judge the "realness" of an experience by how closely it compares to the known world. White-man believes that for this reason the world contacted during the OOBE at first imitates the physical world to which we are accustomed. However, more experienced astral travelers can soon dispense with this crutch and explore the incredible dynamics of the OOB world.

In the summer of 1973 I served as a visiting research consultant at the Psychical Research Foundation in Durham, North Carolina. The main reason for my visit was the happy circumstances that the foundation was working with a young Duke psychology student who could induce the OOB state at will. Blue Harary had offered himself to the foundation, and when I arrived in Durham I found waiting for me a remarkable set of data about his amazing talents. Blue had described targets in closed rooms, affected animals and people during his OOB state, and had even appeared in visible form to several wit-nesses. However, apart from the research work, just talking to Blue about his experiences was an eye-opener. In reply to my question about how it feels to be out of the body so habitually, Blue told me of his many experiences visiting new dimensions, many of which he would not describe. He also told me how he was constantly aware of "presences" about him. Some of these were of the "dead," and others were, as Blue described it to me, "never incarnated." There seems little doubt that the OOBE is a key to new worlds and levels of existence.

Further suggestions that the OOB world can lead to the discovery of new dimensions come from Robert Crookall, a British scientist who gave up his geological work to study the OOBE and who has collected hundreds of spontaneous accounts. Crookall has corroborated the view that even occasional OOBEers can contact other-world dimensions and beings. Analyzing several hundred cases of the experience in his book, *More Astral Projections,* Crookall found that in about 25 per cent of his recorded cases the percipients made contact with supernormal beings. Many of these beings were recognized as the "dead." He further found that while the majority of people found themselves projected to familiar earthly scenes, over 10 per cent found themselves in a new dimension of unparalleled beauty (like Skilton), or in a dingy, misty dimension some 5 per cent of the time.

To many of the hundreds of people who have had the OOBE our earthly life and being is only one of many worlds. And to those rare individuals like Fox, Blue Harary, Monroe, and others, perhaps "this" world is the most insignificant of them all.

YOGI RAMACHARAKA was born in India about 1790. For much of his life he traveled through the East, visiting lamaseries and monasteries, and seeking a better philosophy for living. About 1865 he took an eight-year-old boy, Baba Bharata, as his pupil. Together they retraced the steps of Yogi Ramacharaka's earlier travels while the man taught the boy. In 1893, feeling that his life was drawing to a close, Ramacharaka sent his pupil to carry their beliefs abroad. Arriving in Chicago, where a world exposition was in progress, Baba Bharata was an instant success with his lectures. There he met an English author with whom he collaborated to write many books. The books were attributed to Yogi Ramacharaka as a measure of their respect, and have become classics in translated yogic literature.

THE ASTRAL WORLD

We are confronted with a serious difficulty at the beginning of this lesson, which will be apparent to those of our students who are well advanced in occult studies. We allude to the matter of the description of "planes" of existence. These lessons are intended as elementary studies designed to give the beginner a plain, simple idea of the general principles of occultism, without attempting to lead him into the more complicated stages of the subject. We have tried to avoid technicalities, so far as is possible, and believe that we have at least fairly well accomplished our task of presenting elementary principles in a plain manner, and we know that we have succeeded in interesting many persons in the study, who had heretofore been deterred from taking it up because of the mass of technical description and complicated description of details that met their view upon taking up other works on the subject.

So, in this lesson on the astral world, and the three lessons that follow it, we will be compelled to deal in generalities instead of going into minute and careful descriptions such as would be needed in a work taking up the "higher-grade" work. Instead of endeavoring to describe just what a "plane" is, and then going on to point out the nice little differences between "planes," and "subplanes" we shall treat the whole subject of the higher planes of existence under the general term of "the astral world," making that term include not only the lower divisions of the astral plane, but also some of the higher planes of life. This plan may be objected to by some who have followed other courses of reading on the subject, in which only the lower astral plane has been so styled, the higher planes receiving other names, which has led many to regard the astral plane with but scanty consideration reserving their careful study for the higher planes. But we ask these persons to remember that many of the ancient occultists classed the entire group of the upper planes (at least until the higher spiritual planes were reached) under the general term "the astral world," or similar terms, and we have the best of authority for this general division. There is as much difference between the lowest astral planes and the highest mental or spiritual planes, as there is between a gorilla and an Emerson, but in order to keep the beginner from getting lost in a wilderness of terms, we have treated all the planes above the physical (at least such as our lessons touches upon) under the general style of "the astral world."

It is difficult to convey clearly, in simple terms, the meaning of the word "plane," and we shall use it but little, preferring the word "state," for a plane is really a "state" rather than a place—that is, any one place may be inhabited on several planes. Just as a room may be filled with rays of the sun; light from a lamp; rays from an X-ray apparatus; ordinary magnetic vibrations; air, etc., etc., each acting according to the laws of its being, and yet not affecting the others, so may several planes of being be in full operation in a given space, without interfering with each other. We cannot go into detail regarding the matter, in this elementary lesson, and hope merely to give the student a good working mental conception, in order that he may understand the incidents and phenomena of the several planes comprising "the astral world."

Before going into the subject of the several planes of the astral world, it will be better for us to consider some of the general phenomena classified under the term "astral." We have told you that man (in the body), in addition to his physical senses of sight, hearing, tasting, smelling and feeling, has five *astral* senses (counterparts of the physical senses) operating on the astral plane, by which he may receive sense impressions without the aid of the physical sense organs. He also possesses a "sixth-sense" physical organ (the organ of the "telepathic" sense) which also has a corresponding astral sense.

These astral senses function on the lower astral plane—the plane next removed from the physical plane—and the phenomena of clairvoyance is produced by the use of these astral senses. . . . There are, of course, higher forms of clairvoyance, which operate on planes far above that used in ordinary clairvoyance, but such powers are so rare, and are possessed only by those of high attainment, that we need scarcely do more than mention them here. On this lower astral plane, the clairvoyant sees; the clairaudient hears; the psychometrist feels. On this plane the astral body moves about, and "ghosts" manifest. Disembodied souls living on the higher planes of the astral world, in order to communicate with those on the physical plane, must descend to this lowest plane, and clothe themselves with coarse astral matter in order to accomplish their object. On this plane moves the "astral bodies" of those in the flesh, who have acquired the art of projecting themselves in the astral. It is possible for a person to project his astral body, or travel in his astral body, to any point within the limits of the earth's attraction, and the trained occultist may do so at will, under the proper conditions. Others may occasionally take such trips (without knowing just how they do it, and having, afterward, the remembrance of a particular and very vivid dream); in fact many of us do take such trips, when the physical body is wrapped in sleep, and one often gains much information in this way, upon subjects in which he is interested, by holding astral communication with others interested in the same subject, all unconsciously of course. The conscious acquirement of knowledge in this way, is possible only to those who have progressed quite a way along the path of attainment. The trained occultist merely places himself in the proper mental condition, and then wishes himself at some particular place, and his astral travels there with the rapidity of light, or even more rapidly. The untrained occultist, of course, has no such degree of control over his astral body and is more or less clumsy in his management of it. The astral body is always connected with the physical body (during the life of the latter) by a thin silklike, astral thread, which maintains the communication between the two. Were this cord to be severed the physical body would die, as the connection of the soul with it would be terminated.

On this lower astral plane may also be perceived the auric colors of men. . . . Likewise it is on this plane that the emanations of thought may be observed by the clairvoyant vision, or the astral of one who visits that plane in his astral body. The mind is continually throwing off emanations, which extend some distance from the person, for a time, and which then, if strong enough, gradually pass off, drawn here and there by the corresponding thoughts of others. These thought emanations resemble clouds, some delicate and beautiful, while others are dark and murky. To the psychic or astral vision, places are seen to be filled with this thought-stuff, varying in character and appear-

ance with the quality and nature of the original thought which produced them. Some places are seen to be filled with bright attractive
thought-stuff showing that the general character of the thought of
those who inhabit it is of an uplifting and cheerful character, while
other places are filled with a hazy, murky mass or cloud of thought-
stuff, showing that those who live there (or some visitors) have been
dwelling on the lower planes of thought, and have filled the place
with depressing reminders of their sojourn there. . . .

If people could see but for a few minutes the thought-atmosphere
of groggeries, gambling-rooms, and places of that kind, they would
not care to again visit them. Not only is the atmosphere fairly sat-
urated with degrading thoughts, but the lower class of disembodied
souls flock in large numbers around the congenial scene, striving to
break the narrow bounds which separate them from the physical
plane in such places.

Perhaps the best way to make plain to you the general aspects
and phenomena of the astral world, would be to describe to you an
imaginary trip made by yourself in that world, in charge of an experienced occultist. We will send you, in imagination, on such a trip,
in this lesson, in charge of a competent guide—it being presupposed
that you have made considerable spiritual progress, as otherwise even
the guide could not take you very far, except by adopting heroic and
very unusual methods, which he probably would not see fit to do
in your case. Are you ready for your trip? Well, here is your guide.

You have gone into the silence, and suddenly become aware of
having passed out of your body, and to be now occupying only your
astral body. You stand beside your physical body, and see it sleeping
on the couch, but you realize that you are connected with it by a
bright silvery thread, looking something like a large bit of bright
spider web. You are conscious of the presence of your guide, who
is to conduct you on your journey. He also has left his physical body,
and is in his astral form, which reminds you of a vapory something,
the shape of the human body, but which can be seen through, and
which can move through solid objects at will. Your guide takes your
hand in his and says, "Come," and in an instant you have left your
room and are over the city in which you dwell, floating along as does
a summer cloud. You begin to fear lest you may fall, and as soon
as the thought enters your mind you find yourself sinking. But your
guide places a hand under you and sustains you, saying, "Now just
realize that you cannot sink unless you fear to—hold the thought that
you are buoyant and you will be so." You do so, and are delighted

to find that you may float at will, moving here and there in accordance to your wish or desire.

You see great volumes of thought-clouds arising from the city like great clouds of smoke, rolling along and settling here and there. You also see some finer vapory thought-clouds in certain quarters, which seem to have the property of scattering the dark clouds when they come in contact with them. Here and there you see bright thin lines of bright light, like an electric spark, traveling rapidly through space, which your guide tells you are telepathic messages passing from one person to another, the light being caused by the prana* with which the thought is charged. You see, as you descend toward the ground, that every person is surrounded by an egg-shaped body of color—his aura—in which is reflected his thought and prevailing mental state, the character of the thought being represented by varying colors. Some are surrounded by beautiful auras, while others have around them a black, smoky aura, in which are seen flashes of red light. Some of these auras make you heart-sick to observe, as they give evidence of such base, gross, and animal thoughts, that they cause you pain, as you have become more sensitive now that you are out of your physical body. But you have not much time to spare here, as your trip is but a short one, and your guide bids you come on.

You do not seem to change your place in space, but a change seems to have come over everything—like the lifting of a gauzy curtain in the pantomime. You no longer see the physical world with its astral phenomena, but seem to be in a new world—a land of queer shapes. You see astral "shells" floating about—discarded astral bodies of those who have shed them as they passed on. These are not pleasant to look upon, and you hurry on with your guide, but before you leave this second anteroom to the real astral world, your guide bids you relax your mental dependence upon your astral body, and much to your surprise you find yourself slipping out of it, leaving it in the world of shells, but being still connected with it by a silklike cord, or thread, just as it, in turn, is connected with your physical body, which you have almost forgotten by this time, but to which you are still bound by these almost invisible ties. You pass on clothed in a new body, or rather an inner garment of ethereal matter, for it seems as if you have been merely shedding one cloak, and then another, the *you* part of yourself remains unchanged—you smile now at the recollection that once upon a time you thought that the body was

* A form of nonphysical energy held by the yogic tradition to be the basic life force. *Editors.*

"you." The plane of the "astral shells" fades away, and you seem to have entered a great room of sleeping forms, lying at rest and in peace, the only moving shapes being those from higher spheres who have descended to this plane in order to perform tasks for the good of their humbler brethren. Occasionally some sleeper will show signs of awakening, and at once some of these helpers will cluster around him, and seem to melt away into some other plane with him. But the most wonderful thing about this region seems to be that as the sleeper awakens slowly, his astral body slips away from him just as did yours a little before, and passes out of that plane to the place of "shells," where it slowly disintegrates and is resolved into its original elements. This discarded shell is not connected with the physical body of the sleeping soul, which physical body has been buried or cremated, as it is "dead"; nor is the shell connected with the soul which has gone on, as it has finally discarded it and thrown it off. It is different in your case, for you have merely left it in the anteroom, and will return and resume its use, presently.

The scene again changes, and you find yourself in the regions of the awakened souls, through which you, with your guides, wander backward and forward. You notice that as the awakening souls pass along, they seem to rapidly drop sheath after sheath of their mental bodies (for so these higher forms of ethereal coverings are called), and you notice that as you move toward the higher planes your substance becomes more and more etherealized, and that as you return to the lower planes it becomes coarser and grosser, although always far more etherealized than even the astral body, and infinitely finer than the material physical body. You also notice that each awakening soul is left to finally awaken on some particular plane. Your guide tells you that the particular plane is determined by the spiritual progress and attainment made by the soul in its past lives (for it has had many earthly visits or lives), and that it is practically impossible for a soul to go beyond the plane to which it belongs, although those on the upper planes may freely revisit the lower planes, this being the rule of the astral world—not an arbitrary law, but a law of nature. If the student will pardon the commonplace comparison, he may get an understanding of it, by imagining a large screen, or series of screens, such as used for sorting coal into sizes. The large coal is caught by the first screen, the next size by the second, and so on until the tiny coal is reached. Now the large coal cannot get into the receptacle of the smaller sizes, but the small sizes may easily pass through the screen and join the large sizes, if force be imparted to them. Just so in the astral world, the soul with the greatest amount of materiality, and coarser nature, is stopped by the screen of a certain plane, and cannot pass on the higher ones, while one which has passed on to the higher planes, having cast off more confining sheaths, can easily pass backward and forward among the lower planes. In fact souls often do so, for the purpose of visiting friends on the lower planes, and giving them enjoyment and comfort in this way, and, in cases of a highly developed soul, much spiritual help may be given in this way, by means of advice and instruction, when the soul on the lower plane is ready for it. All of the planes, in fact, have spiritual helpers, from the very highest planes, some devoted souls preferring to so devote their time in the astral world rather than to take a well earned rest, or to pursue certain studies for their own development. Your guide explains these things to you as you pass backward and forward, among the lower set of planes (the reason you do not go higher will be explained to you bye-and-bye), and he also informs you that the only exception to the rule of free passage to the planes below the plane of a soul, is the one which prevents the lower-plane souls from entering the "plane of the sleepers," which plane may not be entered by souls who have awakened on a low plane, but may be freely entered by those pure and exalted souls who have attained a high plane. The plane of the chamber of slumber is sacred to those occupying it, and those higher souls just mentioned, and is in fact in the nature of a distinct and separated state rather than one of the series of planes just mentioned.

The soul awakens on just the plane for which it is fitted—on just the subplane of that plane which its highest desires and tastes naturally select for it. It is surrounded by congenial minds, and is able to pursue that which the heart of the man had longed for during earth-life. It may make considerable progress during this astral world life, and so when it is reborn it is able to take a great step forward, when compared to its last incarnation. There are planes and sub-planes innumerable, and each finds an opportunity to develop and enjoy to the fullest the highest things of which it is capable at that particular period of development, and as we have said it may perfect itself and develop so that it will be born under much more favorable conditions and circumstances in the next earth-life. But, alas, even in this higher world, all do not live up to their best, and instead of making the best of their opportunities, and growing spiritually, they allow their more material nature to draw them downward, and they spend much of their time on the planes beneath them, not to help and assist, but to live the less spiritual life of the denizens of the lower planes—the more material planes. In such cases the soul does not get the benefit of the astral world sojourn and is born back into just about the same condition as the last earth-life—it is sent back to learn its lesson over again.

The very lowest planes of the astral world are filled with souls of a gross type—undeveloped and animal like—who live as near as possible the lives they lived on earth (about the only thing they gain being the possibility of their "living-out" their gross tastes, and becoming sick and tired of it all, and thus allowing to develop a longing for higher things which will manifest in a "better chance" when they are reborn). These undeveloped souls cannot, of course, visit the upper planes, and the only plane below them being the plane of shells and the astral subplane immediately above the material plane (which is one of the so-called anterooms of the astral world) they often flock back as near to earth as is possible. They are able to get so near back to earth that they may become conscious of much that is transpiring there, particularly when the conditions are such that they are in harmony with their own natures. They may be said to be able to practically live on the low material plane, except that they are separated from it by a tantalizing thin veil, which prevents them from actively participating in it except on rare occasions. They may see, but not join in, the earth-life. They hang around the scenes of their old degrading lives, and often take possession of the brain of one of their own kind who may be under the influence of liquor, and thus add to his own low desires. This is an unpleasant subject, and we do not care to dwell upon it—happily it does not concern those who read these lessons, as they have passed beyond this stage of development. Such low souls are so attracted by earth-life, on its lower planes, that their keen desires cause them to speedily reincarnate in similar conditions although there is always at least a slight improvement—there is never a going backward. A soul may make several attempts to advance, in spite of the dragging-back tendencies of its lower nature—but it never slips back quite as far as the place from which it started.

The souls in the higher planes, having far less attraction for earth-life, and having such excellent opportunities for advancement, naturally spend a much longer time in the astral world, the general rule being that the higher the plane, the longer the rest and sojourn. But sooner or later the lesson is fully learned, and the soul yearns for that further advancement that can only come from the experience and action of another earth-life, and through the force of its desires (never against its will, remember) the soul is gradually caught in the current sweeping on toward rebirth, and becoming drowsy, is helped toward the plane of the room of slumber and, then falling into the soul-slumber it gradually "dies" to the astral world, and is reborn into a new earth-life in accordance to its desires and tastes, and for which it is fit at that particular stage of its development. It does not fully awaken upon physical birth, but exists in a dreamy state of gradual awakening during the years of early childhood, its awakening being evidenced by the gradual dawning of intelligence in the child whose brain keeps pace with the demands made upon it. We will go more into detail regarding this matter, in the succeeding chapters.

All of these things, your guide has pointed out to you, and he has shown you examples of all the things we have just mentioned. You have met and talked with friends and loved ones who have passed out of the body and occupy some of the planes through which you have passed. You have noticed with wonder that these souls acted and spoke as if *their* life was the only natural one, and in fact seemed to think that you had come to them from some outside world. You also noticed that while those on each plane were more or less acquainted with the planes beneath them, they often seemed in total ignorance of those above them—excepting in the case of those on the higher planes who had awakened to a *conscious* realization of what it all meant, and knew that they were merely in a class working their way upward. Those on the lower planes seemed more or less unconscious of the real meaning of their existence, not having awakened to the conscious spiritual stage. You also noticed how few changes these souls seemed to have undergone—how very little more they seemed to know about things spiritual and occult than when on earth. You also noticed on the lower planes an old friend, who in earth-life was a pronounced materialist, who did not seem to realize that he was "dead" and who believed that, by some catastrophe of nature, he had been transported to some other planet or physical world, and who was as keen as ever for his argument that "death ended all," and who flew into a rage with the visitors from the higher spheres who told him who they were and from whence they came, calling them rogues and imposters, and demanding that they show him something of their claimed "higher spheres" if they were realities. He claimed that their sudden appearances and disappearances were simply the physical phenomena of the new planet upon which they were living. Passing away from him in the midst of his railing at you for agreeing with the "imposters" and "visionaries," who, to use his expression, were "little better than the spiritualists of the old world," you sadly asked your guide to take you to the highest spheres. Your guide smiled and said, "I will take you as far as you can go," and then took you to a plane which so fitted in with your desires, aspirations, tastes, and development, that you begged him to allow you to remain there, instead of taking you back to earth, as you felt that you had reached the "seventh heaven" of the astral world. He insisted upon your return, but before starting told you that you were still in one of the subplanes of the comparatively lower planes. You seemed to doubt his words, and like the materialist asked to be shown the greater things. He replied, "No, my son, you have progressed just as far as your limitations will allow—you have reached that part of the 'other life' which will be yours when you part with the body, unless you manage to develop still more and thus pass into a higher grade—thus far may you go but no farther. You have your limitations, just as I have mine, still farther on. No soul may travel beyond its spiritual boundaries."

"But," continued your guide, "beyond your plane and beyond mine are plane after plane, connected with our earth, the splendors of which man cannot conceive. And there are likewise many planes around the other planets of our chain—and there are millions of other worlds—and there are chains of universes just as there are chains of planets—and then greater groups of these chains—and so on greater and grander, beyond the power of man to imagine—on and on and on and on, higher and higher to inconceivable heights. An infinity of infinities of worlds are before us. Our world and our planetary chain and our system of suns, and our systems of solar systems, are but as grains of sand on the beach."

"Then what am I—poor mortal thing—lost among all this inconceivable greatness," you cried. "You are that most precious thing—a living soul," replied your guide, "and if you were destroyed the whole system of universes would crumble, for you are as necessary as the greatest part of it—it cannot do without you—you cannot be lost or destroyed—you are a part of it all, and are eternal."

"And beyond all of this of which you have told me," you cried, "what is there, and what is the center of it all?" Your guide's face took on a rapt expression. "The Absolute," he replied.

And when you reached your physical body again—just before your guide faded away—you asked him, "How many million miles away from earth have we been, and how long were we gone?" He replied, "You never left the earth at all—and your body was left alone but a moment of time—time and space belong not to the astral world."

ARTHUR FORD (1896–1971), an ordained minister, was for more than four decades one of the world's most renowned trance mediums. He was catapulted to fame when he "cracked" the code Houdini set up with his wife before he died. The Reverend Ford was also one of the founders of Spiritual Frontiers Fellowship, a national organization of lay people and clergy who encourage the organized churches to encounter and explore the reality of psychic and mystic experience, especially as set forth in the Bible.

JEROME ELLISON is a teacher, journalist, and socially active philosopher. In his writing career he has been an editor for *Reader's Digest, Saturday Evening Post,* and *Collier's.* He left publishing to become a teacher of journalism and literature, and until last year, when he retired, he was a professor of English at the University of New Haven in Connecticut. He has since embarked on another career as founder and chief organizer of The Phenix Club, a national organization to meet the intellectual and spiritual needs of older people. Among his many books are *The Life Beyond Death* (from which this selection comes), *A Serious Call to an American (R)Evolution,* and *The Last Third of Life Club,* which presents the philosophy and organizational principles behind The Phenix Club.

THE REVELATIONS OF FREDERIC MYERS

Arthur Ford, as told to Jerome Ellison

The case of Frederic Myers is of special interest to those of our own time who believe there is a distinct possibility of a life after death and would like to know more about its conditions and quality. This is not only because Myers was an original, energetic, resourceful, dedicated, and highly intelligent psychical researcher for thirty years before his "death" and for thirty years after it. Ancient and modern history, as well as contemporary journalism, offers unnumbered examples of people who had an active curiosity about the life beyond death while in the physical realm and who found means to report back after emerging into the life beyond bone, flesh, and tissue. But most of these people have talked in some idiom other than the language of credence of our time. They may talk in the imagery of poetry, or of religion, or of mythology, or of art, or of common speech. In our time, none of these are believed. When listened to at all, they are not taken seriously or regarded as fact. The language of credence of our day is the idiom of physical or psychological science.

This is Myers' special strength. A highly educated man and professor at Cambridge, one of the world's leading universities, he was a classical scholar best known for his perceptive essays on the Roman poets before he found his life's work in psychical research. He was thoroughly familiar with the physical and theoretical science that led to Einstein's discoveries and with the basic insights of modern psychology up to and including Freud.

Myers began his researches in a deeply skeptical mood. He and his associates were the most ruthless iconoclasts and exposers of fraud ever known. Their standards of evidence were so rigid that some bitterly called his research group, a "society for the suppression of evidence." It was only the relentless pressure of the steadily accumulating evidence that finally persuaded Myers that the survival of human personality beyond death was a fact. After that, he saw the main problem not as establishing truth—this had been done—but of communicating that truth in terms a mass mind sunk deep in the dogma of physical science could comprehend.

No one was more profoundly familiar with the depth and subtleties of the scientific problems of survival research than was Myers. No one was more intimately acquainted with the legitimate basis for scientific skepticism than he was. Immersed as we are in the dogma of physical science from kindergarten, we need to hear new ideas in our familiar language in order to believe them. It is this, rather than its uniqueness, that gives Myers' testimony its special value. He "talks our language."

At the time of Myers' death in 1901, the two great obstacles already mentioned still stood in the way of a general acceptance of the fact of survival. One was the telepathy-of-the-living hypothesis. Once telepathy had been established as a real and continuous phenomenon, there was a rush to explain all communications claiming to originate in the world beyond death as conscious or unconscious fabrications of the medium, who was presumed to gather his information by searching the contents of living human minds. Myers acknowledged this as a legitimate, if improbable, objection. He sought constantly to devise demonstrations which would conclusively rule out every possibility of origin in physical protoplasm. After his "death" he neatly solved the problem in the famous cross correspondences.

The second major difficulty was the lack of any generally accepted theoretical basis on which a materialistically oriented scientist might build a conceptual structure of a continuing and expanding life. This he solved by demonstrating thought energy and thought forms, using language already familiar to psychologists.

It is not necessary to understand scientific terminology in order to understand Myers. We have all heard the expression "He is lost in thought." Myers might ask, "Lost to what?" To be sure, he is lost to the "realities" of the workaday world. But science has shown us that these realities are illusory. The table that looks so solid, the human body that appears so substantial are, science has shown us, mostly empty space. The great relative distances between the small nucleus and the circling electrons of the atom show that all appearance of solidity is illusion in space. The man lost in thought is in a mental world where no such illusions exist. Myers—and a great many other people—would insist that the true case is exactly the opposite. People who never entered the mental realm, these would say, are the truly lost—they are sleepwalking robots. The man "lost" in thought is actually approaching the true and the only reality, since ultimate reality is mental in nature.

The cross correspondences were messages received over Myers' signature by automatic writers in trance after Myers' death. The messages came in fragments so that no one communication through any one medium made any sense. When these fragments were pieced together according to instructions (a matter made easy by the clearinghouse system in use at the time), they made a perfectly clear, consecutive, and sensible communication. Mediums were selected who did not know one another and who had little or no knowledge of the obscure classical sources Myers habitually used, in addition to his signature, to identify himself. The general character, continuity, and governing personality of these messages did not change for a quarter century, though several sets of mediums were used. The early mediums dropped out by death, pressure of circumstance, or other causes and were replaced by new mediums, some of whom had not known of the cross correspondences, all having no understanding of classical literature.

We may take up Myers' elucidation of the circumstances of the life beyond death at a sitting with Mrs. Leonard during which Sir Oliver Lodge had been in communication with his son Raymond.

Lodge had not known Myers in earth life. The great physicist's interest in psychical research began early in this century, shortly after Myers' death. The acquaintance of the two men was entirely "interworld."

Lodge told his son about a statement given by Myers through another medium to the effect that the plane of existence Raymond was now in was what we would call illusion. Lodge wanted to know what Raymond thought of this statement. Raymond explained that Myers, whom he had come to know well enough to address familiarly as "Uncle Fred," was with them at that very moment and that together they would try to clear up the matter. (Difficulties of terminology frequently turn up in such communications; it seems to be rather like explaining what snow and ice are like to a tropical native who has never experienced either.) Raymond explained that there were many parallels between the plane on which he and Myers were living and the plane on which his father was living. On both planes, Raymond said, many of the things we need are created for us by the divine imagination and many more—houses, clothes, jewels, and so on—are created out of our own imaginations. In both cases the necessities are created out of available materials. And in both cases the structures are temporary, meant for use only until the individual had been readied to progress to the next higher plane of life. In earth-side living our objects were made out of what we choose to call matter. In Raymond's sphere the necessities were made out of much finer material created by the power of mind.

"You live in a world of illusions," said Raymond, "—illusions necessary to enable you to do your work. We live in an extension of the illusory world in which you live. The outer rim of it. We are more in touch with the world of reality than you are. Spirit and mind belong to the world of reality. Everything else, that is, external things, are in a sense necessary for a time, but superfluous and only temporary as far as the world of reality goes. Spirit and mind belong to that world and are indestructible."

The bulk of Myers' discourse on the afterworld came through an Irish girl, Geraldine Cummins of Cork. Myers did not begin his serious discussion of after-death living until he had been in his new surroundings for more than twenty years and had completed a great deal of cross correspondence and other work designed to demonstrate the fact of survival. Miss Cummins was not a professional medium. Daughter of a professor, she had no education in science, psychology, or philosophy, but was interested in the theater and had written two plays which had been produced at the Abbey Theater. Her habit when about to write automatically was to sit down, cover her eyes with her left hand, and concentrate on the thought of stillness. This induced a "kind of half-sleep or dream-state." When the automatic writing began, it was "as if an endless telegram were being tapped out" through her arm by a stranger she was willing to help. Her right hand rested on a large pad of paper and someone stood by to remove the pages as they were filled and replace her hand for each new sheet. The writing was very rapid. Normally, Miss Cummins said she would need seven or eight hours to write a short article of perhaps 800 words. In automatic writing she turned out as much as 2,000 words in a little more than an hour. The material seemed to have been organized in advance, for rapid presentation, complete with chapter headings—but without punctuation, paragraphing or spaces between the words, which all ran together continuously. Myers outlined the structure and conditions of life beyond death in considerable detail, transmitting in all, between the years 1924 and 1931, enough to fill an average-size book.

If we are to grasp the full import of Myers' message, it would be well to review at this point the concept which, though never specifically stated by him, permeates the whole of his communication—evolution-of-consciousness or post-Darwinian evolutionary theory. According to this hypothesis, as developed during the twentieth century by Bergson, Bucke, Julian Huxley, Teilhard, Jung, Medawar, and others, the main thrust of evolution is to develop an increasing capacity for breadth and depth of awareness, with the multiplicity of physical forms a mere byproduct of this central evolutionary drive.

Earthworms, clams, and barnacles, possessing "simple consciousness" live in a dim dream, living out their lives in a few cubic feet of earth space, dimly aware of light, dark, heat, cold, hunger, and a need to reproduce. On the reptile, bird, and animal scale, consciousness ascends through a hierarchy of awareness of increasing range. In the human world, the outstanding feature of progression from infancy to adulthood is an extension of the range of things the individual can be aware of. When adulthood is achieved, there still remain vast differences in capacities for—"levels of"—awareness. The consciousness of woman A may be limited to husband, house, children, and shopping centers, while the mind of woman B may encompass all these things and also an appreciation of music, an interest in books, participation in local politics.

The awareness levels of both women may change. Woman A may

suddenly develop an interest in religion which may open her eyes to the predicament of the entire human species and set her off on a serious study of international affairs. Woman B may, in addition to her present interests, develop an intense concern for social justice and thus increase her understanding of social machinery. Both women will have, on this present earth plane, to use a phrase frequently employed by Myers, "progressed to a higher level of consciousness." Similarly, the man obsessed with stock market, family, and fishing may develop an interest in art and languages and thus expand his level of consciousness without ever leaving the earth plane.

The Myers communications assert that the evolutionary thrust toward ever-expanding awareness is cosmic and eternal and hence does not stop at death. The main thrust of creation is not physical forms but mental ones, easily capable of casting off one physical form to take on another or existing in abundant, energetic life with no physical form at all. The wise human being on earth, if he has kept himself mentally alert, progresses toward wisdom through ever-widening and ever-deepening understanding of physical, mental, and spiritual principles.

So, Myers says, do we progress in the life beyond death. In the life on earth, as a byproduct of our growing consciousness, we take on and discard numerous bodies—those of infants, preadolescents, adolescents, young adults, mature adults, and several adult-body replacements. In the life beyond death, not only does the evolutionary thrust toward widening awareness continue, but it is also housed in a sequence of bodies. These life-beyond bodies, however, are made of lighter, finer, more highly energized materials, with an increasing content of mental-spiritual energy as the sequence progresses. The Creator Himself is conceived as pure creative thought-energies source —"The Great Imagination."

Myers, after twenty years of "other-side" experience and observation, conceived the after-death life experience as divided into seven major stages, each with its entry phase, period of development, and period of preparation for the next higher stage. Stage One is, of course, the earth plane. Stage Two is the condition of the individual immediately after death. Myers refers to it variously as "The Life Immediately After Death," "The Intermediate Plane," and "Hades." This stage is brief and is followed by entry into a more stable world Myers calls "The Plane of Illusion" or "The Immediate World After Death."

There follows Stage Four, an indescribably lovely existence called

"The Plane of Color" or "The World of Eidos." Highly qualified souls may not progress to "The Plane of Flame" or "The World of Helios," which is Stage Five. The ultimate stages Six and Seven— "The Plane of Light" and "Timelessness"—are of an advanced spiritual nature, so close to the ultimate essence of creativity that no experience vocabulary has yet been evolved to describe them, and hence they are difficult to communicate to earth-level beings. The situation is roughly analogous to, but far more difficult than, that of the earthside doctor trying to explain the action of the endocrine glands to a kindergarten child whose endocrine glands he is treating.

Myers illustrates this progression with case histories. There should be one further preliminary word before continuing Myers' discourse: on reincarnation. At the time when Myers was writing, both on the earth plane and, through mediums, from the afterlife, the reincarnation theory was not given wide credence among Western psychologists, parapsychologists, and psychical researchers. Since then, and particularly in the light of the very recent investigations of the University of Virginia professor of psychology Ian Stevenson, the likelihood of reincarnation is being taken much more seriously. In this respect, as well as in evolution-of-consciousness theory, Myers proved himself well ahead of his time.

As Myers' first case history, we may consider the instance of "Walter." Walter was one of the four sons of a middle-class family able to live comfortably on the income produced by the father's unimaginative and repetitious occupation. It was a "family-centered" family, dominated by a mother who found adequate life fulfillment in directing the affairs of her children, of whom she was very proud. The family was smug, proud, and aloof, considering themselves somewhat above the general run of humanity and entering hardly at all into human affairs outside the family circle.

Walter was a particular favorite of both his parents. He finally married, but the marriage had a brief life. Walter, so long accustomed to the unqualified praise heaped upon him by his mother, could not adjust to the presence of a woman who assessed him more realistically. There were bitter quarrels and finally a divorce. Walter returned to home and mother, and devoted his surplus energies to making money. An adroit stock manipulator, he was very successful and amassed a great deal of money. After the death of his mother and father, he moved to an expensive and well-appointed city club and there lived out the rest of his earth days enjoying the adulation the earth plane heaps upon the man who has a lot of money. Walter eventually died and entered Stage Two, the "Intermediate Plane" or "Hades."

When a baby emerges from the fetus level of consciousness to earth awareness, he does a good deal of sleeping, dreaming, and resting, while people more accustomed to the earth plane attend to his needs, of which he is but dimly aware. So it is, says Myers, with the entry into Stage Two. In the tradition of folklore, people anticipating immediate death are said to have memories of their entire past lives flash before them. If this is true, it would seem to be a preview of Myers' Intermediate Plane or Hades. During this interval Walter was, when not sleeping, in a resting state of drowsy reverie in which memory pictures of his past life floated through his mind. Apparently it is this state which is referred to in the ancient tradition of "hell." Whether or not it is "hellish," of course, depends upon the memory content of the particular psyche. If this contains sinister episodes and terrifying experiences, these will drift by the dreamer's vision along with the more joyful happenings. Myers designates this interval "The Journey Down the Long Gallery."

During Walter's sleepy journey down this memory path, he rediscovered his old affection for his mother and the pleasant, admiring protective glow of affection with which she had surrounded him. As he became stronger, and his imaginative force more potent, he found himself able to re-create an idealized version of the old home, the old hometown and—in cooperation with the still willing and still possessive psyche of his mother—live happily among circumstances he considered ideal.

In Stage Three—"The Plane of Illusion" or "The Immediate World After Death"—materials are so pliable that they may be shaped by direct action of the imagination. They do not, as in the case of the recalcitrant materials of the earth plane, have to pass through the hands of draftsman, blueprinter, and workman. Walter now had no problems except an excess of time on his hands. Since he had always loved the old game of buying and selling stocks, he looked around for others who might like to play the game with him—and, of course, found them. As on earth, he was very successful and again made a great deal of money. Here, however, the gathering of money did not bring the same admiration and power it had on earth. Since any need could be gratified by the direct action of the imagination, there was no need of money, and few people cared much about it. This produced in Walter a feeling of disappointed restlessness. The feeling was intensified as he began to see that his mother's love for him was childish and possessive. She was a child mother playing with her baby, a little girl playing with her doll.

Nor was his father's admiration of him the same as it had been. The father was one of those who saw little point in making money in a place where it was not needed. Gradually Walter was brought face to face with the fact that, spiritually, he did not amount to much. Trapped between his father's scorn and his mother's suffocating possessiveness, he was driven to a frustrated rage. He felt he had to get out of there. The question was—to where? He longed more and more for the old days of excitement in the stock market, where he was the center of many admiring eyes. He began to feel "what is called the earth pull, the birth pull." He regressed to Stage Two, where he again reviewed his past experience. There he made his decision to return to Stage One, the earth plane. He would be born again as a human baby as soon as appropriate parents could be found and would try again to see what he could learn from further experiences of earth life.

Walter had a brother named Martin who had been killed in a war many years before Walter's death. There had also been a sister, Mary, who had died young. Mary and Martin had wider horizons than their brother Walter or their parents. Both had, through earth-life adventures that had taken them far outside the narrow preoccupations of the family circle, awakened in themselves the possibilities of a loving concern for all humanity.

They, too, after a period in the Stage Two dream rest, had returned to the imaginatively created old-hometown surroundings and enjoyed a family reunion. But their stay at this level of consciousness was brief. They quickly saw the limitations of housekeeping and stock trading, no matter how pleasantly these occupations might be idealized. They longed, not for return to earth life, but for great, awareness-increasing experiences in entirely new dimensions. And so they went on to the "Plane of Color" or "Eidos."

Eventually, all the children gone, even father and mother began to reconsider the hometown situation. The mother, drawn back to earth by her attachment to Walter, would reenter Stage One as an earth baby. There, by living a life of wider awareness and generosity, she would redeem the damage her possessiveness had caused the last time around. The wavering father had no desire to return to earth. At last, with the anonymous help of Martin from Eidos, he was guided along a path that would lead him to strive for the next higher level of consciousness.

Not all experiences on the third plane, Myers says, are as stuffy as those described in the case of this family. The grouping urge, instead of being a family structure, may be a special interest, a religion, a profession, a trade, an art or almost anything that would join people in a joint exercise of their imaginations. Since communication is by direct-image telepathy, there are no language barriers. And since enthusiasms are no respecters of centuries, time is of little account. So it is perfectly possible for a soul to find itself part of a group containing people from other nations and from other centuries.

Though an individual may linger in Stage Three for generations, an eventual decision must be made: The individual either returns to earth or progresses to Stage Four. Before leaving, however, the more enterprising souls may have an opportunity to experience one of the great wonders of this plane of consciousness—a tour through some section of The Great Memory. Just as, on earth, one may go to a film library and see newsreels of important earth events since the invention of the motion-picture camera, so, in Stage Three, one may witness the originals of desire-selected events from the beginning of human experience. Everything that has ever happened has been recorded by the cosmic memory.

"I have journeyed only as far as Eidos, the Fourth Plane," Myers wrote by the hand of Miss Cummins, ". . . so my knowledge is necessarily restricted." Here, as on the earth plane, he sees himself as "an explorer" into the ultimate nature of human life and of the universe and of the relationships between the two. His clear, conscious aim is to penetrate as far as he can into the mystery being successively revealed to him, then, through sensitives, to send back word of newly discovered territories to "the collective mind of man." Gradually he leads us to see a cosmic *process* at work. The traveler who will persevere in the arduous business of increasing the range of his sensitivity and understanding will, stage by stage, find himself growing in perception of ever more extensive ranges of the creative universe.

One receives an impression that it is the aim of the Creator to "take into the firm," as junior partners, as many as can qualify. As soon as earth experience has been thoroughly comprehended—either through one or more return trips to that plane, or through exchange of experience with other travelers met on the third plane—the candidate may proceed to realms beyond the reach of the earth mind. "If you are a soul now," Myers writes "—an intelligent ethically developed soul—you will desire to go up the ladder of consciousness. In most cases, the longing for a physical earth-existence will have been burned into ashes."

Throughout Myers' long series of discourses he emphasizes that what he is talking about is the actual *experience* of other modes of existence rather than mere theorizing about them. "Here on the Fourth Plane one must leave behind all rigid intellectual structures and dogmas, be they scientific, religious, or philosophical." Myers is so insistent on this point that he subtitles the fourth plane "The Breaking of the Image." On "The Plane of Color," Myers finds himself for the first time having difficulty verbalizing in earth terms what he is experiencing. "A human being cannot imagine a new sound, a new color or feeling entirely outside the range of his previous experience. It is impossible for him to conceive the infinite variety of new sounds, colors and feelings experienced by us on the Fourth Plane."

He can, however, communicate certain of its qualities. The demands of the earth body, the presuppositions of earth forms, the effects of their long imprint and conditioning, while still in memory, are now put far behind. A new and more highly energized intellect and spirit find a much wider freedom to function. This new energy requires a new body to give it expression and so creates one. It bears a faint resemblance to the old earth form, but is far more radiant and beautiful and better suited to its new employment. Myers continues:

> Flowers are there, but in shapes unknown to you, exquisite in color, radiant with light. Such colors and lights, not contained within any earthly octave, are expressed by us in thoughts and not in words. Words for us are obsolete. The soul, in this plane of consciousness, must struggle and labor, know sorrow but not earth sorrow. Know ecstasy but not earth ecstasy. Mind expresses itself more directly: we can hear the thoughts of other souls. Experience on the fourth plane leads the soul to the borders of the superterrestrial region.

In this plane, Myers says, everything is unbelievably more intense, more highly energized. Consciousness is continuous; sleep is no longer necessary. Experiences are "indescribably" more intense. Not only love, truth, and beauty are present here but also hostility, hate, and anger. "A hostile mentality may, with a powerful projection of thought, blast and wither some part of your body of light and color. You have to learn how to send out protecting rays. If on earth some other man or woman was your enemy and you hated one another the old emotional memory will awaken when you meet. Love and hate draw you inevitably together in the pattern of your particular designs."

The main work on this plane is toward further understanding of how mind controls energy and life-force, from which all outward appearances emerge. Here one is free from the heavy mechanical restrictions of earth. "I have but to concentrate my thought for what you might call a moment," Myers says, "and I can build up a likeness of myself, send that likeness speeding across our vast world to a friend, to one, that is, in tune with me. Instantly I appear before that friend, though I am remote from him. My likeness holds speech —in thought, remember, not words—with this friend. Yet, all the time, I control it from an enormous distance; and as soon as the interview is concluded I withdraw the life of my thought from that image of myself, and it vanishes."

Since Myers had not progressed beyond the fourth plane at the time of his communication, his accounts of the higher levels of consciousness beyond this are less detailed and more speculative. He seems to have picked up enough hearsay, however, to outline with some confidence the general nature of the further advance.

A death experience and a rebirth are required, he says, as a transition from each stage to the next higher. It is assumed that on the fourth plane the intense experience of "profound despair and inconceivable bliss" has burned away the last vestiges of the cumbersome pettiness and animosities of earth, finally and completely freed the soul from domination by that planet. The spirit is now qualified to experience cosmic ranges beyond earth's confines. In the fifth plane one acquires a body of flame, enabling him to tour the stellar universe without being harmed by its temperatures and turbulence and to return with a fuller experience of these cosmic reaches. The sixth plane is "The Plane of Light." Individuals on this plane are matured spirits, having lived through, with conscious comprehension, all the aspects of the created universe. Myers calls this "The Plane of White Light" and subtitles it "Pure Reason." Souls on this plane are described as follows:

> They bear with them the wisdom of form, the incalculable secret wisdom, gathered only through limitation, harvested from numberless years, garnered from lives passed in myriad forms. . . . They are capable of living now without form, of existing as white light in the pure thought of their creator. They have

joined the immortals . . . fulfilled the final purpose of the evolution of consciousness.

The seventh and final stage—in which the soul enters full partnership with God—is beyond Myers' verbal reach. It "baffles description; it is heartbreaking even to attempt to write of it."

Myers knew that the levels of consciousness in the upper ranges were beyond the insight of the average earth dweller except for intuitive flashes. He gives us such detail about worlds beyond our reach, I believe, simply to assure us that there *are* such worlds. They are attainable to us and to our loved ones whenever the desire to attain them is strong enough. He wanted to remove from the human mind once and for all any fear of death with the assurance that there is no death, only alterations in mode of consciousness.

As a practicing, professional trance medium, I have dealt mainly in those regions designated by Myers as the second and third planes. Only occasionally have the spiritual transactions in which my transmission facilities been utilized tapped the very high regions of spiritual development. These cases I have discussed in other writings. Here I am concerned with those aspects of the life beyond death which assert themselves most frequently and most acceptably to the comprehension of the average earth mind—that is, the second and third planes. Myers gives such abundant insight here that I believe it will be well worth our while to attend to what he has to say about the life-death transactions most familiar to earthside experience.

Though flashes of spirit light may occasionally and briefly illuminate the darkness of the average earth mind, the afterlife business most often brought to its attention concerns only the immediate death transition and the third stage. Very large numbers of average souls remain comfortably in this third stage for very long periods—sometimes many centuries—imagining it to be the ultimate heaven and making no effort to progress further.

When we recall that Myers was writing through Miss Cummins in the early 1930s, we are surprised at the contemporary sound of some of the things he has to say. Population explosion, environmental pollution, military-industrial conspiracies to make war, domination of human spirit by mechanical and political machines, over-attachment to earth possessions—all themes prominent in the more thoughtful press of our time—were subjects of solemn warnings by Myers, writing through Miss Cummins, a generation ago.

It is commonly (and mistakenly) believed that people mysteriously acquire the ability to foretell the future after they have passed into the afterlife. Though they cannot predict events, they can discern trends; this is something a little different. "No man is permitted to know in full the secret of the coming time," Myers wrote. "But we souls who dwell in . . . Eidos dimly see the trend of man's thought and therefore, presage his endeavor in the coming time." His clear observation of these trends evoked his profound concern: "I beg of the men and women of the day to consider the human being apart from machines, to consider life apart from gold. Within the restless jangle of those monstrous cogs and wheels which now turn ceaselessly and bear your so-called civilization upon them, there is little leisure or quiet for the calmness or philosophic meditation out of which knowledge is born. What somber destiny may not awake the children of the morrow if they, too, are caught in the grip of that creature without a soul, the machine—that last and final embodiment of the god of materialism."

Myers points to the dangers of runaway nationalistic feelings which splinter mankind into mutually hating and fearing national groups. This delays the awareness that mankind is one, and its problems cannot be solved until they are solved jointly. "The nations may plunge down the hill into war, or produce and propagate misery by an increase in its millions of human beings." As for environment: "Neither beauty nor health can survive and flourish when nation destroys nation and machine destroys machine." Machine thinking endangers man's spiritual evolution: "A mechanism without a soul should be the servant, not the master, of the thinking human being. The world of today should envisage the ideal of quality, not quantity."

People have often asked me about the status in the afterlife of suicides. Myers' position on suicide is less moralistic than practical. The extreme negative, depressed mental state of the suicide at the time of his self-destructive act carries over into the afterlife, placing him at a great disadvantage in making his adjustment. Many times, upon awakening, he does not realize that he has passed over. He may go into an extreme panic upon discovering that he can no longer control his physical body. Upon reaching full realization that he has in fact killed himself, he may—as in the case of the son of the late Bishop James Pike, in which I was able to be of some help—deeply regret his act.

In the Pike case, the young man committed suicide while undergoing a destructive LSD experience. On discovering his plight, he was desperate. He produced every kind of poltergeist effect within his power—smashing things, disarranging clothing, moving objects, bending and distributing safety pins, moving books that would call attention to his memory—all to attract help in his plight. The bishop finally caught the hint and sought the assistance of mediums, including myself. The boy's whole desperate story then came through, and forces were set going to help him.

"The mood that drives the suicide to self-slaughter," Myers wrote through Miss Cummins, "will envelop him like a cloud from which we may not for a long time be able to give him release. His emotional thoughts, his whole attitude of mind sets up a barrier which can only be broken down by his own strenuous efforts, by a brave control of himself, and above all by the call sent out with all the strength of his soul to higher beings to bestow succour, to grant release."

"Sudden death," mentioned in the famous litany and commonplace in our time of war and highway accident, is another theme that has produced many questions. Again Myers takes the practical view. The disadvantage of a sudden death, he says, lies mainly in the circumstance that the psyche has no time to adjust. A person suddenly killed in his prime may linger among earth scenes for some time before the realization of his new situation reaches him. In this state of mind he is slow to understand the need for the other discarnate beings in making his adjustment and hence is slow to utilize this help. However, there have been many cases in my own experience as a medium in which death which came suddenly has seemingly been handled without great deviation from the normal, comfortable transition. The normal transition, Myers says, is a simple and peaceful going into a pleasant, sometimes even blissful, totally restful sleep. During this period the astral body—that radiant "double" which accompanies our physical body from the fetal stage and which is clearly visible to psychics gifted with the ability to see auras—detaches itself.

This body, though sleeping, is as alive as ever, though now existing exclusively in the consciousness wavelengths allotted to astral bodies. As the rest continues, there may be dreams involving memories of earth life. Upon awakening the soul is usually met and welcomed by friends, vocational associates, and relatives who made this transition before him.

Myers did not disapprove the use of drugs to ease and speed the passage of persons suffering an incurable disease, though he thought several days should be allowed for the transition. "Under these conditions the merciful physician is entirely justified in committing what the law still holds to be murder." A great deal more understanding of disease will come, he says, when doctors begin to see the connection between body and spirit.

What is the effect of brain damage or advanced senility on the afterlife? Here, Myers reminds us that the "double" or astral body, the vehicle of the personality after death, is with us from conception. Everything known to the physical body is also known to the astral body. Brain damage, he says, can only make the individual "unable to *manifest* his intelligence to the visible world of men. He is still intellectually alive . . . after death, the soul finds his fundamental memory center in his astral body. . . . He or she has only withdrawn a little way from you and has no need of your pity."

There has been much speculation about how the body sustains itself without food. Myers explains: "Etheric life is nourished by cosmic rays that splendidly light up our surroundings and—in some manner I do not understand—sustain the life of our bodies." There have been cases of earth dwellers—specifically the famous German mystic Therese Neumann and a saintly old Indian woman known to Yogananda—who were able to utilize these rays for physical nourishment on earth. They sustained themselves without food for many years. Just how this was managed is a secret not understood even by such advanced spirits as Yogananda. It is reported here simply as an empiric fact.

Myers expressed the opinion that other planets carry life resembling ours. He does not believe that the failure of our senses and instrumentation to detect them can be taken as evidence. We perceive, he says, only those wavelengths which our "sets" are tuned to perceive. In electromagnetic reception, a radio or television tuned to a given station will not register messages from another broadcasting station even though this be nearby and broadcasting a powerful signal. He emphasizes that all worlds occupy the same space. Our inability to perceive anything other than earth phenomena affects in no way the fact that superterrestrial, cosmic, and spiritual activity of incredible intensity is at all times in progress around us.

RUDOLF STEINER (1861–1925) was a philosopher, scientist, educator, and artist who developed the world conception known as anthroposophy. He was concerned with describing the path of spiritual development most suited to the modern age, a path emphasizing clarity, objectivity, and inner freedom. This path proceeds from the normal human powers of thinking, feeling, and willing to the higher modes of consciousness that he termed imagination, inspiration, and intuition. Thus the anthroposophical path of knowledge calls upon the whole person, challenging him to harmoniously balance the scientific (thinking), artistic (feeling), and practical (willing) aspects of his nature. This "spiritual science" was the foundation for many developments by Steiner: eurhythmy (a movement artform), biodynamic gardening, the Waldorf schools for child education. Although Steiner himself wrote very little, his works, prepared from his lectures, number nearly three hundred. A good introduction to his thought is *Knowledge of the Higher Worlds and Its Attainment,* from which this selection is taken, and *Occult Science.* Steiner's research, ideas, and teachings are carried on by the Anthroposophical Society, headquartered in Dornach, Switzerland. The Anthroposophical Society in America is located in New York City.

KNOWLEDGE OF THE HIGHER WORLDS

During sleep no impressions are conveyed to the human soul through the instrumentality of the physical sense organs. The impressions from the ordinary outer world do not find their way to the soul when in that condition. In certain respects the soul is actually outside that part of the human being—the so-called physical body—which in waking life is the medium for sense perceptions and thought. The soul is then only connected with the finer bodies (the etheric body and the astral body), which are beyond the scope of physical sense observation. But the activity of these finer bodies does not cease during sleep. Just as the physical body is connected and lives with the things and beings of the physical world, affecting them and being affected by them, so, too, does the soul live in a higher world; only, this life of the soul continues also during sleep. The soul is in full activity during sleep, but we can know nothing of this activity so long as we have no spiritual organs of perception through which to observe what is going on around us and see what we ourselves are doing during sleep, as we observe our daily physical environment with our ordinary senses. The preceding chapters have shown that esoteric training consists in the development of such spiritual sense organs. Now if, as a result of esoteric training, the student's life during sleep is transformed in the manner described in the foregoing chapter, he will, when in that condition, be able to follow consciously everything going on around him. He can at will find his way in his environment as he could, when awake, with his ordinary senses. It should here be noted that a higher degree of clairvoyance is required for the higher perception of ordinary physical environment. . . . In the initial stages of his development the student perceives things pertaining to another world without being able to discern their connection with the objects of his daily physical environment.

These characteristics of life during sleep or in dreams illustrate what is continually taking place in the human being. The soul lives in uninterrupted activity in the higher worlds, ever gathering from them the impulse to act upon the physical body. Ordinarily unconscious of his higher life, the esoteric student renders himself conscious of it, and thereby his whole life becomes transformed. As long as the soul remains unseeing in the higher sense it is guided by superior cosmic beings. And just as the life of a person born blind is changed, through a successful operation, from its previous dependence on a guide, so too is the life of a person changed through esoteric training. He outgrows the principle of being guided by a master and must henceforward undertake to be his own guide. The moment this occurs he is, of course, liable to commit errors totally unknown to ordinary consciousness. He acts now from a world from which, formerly, higher powers unknown to him influenced him. These higher powers are directed by the universal cosmic harmony. The student withdraws from this cosmic harmony, and must now himself accomplish things which were hitherto done for him without his cooperation.

It is for this reason that so much is found in books dealing with these matters concerning the dangers connected with the ascent into higher worlds. The descriptions sometimes given of these dangers may well make timid souls shudder at the prospect of this higher life. Yet the fact is that dangers only arise when the necessary precautions are neglected. If all the measures counseled by true esoteric science are adopted, the ascent will indeed ensue through experiences surpassing in power and magnitude everything the boldest flights of sense-bound fantasy can picture; and yet there can be no question of injury to health or life. The student meets with horrible powers threatening life at every turn and from every side. It will even be possible for him to make use of certain forces and beings existing beyond physical perception, and the temptation is great to control these forces for the furtherance of personal and forbidden interests, or to employ them wrongly out of a deficient knowledge of the higher worlds. Some of these especially important experiences, for instance the meeting with the Guardian of the Threshold, will be described in the following chapters. Yet we must realize that the hostile powers are none the less present, even though we know nothing of them. It is true that in this case their relation to man is ordained by higher powers, and that this relation alters when the human being consciously enters this world hitherto concealed from him. But at the same time his own existence is enhanced and the circle of his life enriched by a great and new field of experience. A real danger can only arise if the student, through impatience or arrogance, assumes too early a certain independence with regard to the experiences of the higher worlds; if he cannot wait to gain really sufficient insight into the supersensible laws. In these spheres, modesty and humility are far less empty words than in ordinary life. If the student possesses these qualities in the very best sense, he may be certain that his ascent into the higher life will be achieved without danger to all that is commonly called health and life. Above all things, no disharmony must ensue between the higher experiences and the events and demands of everyday life. Man's task must be entirely sought for on this earth, and anyone desiring to shirk his earthly task and to escape into another world may be certain he will never reach his goal. Yet what the senses perceive is only part of the world, and it is in the spirit world that the beings dwell who express themselves in the facts of the physical world. Man must become a partaker of the spirit in order to carry its revelations into the physical world. He transforms the earth by implanting in it what he has ascertained in the spiritual world. That is his task. It is only because the physical world is dependent upon the spiritual, and because man can work upon earth, in a true sense, only if he is a participator in those worlds in which the creative forces lie concealed—only for these reasons should he have the desire to ascend to the higher worlds. No one approaching esoteric training with these sentiments, and resolved not to deviate for a moment from these prescribed directions, need fear the slightest danger. No one should allow the prospect of these dangers to deter him from esoteric training; it should rather act as a strong challenge to one and all to acquire those faculties which every true esoteric student must possess. . . .

It has been described . . . how significant for the human being is his meeting with the so-called lesser Guardian of the Threshold by virtue of the fact that he becomes aware of confronting a supersensible being whom he has himself brought into existence, and whose body consists of the hitherto invisible results of the student's own actions, feelings, and thoughts. These unseen forces have become the cause of his destiny and his character, and he realizes how he himself founded the present in the past. He can understand why his inner self, now standing to a certain extent revealed before him, includes particular inclinations and habits, and he can also recognize the origin of certain blows of fate that have befallen him. He perceives why he loves one thing and hates another; why one thing makes him happy and another unhappy. Visible life is explained by the invisible causes. The essential facts of life, too—health and illness, birth and death—unveil themselves before his gaze. He observes how before his birth he wove the causes which necessarily led to his return into life. Henceforth he knows that being within himself which is fashioned with all its imperfections in the visible world, and which can only be brought to its final perfection in this same visible world. For in no other world is an opportunity given to build up and complete this being. Moreover, he recognizes that death cannot sever him forever from this world; for he says to himself: "Once I came into this world because, being what I was, I needed the life it provided to acquire qualities unattainable in any other world. And I must remain bound to this world until I have developed within myself everything that can here be gained. I shall some day become a useful collaborator in another world only by acquiring all the requisite faculties in this physical world."

Thanks to his insight into the supersensible world, the initiate gains a better knowledge and appreciation of the true value of visible nature than was possible before his higher training; and this may be counted among his most important experiences. Anyone not possessing this insight, and perhaps therefore imagining the supersensible regions to be infinitely more valuable, is likely to underestimate the physical world. Yet the possessor of this insight knows that without experience in visible reality he would be totally powerless in that other invisible reality. Before he can live in the latter he must have the requisite faculties and instruments which can only be acquired in the visible world. Consciousness in the invisible world is not possible without spiritual sight, but this power of vision in the higher world is gradually developed through experience in the lower. No one can be born in the spiritual world with spiritual eyes without having first developed them in the physical world, any more than a child could be born with physical eyes, had they not already been formed within the mother's womb.

From this standpoint it will also be readily understood why the Threshold to the supersensible world is watched over by a Guardian. In no case may real insight into those regions be permitted to anyone lacking the requisite faculties; therefore, when at the hour of death anyone enters the other world while still incompetent to work in it, the higher experiences are shrouded from him until he is fit to behold them.

When the student enters the supersensible world, life acquires quite a new meaning for him; he discerns in the physical world the seed-ground of a higher world, so that in a certain sense the higher will appear defective without the lower. Two outlooks are opened before him; the first into the past and the second into the future. His vision extends to a past in which this physical world was not yet existent; for he has long since discarded the prejudice that the supersensible world was developed out of the sense-world. He knows that the former existed first, and that out of it everything physical was evolved. He sees that he himself belonged to a supersensible world before coming for the first time into this sense-world. But this pristine supersensible world needed to pass through the sense-world, for without this passage its further evolution would not have been possible. It can only pursue its course when certain beings will have developed requisite faculties within the realm of the senses. These beings are none other than human beings. They owe their present life to an imperfect stage of spiritual existence and are being led, even within this stage, to that perfection which will make them fit for further work in the higher world. At this point the outlook is directed into the future. A higher stage of the supersensible world is discerned which will contain the fruits matured in the sense-world. The sense-world as such will be overcome, but its results will be embodied in a higher world.

The existence of disease and death in the sense-world is thus explained. Death merely expresses the fact that the original supersensible world reached a point beyond which it could not progress by itself. Universal death must needs have overtaken it, had it not received a fresh life-impulse. Thus this new life has evolved into a battle with universal death. From the remnants of a dying rigid world there sprouted the seeds of a new one. That is why we have death and life in the world. The decaying portion of the old world adheres to the new life blossoming from it, and the process of evolution moves slowly. This comes to expression most clearly in man himself. The sheath he bears is gathered from the preserved remnants of the old world, and within this sheath the germ of that being is matured which will live in the future.

Thus man is twofold: mortal and immortal. The mortal is in its last, the immortal in its first stage. But it is only within this twofold world, which finds its expression in the sense-world, that he can acquire the requisite faculties to lead the world to immortality. Indeed, his task is precisely to gather the fruits of the mortal for the immortal. And as he glances at himself as the result of his own work in the past he cannot but say: "I have in me the elements of a decaying world. They are at work in me, and I can only break their power little by little, thanks to the new immortal elements coming to life within me." This is the path leading man from death to life. Could he but speak to himself with full consciousness at the hour of his death, he would say: "The perishing world was my taskmaster. I am now dying as the result of the entire past in which I am enmeshed. Yet the soil of mortal life has matured the seeds of immortal life. I carry them with me into another world. If it had merely depended on the past, I could never have been born. The life of the past came to an end with birth. Life in the sense-world is wrested from universal death by the newly formed life-germ. The time between birth and death is merely an expression for the sum of values wrested from the dying past by the new life; and illness is nothing but the continued effect of the dying portions of the past."

In the above the answer will be found to the question why man works his way only gradually through error and imperfection to the good and true. His actions, feelings, and thoughts are at first dominated by the perishing and the mortal. The latter gave rise to his sense-organs. For this reason, these organs and all things activating them are doomed to perish. The imperishable will not be found in the instincts, impulses, and passions, or in the organs belonging to them, but only in the work produced by these organs. Man must extract from the perishable everything that can be extracted, and this work alone will enable him to discard the background out of which he has grown, and which finds its expression in the physical sense-world.

Thus the first Guardian confronts man as the counterpart of his two-fold nature in which perishable and imperishable are blended;

and it stands clearly proved how far removed he still is from attaining that sublime luminous figure which may again dwell in the pure, spiritual world. The extent to which he is entangled in the physical sense-world is exposed to the student's view. The presence of instincts, impulses, desires, egotistical wishes and all forms of selfishness, and so forth, expresses itself in this entanglement, as it does further in his membership in a race, a nation, and so forth; for peoples and races are but steps leading to pure humanity. A race or a nation stands so much the higher, the more perfectly its members express the pure, ideal human type, the further they have worked their way from the physical and perishable to the supersensible and imperishable. The evolution of man through the incarnations in ever higher national and racial forms is thus a process of liberation. Man must finally appear in harmonious perfection. In a similar way, the pilgrimage through ever purer forms of morality and religion is a perfecting process; for every moral stage retains the passion for the perishable beside the seeds of an ideal future.

Now, in the Guardian of the Threshold as described above, the product of the past is manifest, containing only so many seeds of the future as could be planted in the course of time. Yet everything that can be extracted from the sense-world must be carried into the supersensible world. Were man to bring with him only what had been woven into his counterpart out of the past, his earthly task would remain but partially accomplished. For this reason the lesser Guardian of the Threshold is joined, after a time, by the greater Guardian. The meeting with the second Guardian will again be described in narrative form.

When the student has recognized all the elements from which he must liberate himself, his way is barred by a sublime luminous being whose beauty is difficult to describe in the words of human language. This encounter takes place when the sundering of the organs of thinking, feeling, and willing extends to the physical body, so that their reciprocal connection is no longer regulated by themselves but by the higher consciousness, which has now entirely liberated itself from physical conditions. The organs of thinking, feeling, and willing will then be controlled from supersensible regions as instruments in the power of the human soul. The latter, thus liberated from all physical bonds, is now confronted by the second Guardian of the Threshold who speaks as follows:

"Thou hast released thyself from the world of the senses. Thou hast won the right to become a citizen of the supersensible world, whence thine activity can now be directed. For thine own sake, thou dost no longer require thy physical body in its present form. If thine intention were merely to acquire the faculties necessary for life in the supersensible world, thou needest no longer return to the sense-world. But now behold me. See how sublimely I tower above all that thou hast made of thyself thus far. Thou hast attained thy present degree of perfection thanks to the faculties thou wert able to develop in the sense-world as long as thou wert still confined to it. But now a new era is to begin, in which thy liberated powers must be applied to further work in the world of the senses. Hitherto thou hast sought only thine own release, but now, having thyself become free, thou canst go forth as a liberator of thy fellows. Until today thou hast striven as an individual, but now seek to co-ordinate thyself with the whole, so that thou mayst bring into the supersensible world not thyself alone, but all things else existing in the world of the senses. Thou wilt some day be able to unite with me, but I cannot be blessed so long as others remain unredeemed. As a separate freed being, thou wouldst fain enter at once the kingdom of the supersensible; yet thou wouldst be forced to look down on the still unredeemed beings in the physical world, having sundered thy destiny from theirs, although thou and they are inseparably united. Ye all did perforce descend into the sense-world to gather powers needed for a higher world. To separate thyself from thy fellows would mean to abuse those very powers which thou couldst not have developed save in their company. Thou couldst not have descended had they not done so; and without them the powers needed for supersensible existence would fail thee. Thou must now share with thy fellows the powers which, together with them, thou didst acquire. I shall therefore bar thine entry into the higher regions of the supersensible world so long as thou hast not applied all the powers thou hast acquired to the liberation of thy companions. With the powers already at thy disposal thou mayst sojourn in the lower regions of the supersensible world; but I stand before the portal of the higher regions as the Cherub with the fiery sword before Paradise, and I bar thine entrance as long as powers unused in the sense-world still remain in thee. And if thou dost refuse to apply thy powers in this world, others will come who will not refuse; and a higher supersensible world will receive all the fruits of the sense-world, while thou wilt lose from under thy feet the very ground in which thou wert rooted. The purified world will develop above and beyond thee, and thou shalt be excluded from it.

Thus thou wouldst tread the *black path,* while the others from whom thou didst sever thyself tread the *white path.*"

With these words the greater Guardian makes his presence known soon after the meeting with the first Guardian has taken place. The initiate knows full well what is in store for him if he yields to the temptation of a premature abode in the supersensible world. An indescribable splendor shines forth from the second Guardian of the Threshold; union with him looms as a far distant ideal before the soul's vision. Yet there is also the certitude that this union will not be possible until all the powers afforded by this world are applied to the task of its liberation and redemption. By fulfilling the demands of the higher light-being the initiate will contribute to the liberation of the human race. He lays his gifts on the sacrificial altar of humanity. Should he prefer his own premature elevation into the supersensible world, the stream of human evolution will flow over and past him. After his liberation he can gain no new powers from the world of the senses; and if he places his work at the world's disposal it will entail his renouncement of any further benefit for himself.

It does not follow that, when called upon to decide, anyone will naturally follow the white path. That depends entirely upon whether he is so far purified at the time of his decision that no trace of self-seeking makes this prospect of felicity appear desirable. For the allurements here are the strongest possible; whereas on the other side no special allurements are evident. Here nothing appeals to his egotism. The gift he receives in the higher regions of the supersensible world is nothing that comes to him, but only something that flows from him, that is, love for the world and for his fellows. Nothing that egotism desires is denied upon the black path, for the latter provides, on the contrary, for the complete gratification of egotism, and will not fail to attract those desiring merely their own felicity, for it is indeed the appropriate path for them. No one therefore should expect the occultists of the white path to give him instruction for the development of his own egotistical self. They do not take the slightest interest in the felicity of the individual man. Each can attain that for himself, and it is not the task of the white occultists to shorten the way; for they are only concerned with the development and liberation of all human beings and all creatures. Their instructions therefore deal only with the development of powers for collaboration in this work. Thus they place selfless devotion and self-sacrifice before all other qualities. They never actually refuse anyone, for even the greatest egotist can purify himself; but no one merely seeking an advantage for himself will ever obtain assistance from the white occultists. Even when they do not refuse their help, he, the seeker, deprives himself of the advantage resulting from their assistance. Anyone, therefore, really following the instructions of the good occultists will, upon crossing the Threshold, understand the demands of the greater Guardian; anyone, however, not following their instructions can never hope to reach the Threshold. Their instructions, if followed, produce good results or no results; for it is no part of their task to lead to egotistical felicity and a mere existence in the supersensible worlds. In fact, it becomes their duty to keep the student away from the supersensible world until he can enter it with the will for selfless collaboration.

V. OTHER UNIVERSES: RETURN TO GODHEAD

V

"That other universes may exist is certainly possible, in the view of [astrophysicist] John Wheeler at Princeton, who has probably pondered such questions as deeply as anyone of our time. Each universe would have its own dimensions, its own physical 'constants' and laws. These universes would have their home in a 'superspace' indefinite in time and space."

These are the words of *New York Times* science editor Walter Sullivan in a 1974 article about black holes in space. Black holes are stars that have collapsed to smaller and smaller volume, eventually disappearing from our universe. According to William J. Kaufmann, director of the Griffith Observatory in Los Angeles, recent astronomical observations suggest the existence of white holes—the time-reversals of black holes—and "worm holes" which connect our universe with a second universe by bridges in space-time. The Theory of Relativity predicts such a possibility, although Einstein thought it would be completely impossible to get from one universe to another. "However," says Kaufmann, "recent calculations have shown that this is not the case. The recently discovered Kerr Solution to Einstein's equation does indeed allow for the possibility of space travel in time backward and forward in time in our own universe!"

Italian scientist Giuseppe Bonfante, writing in the *Journal of Paraphysics* (1969) on "Parallel Universes," stated:

> . . . if we exceed the speed of light we find ourselves outside time and space, the two walls—as Maeterlinck has defined them— formidable and illusory, between which our reason must be confined if we are not to lose it: and then once outside our own universe, we shall find ourselves in another, probably parallel. The theory of parallel universes, that is one interpenetrating

another, has ceased for several years to be solely the province of science fiction: already a number of physicists believe it to be true, and indeed consider it necessary to account for otherwise inexplicable phenomena, as for example the strange behavior of the K meson, which would appear to be influenced by just such forces from another universe, capable of interfering with our own. The existence of one or more parallel universes beyond that investigated by science, has also been the subject of speculation by some famous mathematicians, as for example Luigi Fantappie, who wrote on the subject: "I suggest that the whole of reality is not exhausted with the space-time of our own universe. To be able to explain it all completely, it is necessary therefore to look for a much wider scheme beyond it. So much that seems inexplicable in one universe could fit more satisfactorily into a logical scheme including other universes associated with a group of much wider transformations with a larger number of degrees of freedom."

The late Ivan Sanderson expanded on this mind-boggling topic in 1972 in *Pursuit* magazine. We quote at length from his short note, "Other Universes":

. . . Once you can conceive of this idea of other universes in physical terms, you will be ready to try to understand not only the theories of Jacques Vallee and John Keel regarding UFOs, but a very high percentage of other forteana, like unauthorized things that fall from the sky: out-of-place animals; "monsters" of various kinds; poltergeists; and so on. . . . The key to the whole thing, as we have found after ten years of studying the so-called Bermuda Triangle (which it isn't) and its eleven equally spaced areas of anomaly, disappearances and appearances scattered around the globe, is what we call "Time." This means that these "other universes" could be precisely coincident with ours in space (or anywhere from a tiny bit to infinity off our base), but run on different "times."

It is therefore in no way inconceivable that very high intelligences in other "universes" could devise purely physio-mechanical means of "dropping through" from one space-time continuum to another, or of collecting things from one and dumping things into others. At that level of competence they could possibly create things, animate (monsters) or inanimate (UFOs), to suit their purposes—whatever those might be. Even if our universe is either finite or infinite, there is still an infinity of room for others in time.

If time is the key, we might ask, "How old is the universe?" The most recent observations and calculations, made by Allan Sandage of the Hale Observatories, suggest that it is probably about thirteen billion years old, although it could be as long ago as eighteen billion years when the universe began expanding from a "big bang." Quite a jump from the creation point given by Bishop Ussher of Ireland in 1648, when he calculated the date as 9 A.M. on Sunday, October 23, 4004 B.C.

And what about the end of our universe? Again, the Sandage calculations suggest that the expanding universe will eventually slow down,* stop, and reverse, falling in upon itself until, perhaps seventy billion years from now, it will reach the "big bang" point from which it began—an event, incidentally, that not only fulfills the description of sudden, sharp creation given in the Book of Genesis, but also fulfills the Hindu concept of the creation of the universe as a breathing out and in by the creator: the breath of Brahma.

Part of the key to the societal transformation which we urged in the Introduction must be the acceptance of nonlinear time, a view that time unwinds as a spiral rather than progresses along a straight line/one-two-three kind of unfolding. Man's finite brain with its compulsion to limit, its desire to conceive of a beginning and an ending to everything, seeks to trap time and space into man's marking of history. It is mankind's preoccupation with sunrises and sunsets, springs and winters, that gives birth to rituals and the denouement of the Judgment Day.

There have been many physical, group "Judgment Days." It seems each old age terminates with a period of purgation that purifies those people who live during the transition between ages so that they might be better prepared for the New Age. These "Judgment Days" appear to occur according to some cosmic calendar, some time cycle, approximately every two thousand years. Another two thousand years have run their course on the time spiral since the apostolic era, and our generation closely parallels those days of unrest. Another "Judgment Day" is at hand.

But the crisis moment is always with us on the physical plane. We live always in the Day of Decision. The sons and daughters of men have always been able to attain higher levels of consciousness and obtain the gift of prophecy. Young men have always been able to see visions; old men have always talked to God in their dreams. The

---

* As this book was going to press, Sandage announced his revised view of the universe—a view in which it expands infinitely. *Editors.*

Kingdom Within is always at hand. There has never been a time without the Spirit of God, but Higher Intelligence would seem to shower more and brighter sparks when it is time for mankind to make the transition from one age to another. For each progression from age to age requires a higher level of consciousness, a more intense awareness, a more complete understanding. The great spiritual truths exist in the Eternal Now, valid for all ages, available to everyone, free of all finite boundaries, aloof from all man-imagined beginnings and endings.

And so at last we reach the edge of time and the universe, the far side of reality. Or have we? The preceding sections have shown that reality is apparently multidimensional, many-layered, and filled with lifeforms and civilizations outside the range of ordinary perception. Supersensible realms. Higher and lower planes. Zones of consciousness. Subtle bodies of rarefied matter not yet recognized by science. Forms of energy other than those presently known. What do these mean for our concept of reality? Do we live in a universe, a multiverse of successional universes, or an omniverse of interpenetrating universes? Is there, as Buddha said and Ivan Sanderson notes in his interview in this section, an infinity of universes?

Some so-called occult books ("occult" meaning simply "beyond the bounds of ordinary knowledge") have approached the cosmological problem. The recent book *Uri* by Andrija Puharich describes the experiences of the Israeli psychic Uri Geller and contains this striking passage:

> My story involves three principal agents. The primary agent is not a single being, but a collegium of voices reaching man on Earth. We have, in the beginning, the words of the Nine, who are directly related to man's concept of God. . . . The controllers of the universe operate under the direction of the Nine. Between the controllers and the untold numbers of planetary civilizations in the universe are the messengers. It is the messengers who help to fulfill the destiny of creation by gentle accentuation where and when they are needed. Some of these messengers take the form of spacecraft, which in modern parlance are called unidentified flying objects, or UFOs.

A much more extended mapping of the higher worlds is given in an unusual work, *The Urantia Book,* a 2,000-page volume purportedly written by more than a hundred cosmic entities who dictated it over a twenty-year period through a trance medium living in Chicago during the 1920s and '30s. Urantia is the name for Earth, and according to the book, Urantia

> . . . is one of many similar planets which compromise the local universe of Nebadon. This universe, together with similar creations, makes up the superuniverse of Orvonton (with its capital, Uversa). Orvonton is one of the seven evolutionary superuniverses of time and space which circle the never-beginning, never-ending creation of divine perfection—the central universe of Havona. At the heart of this eternal and central universe is the stationary Isle of Paradise, the geographic center of infinity and the dwelling place of the eternal God.
>
> The seven evolving superuniverses in association with the central and divine universe, we commonly refer to as the grand universe; these are the now organized and inhabited creations. They are all a part of the master universe, which also embraces the uninhabited but mobilizing universes of outer space.

The Urantia Book is indeed worthy of study by cosmologers, astronomers, and physicists, as well as philosophers and theologians. Also worthy are books such as Max Heindl's *A Rosicrucian Cosmo-Conception, The Book of Oahspe,* the works of Rudolf Steiner, Alice Bailey, and H. P. Blavatsky, *The Unobstructed Universe* by Stewart E. White, Guenther Wachsmuth's *The Etheric Formative Forces in the Cosmos, Earth and Man,* and of course the sacred scriptures of the world and the writings of recognized mystics such as Jacob Boehme and Emanuel Swedenborg.

The selections in this section present some of the farthest explorations in consciousness and The Reality Game that ordinary mortals have made. The interview with Ivan Sanderson quite literally speaks for itself of the scope and power of Sanderson's intellect. The work of Emanuel Swedenborg is succinctly presented by Wilson Van Dusen, who makes clear that the highest wisdom always has immediate, pragmatic application to the difficulties and ambiguities of daily living. A synthesis of scientific, philosophic, artistic, and religious knowledge is made by the late philosopher Oliver Reiser, the proponent of Cosmic Humanism whose life was a gentle, fearless quest for synthesis and transcendence along the evolutionary path.

In playing The Reality Game we have moved from orthodox science through occult science to spiritual science in search of omniscience. These moves were necessary. It is fitting that we end with a work of science fiction because, as noted in the Introduction, reality begins in imagination. Imagination, intuition, inspiration: they bring us very close to the source of consciousness. They are pathways for return to godhead, to ultimate reality. Science fiction has a large measure of those qualities, and in nearly forty years Olaf Stapledon's *Star Maker* has been unsurpassed for breadth and power of imagination. Thus this book ends with an inspired work on cosmology. There were several candidates from which to select: Arthur Clarke's *Childhood's End*, Piers Anthony's *Macroscope*, Dane Rudhyar's *Return from No Return*. All are consciousness-expanding experiences to read, as powerful in their form as *2001* or its recent matched pearl, *Zardoz*. But the crowning gem of all science fiction and cosmology is *Star Maker*. It takes us as far as human words ever have into the mind of God and the divine show of creation in which we are audience, actors, and authors of The Reality Game.

IVAN T. SANDERSON (1911-72) was a naturalist, nature writer, and, in the tradition of Charles Fort, an inveterate collector of odd facts and curious events. This last pursuit was formalized in 1965 when he established the Society for Investigation of the Unexplained (SITU) at his home in Columbia, New Jersey. Its official publication, *Pursuit*, proclaims on every cover that "science is the pursuit of the unexplained." Ivan Sanderson appeared frequently on radio and television during the 1940s and '50s, displaying rare wild animals. He was also a prolific writer, publishing twenty-five books and numerous articles in magazines and newspapers. Among his best-known works are *Uninvited Visitors, Invisible Residents, Abominable Snowmen,* and *Investigating the Unexplained.*

MULTIPLE UNIVERSES:
AN INTERVIEW WITH IVAN SANDERSON

Bryce Bond: Mr. Sanderson, do flying saucers exist?

Ivan Sanderson: Certainly, of course they exist.

Bond: Where do they come from?

Sanderson: Who knows! We have no proof; you can't just turn around and say they come from somewhere, but there is one thing I think that comes out of the whole pattern. The scientists who study this—Jacques Vallee, Emile Micheau, Dr. Condon even, and reporters like John Keel—find it's perfectly obvious. It's been known to authorities for forty years now that they do not come to us through our space-time. They don't come from another planet. They come through from another set of dimensions, not another dimension or a fourth dimension, but they come from *another whole universe,* or whole bunch of universes which are interlocked with ours either in space or time. That's why we can't catch one, because they are not really here. They're like projections, but they're three-dimensional and solid projections so they cannot be turned on or turned off. The intelligences behind certain types of them can make them just the way that you, being a New Yorker, might expect in our technological age such a thing to be. Whereas for a primitive tribesman somewhere down in the Grand Cheaco they'll make it look like a thing, probably quite different, more like something he would know about.

They don't really come from anywhere. They come through from somewhere or manywheres!

Bond: How do they come through?

Sanderson: Well, time-wise or space-wise or both. Einstein said that we live in what is called a space-time continuum. Time is a feature of reality's existence in space. Now, space is three-dimensional. Time is not really a fourth dimension; it's another factor of it. See what I mean? Now you can have another whole set of three dimensions plus another time, or our time.

Now, we have antimatter, as you know. We have matter which is going backward in time. It is coming from what is our future, going to our past. Ask any physicist, he can't explain it, but he can prove that this happens.

Bond: What you're saying is that governments, per se, have not captured any of these UFOs or their occupants?

Sanderson: Do you mean the Government of the United States of America?

Bond: Any government, around the world.

Sanderson: Well, they've all been looking. I was introduced to this subject in 1929. In Europe the Swedes, the Danish and, I believe, the British (the British talk less than anybody), and the South Americans, the Chileans, Brazilians, and Argentinos were after them, and the Indians (the British Indian Government and then the Indian Government) long, long before we got into the matter. But, I don't think any of them ever got anything. I don't think we ever will get anything which we can prove comes off what people call a UFO. All kinds of funny things have fallen out of the sky, or appeared suddenly or materialized low in the atmosphere. Whether they're parts of what other people might call a flying saucer, who's to say, lest we catch one itself? But I don't think we ever will. I think we have known this all along. That is what all this coverup is about. The public really would get excited and a little upset if they found out that it is impossible to contact these things. Yet the intelligences behind them can contact us.

Bond: Haven't we been trying for years to make contact with other galaxies, planets, and other beings out in the universe?

Sanderson: Yes, but not our universe. These don't come from our universe!

Bond: Oh, I see! . . . from some other universe.

Sanderson: Entirely different universe . . .

Now if you know about the teacher, Gautama Buddha, the founder of the Buddhist religion, he always stated, just as the early Hebrews did in the Yahwasian religion of which we all are a part (Christians are an outcome) that there is an infinity of other universes. We in the West can't think of infinity. We say, "Well, that's an awfully long time ago. You go that way and there must be an end to it." There is no end going either way—either in space or time, see? The teaching of Gautama Buddha was that there is an infinity of other universes. It's like you can run around and say: "Do you really think that the Loch Ness monster exists?" It's just as if there was one poor wretched animal that had no parents and nothing else. You can't just have *the* or *one* thing. You, who run around saying . . . Well, you asked me the first question: "Do you believe" . . . No, you said UFOs with an "s" on the end, but most people say, "Oh, I saw the flying saucer" practically as if there was only one kind. Now, there are a number of different types of things seen in our sky which we don't know about. Here again it gets even more hairy because we don't know half the natural things which are in our sky. Don't forget it was only a hundred years ago that we admitted that meteorites ever arrived here. Science, as a whole, said it was impossible for pieces of iron and stone to fall out of the sky because there were, obviously, no stones in the sky. So it was only a hundred years ago at that. Now we have these lumps of ice landing all over the place all the time—great, huge things, up to a couple of tons—so they're obviously natural things. They are ice and they *do* come down. So, we don't know what's going on much. What's natural we might accept. Then we have all these other things which seem to be unnatural to us because we have no idea what they are! And, all of them are classed together—as flying saucers or UFOs. But, by golly, UFOs are enormously complicated. Some of them may actually be a form of life themselves; some may come from other planets in other solar systems. Some may come through from another universe or other universes. If you go to the other side of our galaxy and you have a planet—the same as ours, and at our level of intelligence but with a further developed technology, look where we come in two hundred years, with all our modern equipment and everything. Suppose they were just a thousand years ahead of us. They would've probably stumbled across something which actually we really know about, but nobody admits and this is one of our hush-hush things . . . a thing called *teleportation,* which means the instant transference of solid matter through other solid matter, just the same as we pick up sound through radio and two-dimensional pictures in TV. This simply means three-dimension projection. Now we've almost got that in a hologram already. With this photograph you can walk right around and view it from all sides, but it's really a photograph.

I would like to go back to what I nearly finished before: what is the difference in coming here, instantaneously, from the other side of our galaxy in our universe, or dropping out of another universe and coming here instantaneously? This is the point. *We are working up to the immediate transmission of solids.* Radio is airborne, but the actual transmission from the transmitter is instantaneous, just the same as our power. People think you manufacture power and then pipe it from Buffalo down to New York from Niagara Falls. You don't. You use it at the moment it is being made because it's 100 millionths of a second . . . it travels at the speed of light. Exactly the same with the actual broadcast, which is then reconverted back into sound waves. Television is instantaneous. Instantaneous transference of this ashtray, for instance, from here through these walls to my apartment which is about six blocks down the road . . . *that* is teleportation. But, if you can do that within our universe you can do it instantly from any distance in our universe. And, don't forget, our universe is circular. To oversimplify: Einstein said if you can go on to infinity in one direction you will eventually hit the back of your head. Because, actually, our space is curved. There are other curved spaces mixed up in it. You can go from one side of one universe to the other side of the universe instantaneously because you are really there already! It's where you started from! You can also come from another universe and pop in *out* here or *in* there anytime you want once you've got teleportation, or instantaneous projection. I call it ITF—instantaneous transference. This is what we are working up to and this is what scientists—thinking scientists—and all the governments have come to the conclusion is the method by which UFOs appear and disappear and move about and make angular turns and so on.

Bond: From another dimension, in other words.

Sanderson: No, no, not *another* dimension. This is where everybody makes a mistake. There can only be *three* dimensions. The mathematical proof of that appeared just last year in Germany and then, also, in England, and it has now come out in a leading scientific journal here. *You can't have a fourth dimension.* The whole thing would collapse. You can't have any space which is uni-dimensional, or linear or two-dimensional. It's got to have three dimensions, otherwise there will not be a universe. It won't exist in space. Now, there is not a fourth dimension, but *another set of three dimensions* or another set and another set and another set, an infinite number of three dimensions, not a fourth dimension.

What are the UFOs that these people are seeing—the top scientists, the astrologers and the airline pilots and some of the government officials and myself? What am I seeing?

All kinds of things that are coming through from another universe. But, if those are controlled by intelligences you will see what they want you to see and what you expect to see. But, you certainly won't see something that you couldn't imagine and they wouldn't show you anything that they didn't want to show you. In other words, we are all controlled. And, as Charles Fort said, many years ago, "This place is nothing else but a nursery and evolution, which has taken *us* (what we call animal-life) to evolve here four billion years." *Four billion years may be a half hour to people living at a different time cycle and this planet may have been seeded. In fact, the whole blasted earth may have been created by superior intelligence.* And, then we were seeded here and then evolution took place and they watch us and they make a sort of nursery. If we develop intelligences here they take us out and blow up the blasted planet.

Bond: They may have done that before, back in biblical times anyway. One single missile and they blew up a particular place.

Sanderson: Oh, Sodom & Gomorrah and all that stuff! That's just a little punch. I mean disintegrate the whole planet, the whole solar system, the sun and everything converting it from material to pure energy . . . just vanish. That could probably be done by mental (what we call mental) control.

Bond: But what about the reports of the contacts of the so-called "humanoids" walking the earth and people taking rides in UFOs and people being taken aboard them, like Betty and Barney Hill from Exeter, New Hampshire?

Sanderson: All the same. Superior intelligence is coming here and maybe collecting us or studying us to see how we are getting on. Or maybe they are playing games! Maybe they are all mad!

Bond: Then you do agree that there *are* some forms of unidentified aerial objects.

Sanderson: Of course there are!

Bond: What about space animals?

Sanderson: Ditto. After all, they could create a space animal just as much as they could a space machine. They come from Ultra—from another universe. But, we *may* have space animals. We've lots of jelly running around living on space energy. But you can't talk about UFOs as if they were flower pots or houses. Look at the number of different things there are in the North Atlantic Ocean, for instance. I believe there are 140,000 species of fish, and God knows you can go on forever. Sand grains and beer cans and the *Queen Mary!* The universe is a much bigger place than the North Atlantic and the number of things that are in it are infinite and any one of these could dribble through here or a lot of them may live in *our* universe. We haven't the foggiest notion what a quasar is yet, or a pulsar.

Bond: Let's go a bit further. Do you think there are any intelligent beings or human forms living at the bottom of the sea?

Sanderson: I definitely do! I think the majority of what we call UFOs actually come from there. I think that is where their bases are.

Bond: Do you think they are of this planet or some other planet or from this time or universe?

Sanderson: All three, I think.

Bond: It is our planet which I am primarily interested in now.

Sanderson: I think we were evolved here. Life, as we now know it—i.e. you and I, everybody and all the dogs and cats and everything else we know—was evolved on this earth. But everything—all plants and vegetables that live in air, like we do, on land—all originally came out of the sea. They were pretty advanced animals. They had evolved half way up, at least, before they ever came out of the sea. Any animals that didn't come out of the sea have gone on evolving in the sea and they had twice as long there to get where we have got because we had to come out and we had to make all kinds of arrangements to live in a gas. We were evolved, originally, to live in a liquid. So it put us back. Whereas those who never had to do that have had another 250,000,000 years minimum (if not 500,000,000) to go on evolving. I think civilization in water has gotten so far beyond us.

Bond: Is the race evolving, whatever they may be?

Sanderson: Well, I would imagine that 100,000,000 years ago they got to the point where they could dispense with their bodies. This is what we are almost getting to now. This is where your para-psychological stuff comes in, you see!

Bond: An outer intelligence, in other words?

Sanderson: Yes, this is the further evolution of the corporeal body. The mind is beginning to take over. Mental power (what we call mental power) does not run on the electromagnetic band. It has a separate band just as gravity is on another band. And, although you cannot affect the mental band . . . you can't blank it off with electromagnetics. So it seems that the mental evolution comes out of corporeal or material evolution. And when you get to a certain point you can do everything by thinking about it. You don't have to put nuts and bolts together!

Bond: Do the governments of the world know about this? These life forms under the sea?

Sanderson: Well, I can't speak for the governments so I don't know, but I have a very shrewd suspicion that they have known about this all along.

Bond: And, they are keeping it hush-hush.

Sanderson: They have to, really. I have official naval reports which state that thirteen ships on submarine maneuvers latched on by radar* to an underwater device traveling at 250 knots down to 20,000 ft. They had a latch on thirteen ships for four days. Now that's an official Navy document.

Bond: That's fascinating!

Sanderson: The Air Force has thrown out this whole business and Project Blue Book, which consists of four people, and they were never intended to chase moonbeams (they're not scientists). But the Navy went quietly along without making any fuss about it. *They have been doing it all along,* and so have all the navies in the world, particularly the Brazilians. They know there is something going on down there. What the dickens it is they're not, of course, going to come out with. The public really would go balmy if they thought there was a superior civilization indigenous to this earth.

* Sanderson undoubtedly means sonar. *Editors.*

OLIVER REISER (1895–1974) was emeritus professor of philosophy at the University of Pittsburgh. He became emeritus professor in 1966, after teaching there for forty years. Dr. Reiser's lifelong interest was the philosophy of science and exploring the nature of the universe. He authored a dozen books and hundreds of articles and reviews. Among his works are *The Integration of Human Knowledge* (1959), *Cosmic Humanism* (1966), *Cosmic Humanism and World Unity* (1974), and *This Holyest Erthe* (1974). At the time of his death he was completing his magnum opus, *Magnetic Moments in Human History*. "Cosmic humanism" is the term for his pantheistic philosophy of science—a term he adopted after Albert Einstein, for whom the term was invented, assured Dr. Reiser that "your view is very close to my own." Cosmic humanism is a theory of the eight-dimensional cosmos based on integrative principles from science, religion, art, and the humanities. It builds a bridge between cosmology and daily life, providing the intellectual, political, and spiritual foundations for the coming world civilization.

COMETS, SPACEPROBES AND HYPERDIMENSIONS

What is the probability that a comet, taking off from some point near the center of our Milky Way galaxy, where perhaps some of the interstellar matter is being created and where possibly the stars themselves are being formed, would in its trajectory streak through our solar system and say *Hello!* to the unmanned spacecraft *Pioneer 10* as it, in turn, raced toward and within hailing distance of planet Jupiter? The antecedent probability of such a fortuitous conjection of events is close to zero. And yet that is what happened. And both flying objects, having completed their solar system journeys, are now on their way out into the depths of cosmic spaces, carrying information that embodies the astrophysical knowledge about our universe, available to any and all extraterrestrial intelligences who can decipher it.

Pioneer 10's most important mission was to fly by the radioactive planet Jupiter—"twin of the sun"—and radio back to Earth's scientists the information about Jupiter's moons, the iridescent atmosphere, the mysterious magnetosphere, and that fantastic hydrogen-helium Great Red Spot which is larger than Earth. The plaque on the space probe carries a message into the spiral galaxy, a message in the form of the picture of a man and a woman with their human endowments —rational and sexual—all that makes mankind *Homo sapiens*. The comet Kohoutek and the spacecraft are now on their way out into the depths of infinite space, carrying the messages that may survive long after the sun and the planets have died or gone up in cosmic smoke and flames.

As it plunged into the heart of our solar system, comet Kohoutek's visit was visually the more spectacular of the two events. The "orbiting iceberg" reminded those of religious inclinations of the Star of Bethlehem. As Kohoutek traced its path around the sun it followed the course of *Pioneer 10* toward the edge of visibility of manmade radio and visual telescopes, but as both leave the region of man's present habitat they carry their data bank "input" to the cosmic computers "out there" for retrieval and deciphering.

Both events gave scientists unrivaled opportunities to gain knowledge about the external cosmos. One does not need to believe that the radio "voices" from Jupiter are coded messages made by intelligent inhabitants living on Jupiter. However, according to Cosmic Humanism's* far-flung network, Jupiter's Giant Red Spot contains and will ultimately reveal the secrets of the role of helium in the solar system and planetary synergistics. In a similar manner, through the radio signals it emits from electrically excited molecules of methyl cyanide—a gas known to be present in the region of the Milky Way where stars may be aborning—Kohoutek will match *Pioneer 10*'s message to the world telling us that Jupiter's atmosphere contains ammonia and methane, revealing a condition similar to that which prevailed on Earth when life first began. Thus between the two we learn more about the genesis of stars, of life—and of mind.

If we generously extrapolate this fragmentary knowledge we arrive at the captivating conclusion that the mad dance of the "ultimate particles" of the physical universe is not really "mad," since it was predestined to culminate in the nucleic acid strands of meaning embodied in the emergent evolution of life on our planet. Behind the show on the visible stage there is the supporting continuum of the Unmanifest Universe peering through the *Cosmic Lens* whose glow-

---

* The term for Dr. Reiser's philosophic-cosmological stance. *Editors.*

ing eyes show how the Supreme Imagination shines upon us through galaxies, quasars, stars, and our own sun. Perhaps the Cosmic Imagination planned the colonization of the earth and shot the proteins and amino acids, precursors of life, to our planet, with built-in instructions to create the DNA-RNA helices, leaving it to emergent humanity to write (and rewrite) history as the story of man's great and deliberate effort to build spaceships and a guidance system for man's return to the outer galaxy. Already the cosmic heliosphere begins to glow.

We know that helium is a marvelous element. In the sun it is a product of the alchemical transmutation of hydrogen into helium—the hydrogen bomb, in fact. In man's laboratories here on Earth it can be supercooled into the superfluid Helium II, with the "life" and "mind" properties that amaze the philosophers of science. In the present form of Cosmic Humanism the circumglobal heliosphere, six hundred miles in thickness above the earth, functions as an ionized plasma which provides one pole of our bipolar theory of the origin of human consciousness. The other pole, of course, is the human brain. In my book *Cosmic Humanism and World Unity* (Gordon & Breach Publishers, 1974) I have tried to reveal the *how* and the *why* of this bipolar circuitry, i.e., the feedback loops between the heliosphere and the brain waves of the cerebral hemispheres. We now begin to glimpse how the heliosphere (first discovered by the unmanned satellites that orbit the earth) and the *cortex cerebri,* between them and in synergistic coupling, have conspired to generate the light of consciousness which now, through human eyes, sweeps the horizons of the planetary scene and the cosmic panorama. Strange, is it not, that the nuclear power fusion reaction whereby hydrogen transmutes into helium in the sun and on Earth will someday help to drive the spaceships through the heliosphere back to the galactic hydrogen-helium plasma of the Milky Way! It is literally true—so I urge—that liquid helium (Helium II) in the form of a superconducting plasma is the key to the miracle of the *biological* $\rightarrow$ *psychic alchemy* that lights up the phosphorescence of the central nervous system and perhaps even transmutes into a galactic consciousness for our Milky Way —a way "which so gleameth white as to set the very sages questing," as Dante put it so perfectly.

One link of the cosmic DNA helix which twists its way to Earth via the solar wind culminates in the generation of life on Earth and the eventual emergence of man as we know him today. But in the centuries to come another link in the helix chain will synergize the embryogenesis of Cosmic Man with the solar body—astronauts and cosmonauts who will journey back to the galaxy. When we discover the intimacies of the morphology that guide these two intertwined serpents of the galactic caduceus—the yin and yang of cosmic embryogenesis—we will then also comprehend the astroglyphs imprinted on those comets that flash like illuminated Rosetta Stones across the celestial skies and emblazon the pages of human history. Let us prevision this.

Let us start from the fact—or supposition—that comet Kohoutek comes from a region beyond the confines of our spiral arm of the galaxy. Let us also imagine (which may not be the case) that in its earlier career Kohoutek was formed (or at least circulated) in the neighborhood of a quasar ten billion light-years away. If we "look" at that quasar through our Earth telescopes we are not "seeing" that quasar as it is today, but as it "was" ten billion years ago. Since ordinary light (not "tachyons") has a finite velocity, we are really viewing the past, observing ancient history so to speak. Now if it is true, as some astrophysicists are coming to believe, that when we interpret astrophysical data in accordance with the Doppler formula for "red shifts" (by employing the Hubble recession formula), we are not seeing quasars at the "edge of the universe," but are indeed face to face with physical phenomena of a completely unknown nature. That is to say, in these supposedly far-out regions of quasars and radio galaxies astrophysicists are confronting mysteries which, as they propose, defy human ingenuity, i.e., these mysteries are such because they transcend known laws of physics. This is so because, according to astronomer Holton Arp of Cal Tech, our fundamental assumptions are wrong.

If comet Kohoutek comes from the region of a far distant quasar, it brings us news that would take us back ten billion years to acquire by first-hand observation. And if somehow the "strange" laws were ingrained and preserved in the comet's structure—its hydrogen and water vapor, for example—then in effect Kohoutek can function as a data bank for information retrieval in our own solar system.

The trouble is, however, that we must try to understand the above mentioned "completely unknown nature" in terms of presently known modes of operation of the human mind. This seems to constitute a contradiction in terms. A blind alley?

There is another possibility. This is that the cosmic phenomena in the outermost galaxies and metagalaxies point to the overlordship of principles in a domain that is not "way out," but exists in an invisible interpenetrating realm which manifests itself in "paranormal" phenomena here in this our present world. That is to say, the data of paraphysics are evidence of a higher dimensional kingdom—a world of hyperspaces—that has causal connections with our own, but these causal concatenations are not explicable in terms of present knowledge and modes of comprehension. Such psi effects as Uri Geller, Ingo Swann, and other psychics give us in PK and ESP and other paranormal phenomena are manifestations of interpenetrations of influences from outside the $3 + 1$ space-time universe of current physical science. So the knowledge of a world of ten billion years ago that is locked up in the memory box of our celestial visitors may be subject to retrieval only as we explore and understand in accordance with the findings of para-astrophysics!

When I examine the offerings of contemporary cosmologists I find one outstanding scientist who, by virtue of the line of thought he has been developing, will sooner or later come to realize the relevance of hyperspace formulations to astrophysics. This lone scientist is Professor John A. Wheeler, physicist at Princeton University. Perhaps his theory of "superspace" points the way to a resolution of the riddle of the cosmos.

In developing my own world view I shall draw upon Professor Wheeler's cosmology to supply a philosophical framework for the psi-high speculations here presented. This matrix is provided by Wheeler's concepts of "superspace" and "connecting universes," but to explicate my own hypotheses these ideas will have to be reinterpreted in terms of Cosmic Humanism's eight-dimensional cosmos as that has been expounded in my previous book, *Cosmic Humanism* (1966). What is baffling to me about the idea of some astrophysicists that there are other universes, not subject to the laws of "our" universe, is that this cosmology is really not conceivable. How can one think about the unthinkable?

Our own hierarchical cosmos exhibits the architectonics of an eight-dimensional structure—a Jacob's ladder of *toruses*—that are eternally intertwined by interpenetrations. These perfusing hyperspace universes are homomorphic; that is, they have analogous properties and therefore display "thinkable" structures. But one must know something about topological transformations. One can pass from one universe to another of the dimensional rungs by the operation of *circumversion*, a "rounding of the curves of dimensionalities" by toroidal inversion. This is explained more fully in my book *The Integration of Human Knowledge* (1958). A familiar lower-level three-dimensional example of this operation is the smoke-ring type of circumversion known as the torus. That is to say, just as three-dimensional vortex rings can move through each other quite easily, so in a toroidal circumversible ionized plasma this and other types of wave phenomena, such as longitudinal, transverse, and nonlinear frequency waves, can interpenetrate and pass through each other. Wonderful!

Now back to Professor Wheeler and his version of the cosmos.

As indicated, this cosmologist is working out the profound implications of Einstein's general relativity theory. Among such implications is the idea that stellar systems may undergo a kind of life cycle that oscillates between a period of expansion outward until a point is reached where a contraction period takes over, which ends when the system condenses under a gravitational attraction that ends with the creation of a "black hole." By applying this to the whole universe, Wheeler concludes that forty billion years from "now" the entire universe will collapse into an immense black hole. In this collapse the laws of the universe as we know them are superseded. Perhaps, as some have surmised, there is a "white hole" in a neighboring universe, so that matter which vanishes into the black hole reappears elsewhere to restore a balance. In this expansion-contraction cycle the universe in some incredible way turns itself inside-out. And here we note: This last idea hits pretty close to the "circumversion" of dimensionalities of Cosmic Humanism's hierarchical cosmos—as will appear in a moment.

Professor Wheeler's idea is that a universe can end up as a "drop out" from the three-space cosmos and that this in fact may be the source of the prodigious energies that issue from the quasistellar sources (quasars). It could also be the explanation of the space-time puckers of such immense densities that even space-time is inverted.

The context within which the black hole hypothesis has developed is part of the total situation which Professor Wheeler has described as constituting the "greatest crisis of the physics of our time." The satisfactory explanation of the interchangeability of space and time, matter and energy and light, requires new ways of thinking. And yet, surprisingly enough, the "crisis" marks a return to some primitive and supposedly obsolete view about man and the universe. Specifically the idea that there is a central mechanism of the universe which supports the vision of a cosmos "peculiarly tuned to man" restores a presumably discredited anthropomorphism. Man once more becomes an integral part of the totality—but now we find a magnificent harmony between us and the one cosmic environment such as was not foreseen even in the "special creation" story of Genesis.

This harmony is conceived to exist in the presence of another component of Wheeler's cosmology. This is the proposal that the arena for the cosmic drama requires a "superspace," an arena endowed with an infinite number of dimensions. In this total setting the rhythm of contraction and expansion, the ebb and flow, is sustained by a dynamics that changes, but which in its subcycles does not repeat itself. This is Wheeler's version of General Relativity—or geometro-dynamics, as he terms it.

Now for a brief digression. Anyone who engages in the game of building a universe must sooner or later come to terms with what is known as the "cosmological postulate." So let us make our peace with it.

The most general form of the "cosmological principle" states that the view of the universe obtained from one point of view (from a spiral nebula such as ours, for example) is the same as the view from any other. This postulate of temporal uniformity is an integral part of the "steady state" theory of the universe as advocated by Fred Hoyle and his colleagues. How this fits in with our own cosmology has been discussed in the *Integration* book. Here we show how our version of the postulate is related to that presented by Giordano Bruno and the later and contemporary theorists.

The critics of the postulate have argued that the universe as it appears in the findings revealed by studies of quasars, radio stars, and pulsars seems not to be in accord with this principle. But as Cosmic Humanism interprets the "findings," the study of quasars can be interpreted as tending to confirm our own version of the hierarchical universe. We suggest that the prodigious display of energies from quasars may be evidence of influxes of superenergies from the hyper-space of a multidimensional cosmos—these energies "leaking down" from a fifth dimension into the four-dimensional space-time universe of conventional physics and relativity theory. This would be comparable to Wheeler's theory of space changing into time (or conversely) in a black hole. This means, in our scheme, that what is called "farther out in space" than the quasars may only be "higher up" in the multidimensionality. In that case the paradox subsides. And what exists in this invisible hyperdimensional hierarchy is really closer than hands and feet—or better yet, than brains and heart.

This idea seems to be in harmony with Wheeler's cosmology. As already indicated, one of the unusual features of his cosmo-conception is the manner in which his synthesis restores man to a position of centrality in an incredible cosmos of billions of billions of stars in hundreds of billions of galaxies. Behold: The universe is not independent of man; indeed, its existence is somehow connected with our existence. Man is not merely an observer—he is a participant —and his unfolding self-consciousness is leading him on his journey to an understanding of the meaning of his own existence.

While Professor Wheeler does not say this, it is as if Kohoutek comes into the realm of man's own miniscule solar system to say, *Hello Man! You are on your way. Follow me into the great beyond . . . through the black hole into the white hole.* And as you pass the radioactive planet Jupiter on the way out, synergize your helium bulb of consciousness with the light of supermind and join the clavilux symphony of celestial music. Join the chorus of Pythagoras, Copernicus, Galileo, Newton, and Einstein, in the beatific crescendo of the cosmic hyperspace consonance.

References

For a discussion of "black holes" and "connecting universes" see the articles: "The Dynamics of Space-Time," by John A. Wheeler and Seymour Tilson, *International Science and Technology,* Dec. 1963; "Introducing the Black Hole," by Remo Ruffini and John A. Wheeler, *Physics Today,* Jan. 1971; "Black Holes and Gravitational Theory," by Roger Penrose, *Nature,* Vol. 236, 1972, 377–80; "Gravitational Collapse and the Death of a Star," by Kip S. Thorne, *Science,* Vol. 150, 1965, 1671–79; "The Black Hole of the Universe," by Laurence B. Chase, *Intellectual Digest,* Dec. 1972, p. 83 ff.

WILSON VAN DUSEN is a clinical psychologist, Merchant Marine officer, and yachtsman. For many years he served as chief psychologist in a California state mental hospital. Dr. Van Dusen reports that after much wandering he has learned that his own natural inclination is toward scholarly work and especially phenomenology, the very accurate description of human experience. He finds human experience a vast and curious terrain—much traveled but little known. He is the author of two books, *The Natural Depth in Man* and *The Presence of Other Worlds*. The latter deals with Swedenborg's life. Dr. Van Dusen is presently engaged in the restoration of yachts through The Redwood Foundation, which he directs.

A JOURNEY THROUGH THE HEAVENS AND HELLS

Emanuel Swedenborg (1688–1772) was a mystic whose findings were so incredible that they have been little accepted even though he had impeccable credentials. He was one of the greatest living scientists; he wrote 160 works on every known science, and founded six new sciences. His spiritual claims were presented without aggrandizement; he kept his authorship secret through most of his life. They were backed by his almost miraculous powers, reported by his friends and enemies because he himself didn't think they were worth noting. He freely explored all the heavens and hells for 32 years and described this exploration in works such as *Heaven and Hell, Divine Providence, Divine Love and Wisdom,* and his 12-volume *Arcana Coelestia.* To top it off, his findings fit with biblical revelation and modern psychology. Those who have a superficial acquaintance with this man don't know whether he was very gifted or quite mad, for it truly may be said he found too much.

Swedenborg was a modest, brilliant man who simply wanted to know everything. He was probably the last of the universal renaissance men. By the time he was fifty he had surveyed the whole of the outer world and, as one of the greatest anatomists of his time, the body of man himself. His work, however, was very academic—intellectual, careful, searching, and dry.

Having grasped all known knowledge in an attempt to learn the secrets of life, he took a reasonable next step. If life was not to be captured by anatomy, he would look directly at life processes, the operation of the mind itself. He surveyed all of the psychology of his day and summarized it in three volumes. The psychology of his day was mostly philosophical speculation on the factors of mind, will, intellect, etc. and their interaction. It was based remarkably little on direct observation. Swedenborg was a genius for getting at the substance of things. He did direct observation on what his mind did in meditation, near-sleep, and in dreams. These areas were ones in which mind tended to show its own processes unimpeded by philosophical rationalizations. Swedenborg's *Journal of Dreams* is still available, though it is a rare volume.

By focusing his whole being on inner processes, in an intense meditation, he began to glimpse and understand the natural symbolic inner processes. As was his habit, he mastered all of the states in this area, meditation, the hypnogogic (between sleep and waking), trance, and dreams. His knowledge of the hypnogogic state remains, even today, two centuries later, superior to ours. His interpretation of dreams still appears to us to be sensitive and accurate. The central problem appearing in his dreams lay in the encounter of this brilliant intellect with the sea of feeling and the vagaries of the unconscious symbolism. With difficulty he integrated his own feeling side. His meditative and trance states became mixed with religious visions. The inner process guided him he knew not quite where. He felt he must be encountering the god within, but he wasn't always sure. The whole focus of his values and of his life shifted away from a very academic intellect to a more feelingful ease with inner processes. He had fleeting encounters with what seemed to be other spiritual beings, an experience available to anyone who carefully studies the hypnogogic state.*

A precognitive dream came to him. He missed its meaning because he did not guess that it was factually reporting what was to happen to him.

I beheld the gable-end of the most beautiful palace that anyone could see and the midst of it was shining like the sun. I was told that it had been resolved in the society that I was to become a member, as it were an immortal, which no one had ever been before, unless he had died and lived again: others said that

* See Dr. Van Dusen's *The Natural Depth in Man.* Editors.

there were several in that state. The thought occurred, whether it is not the most important to be with God, and thus to live. (*Journal of Dreams* 243.)

He had used the gable end of a house before in dreams as though it meant "I am in an ideal place." The society that he was to join was heaven and hell. No one had ever been there before unless they had died and lived on in that world. The "several" in that state were all those who had died.

This great searcher had finally found his way in the very unknown inner world to the spiritual worlds beyond. His whole style of living shifted to a very feelingful orientation that reflected strikingly in his writings from that time onward. With the long perspective of late years he felt that his whole long quest through all the sciences was merely preparation for this journey through this inner world to the spiritual worlds beyond. He had been trained to look and report accurately. This inner penetration required his mastery of trances even to the point of very minimal breathing or possibly the cessation of breathing altogether. His near deep visionary experiences became more common in the waking state. Shortly after the dream mentioned above, he met the Lord in a waking state and was introduced into heaven and hell. With this impressive experience at the age of fifty-four his scientific work was put aside.

There followed more than thirty years of free access to the heavens and hells and his usual careful note taking and reporting in his five-volume *Spiritual Diary*. Through most of the rest of his life these, his richest and most important spiritual and psychological works, appeared anonymously as "Servant of the Lord Jesus Christ." Only late in life was this anonymity removed after his miraculous powers were discovered and people learned of his full knowledge of the spiritual worlds. The Emanuel Swedenborg so concerned with better mining machinery for the economic extraction of minerals, and the Swedenborg who mastered all the sciences, was the same man who reported as fully and faithfully as he could the real nature of the spiritual worlds beyond this one. The only real difference was that it was a much more sensitive, feelingful, loving, and humble man who reported on the spiritual worlds. There was no pride apparent. It is true he could easily see through time, see events at a distance, and contact loved ones in the spiritual worlds, but these feats he considered so minor that he didn't bother to note these powers in his own writings. They were reported by friends and enemies and became the subject of much gossip. I'll just briefly touch on these powers.

Although Swedenborg first explored the worlds beyond this one
only in deep trances, he became more and more easily able to enter
these worlds through light trances and later could apparently experience heaven and hell while carrying on his ordinary affairs in the
world. He could easily see and communicate with the angels and
spirits that were with him all the time and, he said, are with everyone.
It appears that angels would give him intelligence of matters that
concerned him. The first publicly known incident occurred when he
was at a social gathering some two hundred miles from his home in
Stockholm. He saw a fire start, and watched its progress toward his
own home with evident agitation while at a gathering of friends. When
they asked him what was wrong he described the fire in detail some
days before a horseback messenger could bring confirmation. On another occasion he was at the home of a friend when he brusquely
ordered the friend to go to his cloth mill because it was about to
catch fire. He became known for these powers but he would contact
the spiritual world only for serious matters. In one of these a woman
was being sued for the cost of an expensive silver set she was sure
her deceased husband had paid for. Swedenborg contacted the husband and accurately reported that the receipt was hidden in the false
back of a drawer along with some other missing papers. The capstone
of the ten known incidents came when Swedenborg shocked John
Wesley, the founder of Methodism. Swedenborg wrote Wesley saying
that he had learned in heaven that Wesley wished to see him. In the
company of coworkers Wesley opened the note and expressed surprise that Swedenborg knew this. Wesley arranged a meeting months
later because he was to go on tour. Swedenborg answered simply
that he could not keep the appointment because he was due to die on
a given date, which, of course, he did.

The main reason Swedenborg didn't accentuate these powers was
that he felt miracles tended to coerce belief. He was dealing with
spiritual truth, which the individual had to be free to choose. Besides, he was no showman in any sense. If you asked a serious question of the nature of the spiritual worlds he would answer frankly in
terms of his experience, but he never lectured, never preached, never
cared to show his powers. The golden gem of his work lay in his carefully prepared writings and these he made available at cost or less
for anyone.

In his explorations Swedenborg was ushered several times through
the portals of death by angels before he went, with almost childlike
joy, to meet his own real predicted death. He described this process,

that all will be able to confirm eventually in his *Heaven and Hell*. He describes how those who have died awaken in three days in a spiritual world in which life looks, at first, so much like this one that newly entered spirits need to be instructed that they have died. The essentials of a person are his whole inner livingness, which is, in some respects, liberated by death. The new spirit is a person with all his senses and attributes as before. The physical body is the image or representation, or the vehicle of the life of the person. It is not its cause. Rather the life is the cause of the body and Swedenborg reflects his mastery of anatomy in his knowledge of the psychosomatic implications of the way the body, and its organs and functions represent the real nature of the spirit.

The new spirit is gradually let into his own real nature and tendencies. The person becomes acquainted with his own Book of Lives, or the full nature of his own tendencies. In even the beginning spiritual world it is not possible to pretend to be one thing and actually be another. As the person is opened to his nature, he drifts toward what he really is, over and above the minor accidents of birth, culture, and personal life circumstances. Swedenborg comments that some who were insane in the world become rational when they die, and some who looked so impressive in the world become madmen when the outer shell is taken away. The spiritual judgment is quite real and it consists essentially in the person drifting toward the spiritual world that reflects his real nature. In effect, by all our free acts in this world we've hammered out what we are. The spiritual worlds are more psychic or psychological and drift toward the real. The choice between heaven and hell is made by the individual. No one is condemned by God. The person drifts toward the society in heaven or hell that suits the real person.

Swedenborg described in many ways the essential difference between the hierarchy of the three hells and the three heavens. Those who have aimed themselves for hell have, by a lifetime of choices, tended toward a me-over-others, selfish orientation. Heaven reflects a me-with-others orientation. All of the basic tenets of all the religions revolve around this point of choice. Those in heaven have work to do that reflects their nature and interests. They live in societies of like people though all are free to explore other realms. Those in the hells find the light of heaven blinding and uncomfortable and are pleased to return to their own place. Those in heaven see the real nature of the hells and find them dark, stressful, and cut-off places, and are pleased to return to their own place. Heaven is marked by a shared quality, a place where the "joy of one is the joy of all." It must be a very feelingful, with-people, shared place.

In the two lowest heavens the orientation is basically love toward the neighbor. The third, highest, celestial heaven is marked by love of the Lord. Everyone works in heaven, along the lines of his own disposition, for whatever contributes to the common good. Swedenborg does not describe a heaven where winged angels strum harps and drift about on clouds. People are people as they have always been, but only more so as they act out more truly what they really are. There are countries and cities, much to be done, marrying, sharing, learning.

But heaven is not a simple extension of the outer world we know here. For one thing, a person's surroundings, home, clothes, and circumstances reflect the truth of what he is inwardly. A rich, heavenly way of living reflects in the beauty of one's surroundings. The tendency in this world to experience other worlds, circumstances and even the beauty and significance of our surroundings depending upon how we feel within, is even truer in heaven. Also, there is no real time or space there. Instead they experience what corresponds inwardly as psychological time and space. There is change of state which is a looser correspondent of the inevitable measured clock time. Swedenborg's description of heaven and hell reflects so accurately the inner qualities of human life that *Heaven and Hell* can equally well be read to understand the inner nature of our human experience of *this world*. Even if there were no heaven and hell this would be a profoundly valuable work. But, taken the other way, it seems reasonable to me that heaven and hell, the eternal aspect of our life, should reflect in our experience here. Swedenborg says, simply, that those who think that heaven should be blissful indolence are allowed to experience this to see how meaningless and boring it is. Besides, if all wanted to be cared for, who would do the caring? Heaven is a place where each contributes to the common good, in his own way, which is what makes it heavenly.

In one of his leaps beyond our ordinary understanding Swedenborg described the whole of heaven arranged as the Grand Man. The various societies and their functions are like organs of this cosmic man, which is the appearance of the Lord's humanness, of which we are each minor editions. The heavens are in the form of the Grand Man because the Lord is the Very Human, a statement which echoes through the halls of our own nature but stretches beyond the bounds of our understanding. We are the microcosm, the little universe that echoes in all aspects the macrocosm, the total universe. It is the One, which is the Only, that searches through the clouds of our understanding. Even the angelic spirits, who are very advanced in the quality of their life, can be brought down in vastation, which is the equivalent of depression and human stress in this world. Our stress is part of heaven's guidance, which pokes and prods us to learn and yet leaves us free to choose.

The whole is created out of the One, which is the Only. All existence is arranged in hierarchies which reflect the total possibilities of the One. The heavens reflect the possibilities of at-oneness (with the Lord, the neighbor, and one's self). The hells reflect the possibilities of lostness. Our lives in this world are precisely the beginning experience of these possibilities. How we do everything makes a spiritual difference. The shoemaker who repairs shoes well for a fair price serves himself and his neighbor and is preparing himself for an eternity of with-others experience. The shoemaker who does the work poorly at an unfair price is cutting himself off from the real quality of life and is building an eternity of similar experiences. It is as though the other person is a real part of the self and cutting off the other cuts off one from life. This cutting-off reflects in the tormented, alienated world of fantasy in hell, which contrasts with the peaceful reality of heaven.

However far Swedenborg journeyed in spiritual insight, he never departed from the real root qualities of human experience. The whole profound design and beauty of all the spiritual worlds (including hell, which nicely illustrates human stupidity) comes to rest in Swedenborg's idea of uses. We tend to think of certain human functions as higher than others—e.g., the statesman who resolves a war as greater than the shoemaker. The turning point between heaven and hell is in such a simple matter as how a sole is put on a shoe. Whatever the Lord and the three heavens might be, the whole comes to Earth in the uses the individual serves. In setting a fair price for soling shoes, the shoemaker makes a difficult decision between his own reasonable and heaven-sent needs and the needs of his customer. We decide as well as we can, and eternity mirrors the result. Moreover, Swedenborg's idea of uses gives much latitude to individual differences. Each works at his eternal destiny through whatever uses come to hand. Part of the beauty of the spiritual worlds lies in the unity of the infinite differences there, which is illustrated by watching the endless differences in the faces of passersby in this world. Through use, the essential thrust of the good of heaven comes to Earth as the real. The good person, open to the possibilities of existence, senses that he is an instrument acted through. Do you want to know heaven? Then become accustomed to acting with others by the uses that come to your hand. How cosmically reasonable! Do you want to know all the worlds beyond this? Then look closely and carefully at your experiences and the experiences of others. It is all shown here.

Being a very practical and down-to-earth man, Swedenborg was opposed to the religions that emphasize faith as a kind of intellectual leap into heaven. Faith that doesn't come to Earth in good acts, uses, is simply self-serving fantasy. The fulcrum of your journey through the worlds is in what you do, not in fancy intellectual perambulations. Faith, hope, and charity are the most important things, and the greatest of these is charity, what you do.

Swedenborg also clarified the whole structure of mind and its relationship to the spiritual worlds. Love is the life of existence, truth or understanding its form. Love, feeling, affects are the inner aspect of mind and thought, the outer form which corresponds to the inner. In many ways Swedenborg is dealing with levels of the unconscious. There is a natural drift to the innermost of each which he calls the love of the life. This is the unique ruling tendency of each that brings into order and subordination all other tendencies. Understand the love of the life of another and you understand myriads of individual acts. By divesting the outer shell, spirits become primarily affective tendencies. Good and evil spirits are with us at this subconscious level of the affects. The good and evil spirits with us are like our innermost tendencies. Each individual is a living choice point.

When examined closely Swedenborg leaves little or no room for ego. In this respect he fits with the no-mind aspect of Zen. What good we do is the Lord acting through the heavens and through the affective levels of mind, and through us. The evil we do is the hells acting through us because we think we act of ourselves, and thereby close out the openness of heaven. We are the fulcrum of the spiritual worlds. The Lord's love gives us the feeling that we act of ourselves. Yet the vaunted-up illusion that we are the real doer cuts us off from heaven, the enlarging experience of existence.

Even freedom is mysteriously simple. We feel freest when we act out of innermost love, which is to be an instrument of heaven. Freedom lies in the direction of love and oneness with all. The cut-off, fighting-it-alone self is imprisoned in its own conception. To act out of one's deepest love is to express heaven. This accords one the greatest sense of freedom and self-awareness while at the same time opening the vistas of heaven, for the Lord is the ultimate freedom.

Around these issues Swedenborg is very psychological and spiritual at the same time. Both have to do with life, but spiritual knowledge is the ultimate aspect of psychological knowledge or personal experience.

Swedenborg clearly lived, thought and wrote in Christian terms. In the eighteenth century he had little contact with non-Christian religions or the other great bibles of the world. Several small Christian sects have sprung up in his name. Yet in his clear emphasis on uses and the good people do he appeared to have transcended the cultural and sectarian differences of religions. He said that all who acted by the good they know would be saved (that is, experience the enlarging nature of reality). In a casual remark he mentioned that the then-primitive, non-Christian blacks of Africa were favored in heaven because they were so easy to instruct, in contrast to learned bishops and potentates of this world. He indicated that the Lord was easily master of all scenes and all were guided from heaven. In a beautiful passage he transcended the conflicts of religions:

> . . . it is plain that the church of the Lord is not here, nor there, but that it is everywhere, both within those kingdoms where the church is, and outside them, where men live according to the precepts of charity. Hence it is that the church of the Lord is scattered through the whole world, and yet it is one; for when life makes the church, and not doctrine separate from life, then the church is one, but when doctrine makes the church, then there are many. (*Arcana Coelestia* 8152)

The key to Swedenborg lies in his concept of the human. Because we are human we have access to all the potentialities of the human. Mind or man's experience is deliberately made as a microcosm that reflects the macrocosm of the universe. The inner, more affective and less conscious, layers of mind correspond to the heavens and hells. We have access to all the potentialities of the universe. It seems, at first sight, that Swedenborg departs from modern psychology when he says that everyone has good and evil spirits associated with them. But since the spirits associated with us are like us ("The enthusiastic are possessed by enthusiastic spirits.") there is no fundamental way of distinguishing their nature and ours. Moreover, when the bodily shell of spirits is removed, they are more thoroughly affective or emotional in nature, just as are the more unconscious levels of mind.

In a practical sense, what Swedenborg described as spirits interacting with us is much the same as the modern conception of the unconscious. The human experience would be the same whether we are inwardly constituted as in modern psychology of the unconscious or in Swedenborg's conception. The real difference lies in the fact that Swedenborg cannot and will not leave out the other spiritual worlds in which we already participate and which are our ultimate destiny. On the other hand, most modern psychologists cannot include these worlds. Their conception is cut off at the level of the individual with perhaps the introjection of a few relatives and friends.

A mystical implication in Swedenborg's works is that we are a part of everyone else. The unity of a society of myriads of people acting like a single psychological organ of the Grand Man, the image of all mankind, is a real unity which we will grow to know. Pressed just a bit further, Swedenborg says that there really is just One Life. Our concern over possible good and evil spirits interacting in the less conscious affective levels of mind is just a beginning understanding of the One Life.

Swedenborg then describes the inner tickings of mind in much the same way as the analysts with a richer understanding of symbolism than all except perhaps Jung. His hell aspect lies across the domain of Freud and his heaven aspect is closer to Jung. He differs in that he is thoroughly empirical or phenomenological, and he sees the relationship of man to all the world as essential. That he is only describing just what he experienced, with no theorizing, would be especially difficult for modern psychologists to accept, since they mostly reject the reality of the spiritual worlds. These worlds are essential to Swedenborg in several senses. In an immediate, here-and-now sense they represent the full scope of our potentialities as humans. They also represent the design of the subtle inner aspects of mind. In a larger sense they are our ultimate destiny. When asked, "Why is there man?," Swedenborg answered, "That there might be a heaven." But in the largest sense of all, both the design of our mind and of the spiritual worlds beyond this one are only images of the potentialities of the Divine. The whole show of existence is the One Divine endlessly creating and experiencing itself through creation. It is the Divine itself that searches through the clouds of our understanding, but we fear it is only us!

Swedenborg's aim was to find it all and the comprehensiveness of his understanding implies that he did. Yet this very comprehensiveness will cause him to remain little known. He stretches across too many realms. He attained heaven and hell by personally penetrating the inner experience of hypnogogic states, dreams, and trances.

What other theologian will follow this way? His mastery of biblical symbolism rests on these personal symbolic experiences and the direct guidance of heaven. How many biblical scholars are like this? His knowledge of psychology takes in the whole design of all the spiritual worlds. But it is not a matter of his works simply being too rich. Many very ordinary people are captivated by him. The blind, deaf mute Helen Keller was put into ecstasy by his works. He is speaking of too much to be tested out in any laboratory of retorts and instruments. But he isn't speaking of too much to be tested out in the ultimate laboratory of any human's experience. For we are, after all, the image of all there is, which is not a prideful position but one of great responsibility. We are the hinge or fulcrum of existence, each the fulcrum of all the spiritual worlds.

OLAF STAPLEDON (1886–1950) was a noted British philosopher and novelist. He studied psychology and philosophy at the University of Liverpool, where he earned his Ph.D. His academic career gave way to that of a novelist, *Star Maker* (published in 1937) being his best known and the one Stapledon himself considered the best. Among his other works are *Last and First Men* (1930), *Odd John* (1935), *Sirius* (1944), and his posthumous spiritual autobiography, *The Opening of the Eyes*. In 1949 he was a delegate to a conference on world peace. Although he became known in his time for his description of a cosmic disaster envisioned to engulf the universe in two billion years, he felt that man's "whole future . . . depends on the turn which events may take in the next half century." Stapledon's visionary account of the end of a universe and the birth of future universes is one of the high points in all human thought.

FROM *STAR MAKER*

The Supreme Moment and After

In the supreme moment of the cosmos I, as the cosmical mind, seemed to myself to be confronted with the source and the goal of all finite things.

I did not, of course, in that moment sensuously perceive the infinite spirit, the Star Maker. Sensuously I perceived nothing but what I had perceived before, the populous interiors of many dying stellar worlds. But through the medium which in this book is called telepathic I was now given a more inward perception. I felt the immediate presence of the Star Maker. Latterly, as I have said, I had already been powerfully seized by a sense of the veiled presence of some being other than myself, other than my cosmical body and conscious mind, other than my living members and the swarms of the burnt-out stars. But now the veil trembled and grew half-transparent to the mental vision. The source and goal of all, the Star Maker, was obscurely revealed to me as a being indeed other than my conscious self, objective to my vision, yet as in the depth of my own nature; as, indeed, myself, though infinitely more than myself.

It seemed to me that I now saw the Star Maker in two aspects: as the spirit's particular creative mode that had given rise to me, the cosmos; and also, most dreadfully, as something incomparably greater than creativity, namely as the eternally achieved perfection of the absolute spirit.

Barren, barren and trivial are these words. But not barren the experience.

Confronted with this infinity that lay deeper than my deepest roots and higher than my topmost reach, I, the cosmical mind, the flower of all the stars and worlds, was appalled, as any savage is appalled by the lightning and the thunder. And as I fell abject before the Star Maker, my mind was flooded with a spate of images. The fictitious deities of all races in all worlds once more crowded themselves upon me, symbols of majesty and tenderness, of ruthless power, of blind creativity, and of all-seeing wisdom. And though these images were but the fantasies of created minds, it seemed to me that one and all did indeed embody some true feature of the Star Maker's impact upon the creatures.

As I contemplated the host of deities that rose to me like a smoke cloud from the many worlds, a new image, a new symbol of the infinite spirit, took shape in my mind. Though born of my own cosmical imagination, it was begotten by a greater than I. To the human writer of this book little remains of that vision which so abashed and exalted me as the cosmical mind. But I must strive to recapture it in a feeble net of words as best I may.

It seemed to me that I had reached back through time to the moment of creation. I watched the birth of the cosmos.

The spirit brooded. Though infinite and eternal, it had limited itself with finite and temporal being, and it brooded on a past that pleased it not. It was dissatisfied with some past creation, hidden from me; and it was dissatisfied also with its own passing nature. Discontent goaded the spirit into fresh creation.

But now, according to the fantasy that my cosmical mind conceived, the absolute spirit, self-limited for creativity, objectified from itself an atom of its infinite potentiality.

This microcosm was pregnant with the germ of a proper time and space, and all the kinds of cosmical beings.

Within this punctual cosmos the myriad but not unnumbered physical centers of power, which men conceive vaguely as electrons, protons, and the rest, were at first coincident with one another. And they were dormant. The matter of ten million galaxies lay dormant in a point.

Then the Star Maker said, "Let there be light." And there was light.

From all the coincident and punctual centers of power, light leapt and blazed. The cosmos exploded, actualizing its potentiality of space and time. The centers of power, like fragments of a bursting bomb, were hurled apart. But each one retained in itself, as a memory and a longing, the single spirit of the whole; and each mirrored in itself aspects of all others throughout all the cosmical space and time.

No longer punctual, the cosmos was now a volume of inconceivably dense matter and inconceivably violent radiation, constantly expanding. And it was a sleeping and infinitely dissociated spirit.

But to say that the cosmos was expanding is equally to say that its members were contracting. The ultimate centers of power, each at first coincident with the punctual cosmos, themselves generated the cosmical space by their disengagement from each other. The expansion of the whole cosmos was but the shrinkage of all its physical units and of the wavelengths of its light.

Though the cosmos was ever of finite bulk, in relation to its minutiae of light-waves, it was boundless and centerless. As the surface of a swelling sphere lacks boundary and center, so the swelling volume of the cosmos was boundless and centerless. But as the spherical surface is centered on a point foreign to it, in a "third dimension," so the volume of the cosmos was centered in a point foreign to it, in a "fourth dimension."

The congested and exploding cloud of fire swelled till it was of a planet's size, a star's size, the size of a whole galaxy, and of ten million galaxies. And in swelling it became more tenuous, less brilliant, less turbulent.

Presently the cosmical cloud was disrupted by the stress of its expansion in conflict with the mutual clinging of its parts, disrupted into many million cloudlets, the swarm of the great nebulae.

For a while these were as close to one another in relation to their bulk as the flocculations of a mottled sky. But the channels between them widened, till they were separated as flowers on a bush, as bees in a flying swarm, as birds migrating, as ships on the sea. More and more rapidly they retreated from one another; and at the same time each cloud contracted, becoming first a ball of down and then a spinning lens and then a featured whirl of star-streams.

Still the cosmos expanded, till the galaxies that were most remote from one another were flying apart so swiftly that the creeping light of the cosmos could no longer bridge the gulf between them.

But I, with imaginative vision, retained sight of them all. It was as though some other, some hypercosmical and instantaneous light, issuing from nowhere in the cosmical space, illuminated all things inwardly.

Once more, but in a new and cold and penetrating light, I watched all the lives of stars and worlds, and of the galactic communities, and of myself, up to the moment wherein now I stood, confronted by the infinity that men call God, and conceive according to their human cravings.

I, too, now sought to capture the infinite spirit, the Star Maker, in an image spun by my own finite though cosmical nature. For now it seemed to me, it seemed, that I suddenly outgrew the three-dimensional vision proper to all creatures, and that I saw with physical sight the Star Maker. I saw, though nowhere in cosmical space, the blazing source of the hypercosmical light, as though it were an overwhelmingly brilliant point, a star, a sun more powerful than all suns together. It seemed to me that this effulgent star was the center of a four-dimensional sphere whose curved surface was the three-dimensional cosmos. This star of stars, this star that was indeed the Star Maker, was perceived by me, its cosmical creature, for one moment before its splendor seared my vision. And in that moment I knew that I had indeed seen the very source of all cosmical light and life and mind; and of how much else besides I had as yet no knowledge.

But this image, this symbol that my cosmical mind had conceived under the stress of inconceivable experience, broke and was transformed in the very act of my conceiving it, so inadequate was it to the actuality of the experience. Harking back in my blindness to the moment of my vision, I now conceived that the star which was the Star Maker, and the immanent center of all existence, had been perceived as looking down on me, his creature, from the height of his infinitude; and that when I saw him I immediately spread the poor wings of my spirit to soar up to him, only to be blinded and seared and struck down. It had seemed to me in the moment of my vision that all the longing and hope of all finite spirits for union with the infinite spirit were strength to my wings. It seemed to me that the Star, my Maker, must surely stoop to meet me and raise me and enfold me in his radiance. For it seemed to me that I, the spirit of so many worlds, the flower of so many ages, was the Church Cosmical, fit at last to be the bride of God. But instead I was blinded and seared and struck down by terrible light.

It was not only physical effulgence that struck me down in that supreme moment of my life. In that moment I guessed what mood it was of the infinite spirit that had in fact made the cosmos, and constantly supported it, watching its tortured growth. And it was that discovery which felled me.

For I had been confronted not by welcoming and kindly love, but by a very different spirit. And at once I knew that the Star Maker had made me not to be his bride, nor yet his treasured child, but for some other end.

It seemed to me that he gazed down on me from the height of his divinity with the aloof though passionate attention of an artist judging his finished work; calmly rejoicing in its achievement, but recognizing at last the irrevocable flaws in its initial conception, and already lusting for fresh creation.

His gaze anatomized me with calm skill, dismissing my imperfections, and absorbing for his own enrichment all the little excellence that I had won in the struggle of the ages.

In my agony I cried out against my ruthless maker. I cried out that, after all, the creature was nobler than the creator; for the creature loved and craved love, even from the star that was the Star Maker; but the creator, the Star Maker, neither loved nor had need of love.

But no sooner had I, in my blinded misery, cried out, than I was struck dumb with shame. For suddenly it was clear to me that virtue in the creator is not the same as virtue in the creature. For the creator, if he should love his creature, would be loving only a part of himself; but the creature, praising the creator, praises an infinity beyond himself. I saw that the virtue of the creature was to love and to worship, but the virtue of the creator was to create, and to be the infinite, the unrealizable and incomprehensible goal of worshipping creatures.

Once more, but in shame and adoration, I cried out to my maker. I said, "It is enough, and far more than enough, to be the creature of so dread and lovely a spirit, whose potency is infinite, whose nature passes the comprehension even of a minded cosmos. It is enough to have been created, to have embodied for a moment the infinite and tumultuously creative spirit. It is infinitely more than enough to have been used, to have been the rough sketch for some perfected creation."

And so there came upon me a strange peace and a strange joy.

Looking into the future, I saw without sorrow, rather with quiet interest, my own decline and fall. I saw the populations of the stellar worlds use up more and more of their resources for the maintenance of their frugal civilizations. So much of the interior matter of the stars did they disintegrate, that their worlds were in danger of collapse. Some worlds did indeed crash in fragments upon their hollow centers, destroying the indwelling peoples. Most, before the critical point was reached, were remade, patiently taken to pieces and rebuilt upon a smaller scale. One by one, each star was turned into a world of merely planetary size. Some were no bigger than the moon. The populations themselves were reduced to a mere millionth of their original numbers, maintaining within each little hollow grain a mere skeleton civilization in conditions that became increasingly penurious.

Looking into the future eons from the supreme moment of the cosmos, I saw the populations still with all their strength maintaining the essentials of their ancient culture, still living their personal lives in zest and endless novelty of action, still practicing telepathic intercourse between worlds, still telepathically sharing all that was of value in their respective world-spirits, still supporting a truly cosmical community with its single cosmical mind. I saw myself still preserving, though with increasing difficulty, my lucid consciousness; battling against the onset of drowsiness and senility, no longer in the hope of winning through to any more glorious state than that which I had already known, or of laying a less inadequate jewel of worship before the Star Maker, but simply out of sheer hunger for experience, and out of loyalty to the spirit.

But inevitably decay overtook me. World after world, battling with increasing economic difficulties, was forced to reduce its population below the numbers needed for the functioning of its own communal mentality. Then, like a degenerating brain center, it could no longer fulfill its part in the cosmical experience.

Looking forward from my station in the supreme moment of the cosmos, I saw myself, the cosmical mind, sink steadily toward death. But in this my last eon, when all my powers were waning, and the burden of my decaying body pressed heavily on my enfeebled courage, an obscure memory of past lucidity still consoled me. For confusedly I knew that even in this my last, most piteous age I was still under the zestful though remote gaze of the Star Maker.

Still probing the future, from the moment of my supreme unwithered maturity, I saw my death, the final breaking of those telepathic contacts on which my being depended. Thereafter the few surviving worlds lived on in absolute isolation, and in that barbarian condition which men call civilized. Then in world after world the basic skills of material civilization began to fail; and in particular the techniques of atomic disintegration and photosynthesis. World after world either accidentally exploded its little remaining store of matter, and was turned into a spreading, fading sphere of light-waves in the immense darkness; or else died miserably of starvation and cold. Presently nothing was left in the whole cosmos but darkness and the dark whiffs of dust that once were galaxies. Eons incalculable passed. Little by little each whiff of dust-grains contracted upon itself through the gravitational influence of its parts; till at last, not without fiery collisions between wandering grains, all the matter in each whiff was concentrated to become a single lump. The pressure of the huge outer regions heated the center of each lump to incandescence and even to explosive activity. But little by little the last resources of the cosmos were radiated away from the cooling lumps, and nothing was left but rock and the inconceivably faint ripples of radiation that crept in all directions throughout the ever "expanding" cosmos, far too slowly to bridge the increasing gulfs between the islanded grains of rock.

Meanwhile, since each rocky sphere that had once been a galaxy had been borne beyond every possible physical influence of its fellows, and there were no minds to maintain telepathic contact between them, each was in effect a wholly distinct universe. And since all change had ceased, the proper time of each barren universe had also ceased.

Since this apparently was to be the static and eternal end, I withdrew my fatigued attention back once more to the supreme moment which was in fact my present, or rather my immediate past. And with the whole mature power of my mind I tried to see more clearly what it was that had been present to me in that immediate past. For in that instant when I had seen the blazing star that was the Star Maker, I had glimpsed, in the very eye of that splendor, strange vistas of being; as though in the depths of the hypercosmical past and the hypercosmical future also, yet coexistent in eternity, lay cosmos beyond cosmos. . . .

Mature Creating

According to the myth that my mind conceived when the supreme moment of my cosmical experience had passed, the Star Maker at length entered into a state of rapt meditation in which his own nature suffered a revolutionary change. So at least I judged from the great change that now came over his creative activity.

After he had reviewed with new eyes all his earlier works, dismissing each, as it seemed to me, with mingled respect and impatience, he discovered in himself a new and pregnant conception.

The cosmos which he now created was that which contains the readers and the writer of this book. In its making he used, but with more cunning art, many of the principles which had already served him in earlier creations; and he wove them together to form a more subtle and more capacious unity than ever before.

It seemed to me, in my fantasy, that he approached this new enterprise in a new mood. Each earlier cosmos appeared to have been fashioned with conscious will to embody certain principles, physical, biological, psychological. As has already been reported, there often appeared a conflict between his intellectual purpose and the raw nature which he had evoked for his creature out of the depth of his own obscure being. This time, however, he dealt more sensitively with the medium of his creation. The crude spiritual "material" which he objectified from his own hidden depth for the formation of his new creature was moulded to his still tentative purpose with more sympathetic intelligence, with more respect for its nature and its potentiality, though with detachment from its more extravagant demands.

To speak thus of the universal creative spirit is almost childishly anthropomorphic. For the life of such a spirit, if it exists at all, must be utterly different from human mentality, and utterly inconceivable to man. Nevertheless, since this childish symbolism did force itself upon me, I record it. In spite of its crudity, perhaps it does contain some genuine reflection of the truth, however distorted.

In the new creation there occurred a strange kind of discrepancy between the Star Maker's own time and the time proper to the cosmos itself. Hitherto, though he could detach himself from the cosmical time when the cosmical history had completed itself, and observe all the cosmical ages as present, he could not actually create the later phases of a cosmos before he had created the earlier. In his new creation he was not thus limited.

Thus although this new cosmos was my own cosmos, I regarded it from a surprising angle of vision. No longer did it appear as a familiar sequence of historical events beginning with the initial physical explosion and advancing to the final death. I saw it now not from within the flux of the cosmical time but quite otherwise. I watched the fashioning of the cosmos in the time proper to the Star Maker; and the sequence of the Star Maker's creative acts was very different from the sequence of historical events.

First he conceived from the depth of his own being a something, neither mind nor matter, but rich in potentiality, and in suggestive traits, gleams, hints for his creative imagination. Over this fine substance for a long while he pondered. It was a medium in which the one and the many demanded to be most subtly dependent upon one another; in which all parts and all characters must pervade and be pervaded by all other parts and all other characters; in which each thing must seemingly be but an influence in all other things; and yet the whole must be no other than the sum of all its parts, and each part an all-pervading determination of the whole. It was a cosmical substance in which any individual spirit must be, mysteriously, at once an absolute self and a mere figment of the whole.

This most subtle medium the Star Maker now rough-hewed into the general form of a cosmos. Thus he fashioned a still indeterminate space-time, as yet quite ungeometrized; an amorphous physicality with no clear quality or direction, no intricacy of physical laws; a more distinctly conceived vital trend and epic adventure of mentality; and a surprisingly definite climax and crown of spiritual lucidity. This last, though its situation in the cosmical time was for the most part late, was given a certain precision of outline earlier in the sequence of creative work than any other factor in the cosmos. And it seemed to me that this was so because the initial substance itself so clearly exposed its own potentiality for some such spiritual form. Thus it was that the Star Maker at first almost neglected the physical minutiae of his work, neglected also the earlier ages of cosmical history, and devoted his skill at first almost entirely to shaping the spiritual climax of the whole creature.

Not till he had blocked in unmistakably the most awakened phase of the cosmical spirit did he trace any of the variegated psychological trends which, in the cosmical time, should lead up to it. Not till he had given outline to the incredibly diverse themes of mental growth did he give attention fully to constructing the biological evolutions and the physical and geometrical intricacy which could best evoke the more subtle potentialities of his still rough-hewn cosmical spirit.

But, as he geometrized, he also intermittently turned again to modify and elucidate the spiritual climax itself. Not till the physical and geometrical form of the cosmos was almost completely fashioned could he endow the spiritual climax with fully concrete individuality.

While he was still working upon the detail of the countless, poignant individual lives, upon the fortunes of men, of ichthyoids, of nautiloids, and the rest, I became convinced that his attitude to his

creatures was very different from what it had been for any other cosmos. For he was neither cold to them nor yet simply in love with them.
In love with them, indeed, he still was; but he had seemingly out-
grown all desire to save them from the consequences of their finitude
and from the cruel impact of the environment. He loved them without
pity. For he saw that their distinctive virtue lay in their finitude, their
minute particularity, their tortured balance between dullness and
lucidity; and that to save them from these would be to annihilate
them.

When he had given the last touches to all the cosmical ages from
the supreme moment back to the initial explosion and on to the final
death, the Star Maker contemplated his work. And he saw that it was
good.

As he lovingly, though critically, reviewed our cosmos in all its
infinite diversity and in its brief moment of lucidity, I felt that he was
suddenly filled with reverence for the creature that he had made, or
that he had ushered out of his own secret depth by a kind of divine
self-midwifery. He knew that this creature, though imperfect, though
a mere creature, a mere figment of his own creative power, was yet
in a manner more real than himself. For beside this concrete splendor
what was he but a mere abstract potency of creation? Moreover in
another respect the thing that he had made was his superior, and his
teacher. For as he contemplated this the loveliest and subtlest of all
his works with exultation, even with awe, its impact upon him
changed him, clarifying and deepening his will. As he discriminated
its virtue and its weakness, his own perception and his own skill matured. So at least it seemed to my bewildered, awe-stricken mind.

Thus, little by little, it came about, as so often before, that the Star
Maker outgrew his creature. Increasingly he frowned upon the loveliness that he still cherished. Then, seemingly with a conflict of reverence and impatience, he set our cosmos in its place among his other
works.

Once more he sank into deep meditation. Once more the creative
urge possessed him.

Of the many creations which followed I must perforce say almost
nothing, for in most respects they lay beyond my mental reach. I could
not have any cognizance of them save in so far as they contained,
along with much that was inconceivable, some features that were but
fantastic embodiments of principles which I had already encountered.
Thus all their most vital novelty escaped me.

I can, indeed, say of all these creations that, like our own cosmos, they were immensely capacious, immensely subtle; and that, in some alien manner or other, every one of them had both a physical and a mental aspect; though in many the physical, however crucial to the spirit's growth, was more transparent, more patently phantasmal than in our own cosmos. In some cases this was true equally of the mental, for the beings were often far less deceived by the opacity of their individual mental processes, and more sensitive to their underlying unity.

I can say too that in all these creations the goal which, as it seemed to me, the Star Maker sought to realize was richness, delicacy, depth and harmoniousness of being. But what these words in detail mean I should find it hard to say. It seemed to me that in some cases, as in our own cosmos, he pursued this end by means of an evolutionary process crowned by an awakened cosmical mind, which strove to gather into its own awareness the whole wealth of the cosmical existence, and by creative action to increase it. But in many cases this goal was achieved with incomparably greater economy of effort and suffering on the part of the creatures, and without the huge dead loss of utterly wasted, ineffective lives which is to us so heart-rending. Yet in other creations suffering seemed at least as grave and widespread as in our own cosmos.

In his maturity the Star Maker conceived many strange forms of time. For instance, some of the later creations were designed with two or more temporal dimensions, and the lives of the creatures were temporal sequences in one or other dimension of the temporal "area" or "volume." These beings experienced their cosmos in a very odd manner. Living for a brief period along one dimension, each perceived at every moment of its life a simultaneous vista which, though of course fragmentary and obscure, was actually a view of a whole unique "transverse" cosmical evolution in the other dimension. In some cases a creature had an active life in every temporal dimension of the cosmos. The divine skill which arranged the whole temporal "volume" in such a manner that all the infinite spontaneous acts of all the creatures should fit together to produce a coherent system of transverse evolutions far surpassed even the ingenuity of the earlier experiment in "pre-established harmony."

In other creations a creature was given only one life, but this was a "zigzag line," alternating from one temporal dimension to another according to the quality of the choices that the creature made. Strong or moral choices led in one temporal direction, weak or immoral choices in another.

In one inconceivably complex cosmos, whenever a creature was faced with several possible courses of action, it took them all, thereby creating many distinct temporal dimensions and distinct histories of the cosmos. Since in every evolutionary sequence of the cosmos there were very many creatures, and each was constantly faced with many possible courses, and the combinations of all their courses were innumerable, an infinity of distinct universes exfoliated from every moment of every temporal sequence in this cosmos.

In some creations each being had sensory perception of the whole physical cosmos from many spatial points of view, or even from every possible point of view. In the latter case, of course, the perception of every mind was identical in spatial range, but it varied from mind to mind in respect of penetration or insight. This depended on the mental caliber and disposition of particular minds. Sometimes these beings had not only omnipresent perception but omnipresent volition. They could take action in every region of space, though with varying precision and vigor according to their mental caliber. In a manner they were disembodied spirits, striving over the physical cosmos like chess-players, or like Greek gods over the Trojan Plain.

In other creations, though there was indeed a physical aspect, there was nothing corresponding to the familiar systematic physical universe. The physical experience of the beings was wholly determined by their mutual impact on one another. Each flooded its fellows with sensory "images," the quality and sequence of which were determined according to psychological laws of the impact of mind on mind.

In other creations the processes of perception, memory, intellection, and even desire and feeling were so different from ours as to constitute in fact a mentality of an entirely different order. Of these minds, though I seemed to catch remote echoes of them, I cannot say anything.

Or rather, though I cannot speak of the alien psychical modes of these beings, one very striking fact about them I can record. However incomprehensible their basic mental fibers and the patterns into which these were woven, in one respect all these beings came fleetingly within my comprehension. However foreign to me their lives, in one respect they were my kin. For all these cosmical creatures, senior to me, and more richly endowed, constantly faced existence in the manner that I myself still haltingly strove to learn. Even in pain and grief, even in the very act of moral striving and of white-hot pity, they met fate's issue with joy. Perhaps the most surprising and heartening fact that emerged from all my cosmical and hypercosmical experience was this kinship and mutual intelligibility of the most alien beings in respect of the pure spiritual experience. But I was soon to discover that in this connection I had still much to learn.

The Ultimate Cosmos and the Eternal Spirit

In vain my fatigued, my tortured attention strained to follow the increasingly subtle creations which, according to my dream, the Star Maker conceived. Cosmos after cosmos issued from his fervent imagination, each one with a distinctive spirit infinitely diversified, each in its fullest attainment more awakened than the last; but each one less comprehensible to me.

At length, so my dream, my myth, declared, the Star Maker created his ultimate and most subtle cosmos, for which all others were but tentative preparations. Of this final creature I can say only that it embraced within its own organic texture the essences of all its predecessors; and far more besides. It was like the last movement of a symphony, which may embrace, by the significance of its themes, the essence of the earlier movements; and far more besides.

This metaphor extravagantly understates the subtlety and complexity of the ultimate cosmos. I was gradually forced to believe that its relation to each earlier cosmos was approximately that of our own cosmos to a human being, nay to a single physical atom. Every cosmos that I had hitherto observed now turned out to be but a single example of a myriad-fold class, like a biological species, or the class of all the atoms of a single element. The internal life of each "atomic" cosmos had seemingly the same kind of relevance (and the same kind of irrelevance) to the life of the ultimate cosmos as the events within a brain cell, or in one of its atoms, to the life of a human mind. Yet in spite of this huge discrepancy I seemed to sense throughout the whole dizzying hierarchy of creations a striking identity of spirit. In all, the goal was conceived, in the end, to include community and the lucid and creative mind.

I strained my fainting intelligence to capture something of the form of the ultimate cosmos. With mingled admiration and protest I haltingly glimpsed the final subtleties of world and flesh and spirit, and of the community of those most diverse and individual beings, awakened to full self-knowledge and mutual insight. But as I strove to hear more inwardly into that music of concrete spirits in countless worlds, I caught echoes not merely of joys unspeakable, but of griefs inconsolable. For some of these ultimate beings not only suffered, but suffered in darkness. Though gifted with full power of insight, their power was barren. The vision was withheld from them. They suffered as lesser spirits would never suffer. Such intensity of harsh experience was intolerable to me, the frail spirit of a lowly cosmos. In an agony of horror and pity I despairingly stopped the ears of my mind. In my littleness I cried out against my maker that no glory of the eternal and absolute could redeem such agony in the creatures. Even if the misery that I had glimpsed was in fact but a few dark strands woven into the golden tapestry to enrich it, and all the rest was bliss, yet such desolation of awakened spirits, I cried, ought not, ought never to be. By what diabolical malice, I demanded, were these glorious beings not merely tortured but deprived of the supreme consolation, the ecstasy of contemplation and praise which is the birthright of all fully awakened spirits?

There had been a time when I myself, as the communal mind of a lowly cosmos, had looked upon the frustration and sorrow of my little members with equanimity, conscious that the suffering of these drowsy beings was no great price to pay for the lucidity that I myself contributed to reality. But the suffering individuals within the ultimate cosmos, though in comparison with the hosts of happy creatures they were few, were beings, it seemed to me, of my own, cosmical, mental stature, not the frail, shadowy existences that had contributed their dull griefs to my making. And this I could not endure.

Yet obscurely I saw that the ultimate cosmos was nevertheless lovely, and perfectly formed; and that every frustration and agony within it, however cruel to the sufferer, issued finally, without any miscarriage in the enhanced lucidity of the cosmical spirit itself. In this sense at least no individual tragedy was vain.

But this was nothing. And now, as through tears of compassion and hot protest, I seemed to see the spirit of the ultimate and perfected cosmos face her maker. In her, it seemed, compassion and indignation were subdued by praise. And the Star Maker, that dark power and lucid intelligence, found in the concrete loveliness of his creature the fulfillment of desire. And in the mutual joy of the Star Maker and the ultimate cosmos was conceived, most strangely, the absolute spirit itself, in which all times are present and all being is comprised; for the spirit which was the issue of this union confronted my reeling intelligence as being at once the ground and the issue of all temporal and finite things.

But to me this mystical and remote perfection was nothing. In pity of the ultimate tortured beings, in human shame and rage, I scorned my birthright of ecstasy in that inhuman perfection, and yearned back to my lowly cosmos, to my own human and floundering world, there to stand shoulder to shoulder with my own half animal kind against the powers of darkness; yes, and against the indifferent, the ruthless, the invincible tyrant whose mere thoughts are sentient and tortured worlds.

Then, in the very act of this defiant gesture, as I slammed and bolted the door of the little dark cell of my separate self, my walls were all shattered and crushed inwards by the pressure of irresistible light, and my naked vision was once more seared by lucidity beyond its endurance.

Once more? No. I had but reverted in my interpretative dream to the identical moment of illumination, closed by blindness, when I had seemed to spread wing to meet the Star Maker, and was struck down by terrible light. But now I conceived more clearly what it was that had overwhelmed me.

I was indeed confronted by the Star Maker, but the Star Maker was now revealed as more than the creative and therefore finite spirit. He now appeared as the eternal and perfect spirit which comprises all things and all times, and contemplates timelessly the infinitely diverse host which it comprises. The illumination which flooded in on me and struck me down to blind worship was a glimmer, so it seemed to me, of the eternal spirit's own all-penetrating experience.

It was with anguish and horror, and yet with acquiescence, even with praise, that I felt or seemed to feel something of the eternal spirit's temper as it apprehended in one intuitive and timeless vision all our lives. Here was no pity, no proffer of salvation, no kindly aid. Or here were all pity and all love, but mastered by a frosty ecstasy. Our broken lives, our loves, our follies, our betrayals, our forlorn and gallant defenses, were one and all calmly anatomized, assessed, and placed. True, they were one and all lived through with complete understanding, with insight and full sympathy, even with passion. But sympathy was not ultimate in the temper of the eternal spirit; contemplation was. Love was not absolute; contemplation was. And though there was love, there was also hate comprised within the spirit's temper, for there was cruel delight in the contemplation of every horror, and glee in the downfall of the virtuous. All passions, it seemed, were comprised within the spirit's temper; but mastered, icily gripped within the cold, clear, crystal ecstasy of contemplation.

That this should be the upshot of all our lives, this scientist's, no, artist's, keen appraisal! And yet I worshipped!

But this was not the worst. For in saying that the spirit's temper was contemplation, I imputed to it a finite human experience, and an emotion; thereby comforting myself, even though with cold comfort. But in truth the eternal spirit was ineffable. Nothing whatever could be truly said about it. Even to name it "spirit" was perhaps to say more than was justified. Yet to deny it that name would be no less mistaken; for whatever it was, it was more, not less, than spirit, more, not less, than any possible human meaning of that word. And from the human level, even from the level of a cosmical mind, this "more," obscurely and agonizingly glimpsed, was a dread mystery, compelling adoration.

SUGGESTIONS FOR FURTHER EXPLORATION

I. OTHER WORLDS: THE SEARCH FOR EXTRATERRESTRIAL LIFE

Angrist, Stanley W. *Other Worlds, Other Beings*. T. Y. Crowell, 1973.

Barbour, Ian G. *Issues in Science and Religion*. Prentice-Hall, 1966.

Sagan, Carl, *The Cosmic Connection*. Doubleday, 1974.

Sagan, Carl and I. S. Shklovskii. *Intelligent Life in the Universe*. Delta, 1968.

Sullivan, Walter. *We Are Not Alone*. Signet, 1966.

II. OTHER CIVILIZATIONS: THE PREHISTORY OF EARTH

Berlitz, Charles. *The Mystery of Atlantis*. Grosset & Dunlap, 1969.

Besant, Annie and C. W. Leadbeater. *Man: Whence, How & Whither*. Theosophical Publishing House, 1913 (Adhyar, India).

Charroux, Robert. *Forgotten Worlds*. Walker, 1973.

Churchward, James. *The Lost Continent of Mu*. Ives Washburn, 1931.

Donnelly, Ignatius. *Atlantis: The Antediluvian World*. Gramercy, 1949.

Hansen, L. Taylor. *The Ancient Atlantic*. Amherst Press, 1969.

Michell, John. *City of Revelation*. David McKay, 1972.

Reiser, Oliver. *This Holyest Erthe*. Perennial Press (England), 1975.

Robertson, Lytle. *Edgar Cayce's Story of the Origin and Destiny of Man*. Coward-McCann, 1972.

Sanderson, Ivan. *Invisible Residents*. Avon, 1970.

Steiner, Rudolf. *Cosmic Memory*. Multimedia-Biograf, 1971.

Wauchope, Robert. *Lost Tribes and Sunken Continents*. University of Chicago Press, 1962.

III. OTHER LIFEFORMS: A LOOK AT UFOs

Bergier, Jacques. *Extraterrestrial Visitations from Prehistoric Times to the Present*. Regnery, 1973.

Blum, Ralph and Judy Blum. *Beyond Earth: Man's Contact with UFOs*. Bantam, 1974.

Fuller, John G. *Interrupted Journey*. Dell, 1967.

Hynek, J. Allen. *The UFO Experience*. Regnery, 1972.

Lorenzon, Coral and Jim Lorenzon. *Flying Saucer Occupants*. Signet, 1967.

Sanderson, Ivan. *Uninvited Visitors*. Cowles, 1967.

Thomas, Paul. *Flying Saucers Through the Ages*. Wehman, 1965.

Trench, Brinsley Le Poer. *Mysterious Visitors*. Stein and Day, 1973.

IV. OTHER DIMENSIONS: THE ASTRAL PLANE AND BEYOND

Baba, Pagal and Edward Rice. *Temple of the Phallic King: The Mind of India*. Simon and Schuster, 1973.

Bach, Marcus. *The Inner Ecstasy*. World Publishing, 1969.

Castaneda, Carlos. *The Teaching of Don Juan*. Ballantine, 1969.

David-Neel, Alexandra. *Magic and Mystery in Tibet*. Dover, 1971.

Eliade, Mircea. *Cosmos and History*. Harper Torchbooks, 1959.

Jacobson, Nils. *Life Without Death?* Delacorte, 1973.

Johnson, Raynor C. *Watcher on the Hills*. Hodder & Stoughton (London), 1959.

Keel, John A. *Our Haunted Planet*. Fawcett, 1971.

Leadbeater, C. W. *The Astral Plane*. Theosophical Publishing House, 1970.

Roberts, Jane. *The Seth Material*. Prentice-Hall, 1970.

Steiger, Brad. *The Mind Travellers*. Award Books, 1968.

V. OTHER UNIVERSES: RETURN TO GODHEAD

Krishna, Gopi. *Higher Consciousness*. Julian Press, 1974.

Potter, Charles. *The Great Religious Leaders*. Simon and Schuster, 1958.

Satprem. *Sri Aurobindo or The Adventure of Consciousness*. Sri Aurobindo Ashram Press (India), 1970.

Spalding, Baird T. *Life and Teachings of the Masters of the Far East,* Vol. 1. DeVorss, 1937.

Stace, Walter T. *The Teachings of the Mystics.* New American Library, 1960.

William, Michael. *They Walked with God.* Fawcett, 1962.